CLIVE BARKER'S
HELLRAISER

THE DARK WATCH

BOOM!
S T U D I O S

ROSS RICHIE CEO & Founder • JACK CUMMINS President • MARK SMYLIE Chief Creative Officer • MATT GAGNON Editor-in-Chief • FILIP SABLIK VP of Publishing & Marketing • STEPHEN CHRISTY VP of Development
LANCE KREITER VP of Licensing & Merchandising • PHIL BARBARO VP of Finance • BRYCE CARLSON Managing Editor • MEL CAYLO Marketing Manager • SCOTT NEWMAN Production Design Manager • DAFNA PLEBAN Editor • SHANNON WATTERS Editor
ERIC HARBURN Editor • REBECCA TAYLOR Editor • CHRIS ROSA Assistant Editor • ALEX GALER Assistant Editor • WHITNEY LEOPARD Assistant Editor • JASMINE AMIRI Assistant Editor • MIKE LOPEZ Production Designer
HANNAH NANCE PARTLOW Production Designer • DEVIN FUNCHES E-Commerce & Inventory Coordinator • BRIANNA HART Executive Assistant • AARON FERRARA Operations Assistant • JOSE MEZA Sales Assistant

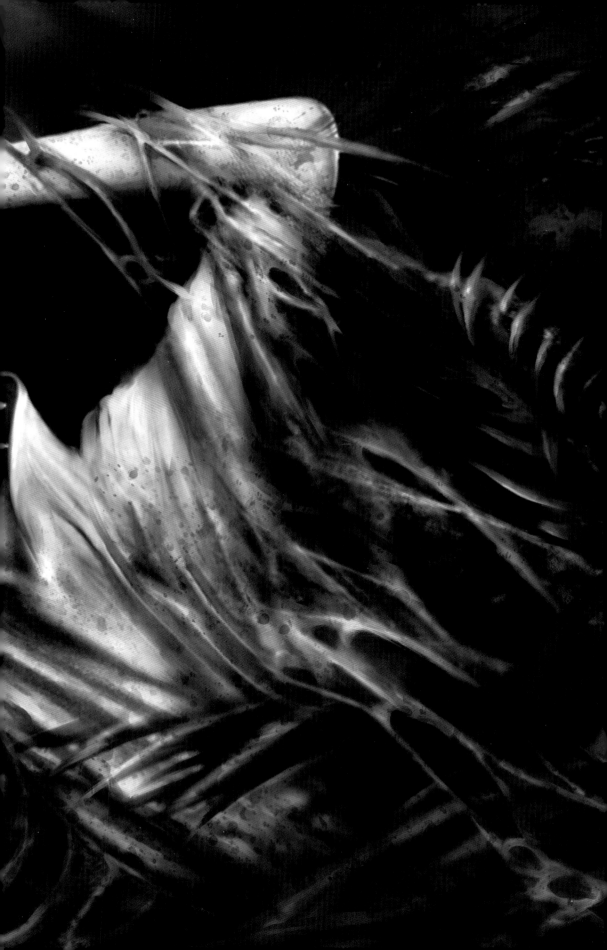

WRITTEN BY

CLIVE BARKER AND BRANDON SEIFERT

ART BY

TOM GARCIA

WITH KORKUT ÖZTEKIN

COLORS BY

VLADIMIR POPOV

LETTERING BY

TRAVIS LANHAM

ASSISTANT EDITOR

CHRIS ROSA

EDITORS

DAFNA PLEBAN
MATT GAGNON

COVER BY

FRAZER IRVING

TRADE DESIGN

MIKE LOPEZ

SPECIAL THANKS TO MARK MILLER AND BEN MEARES

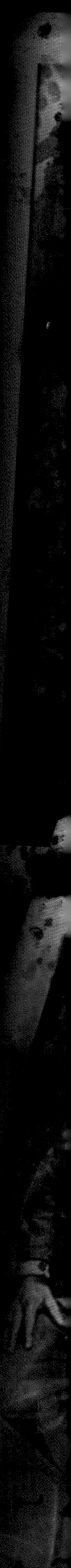

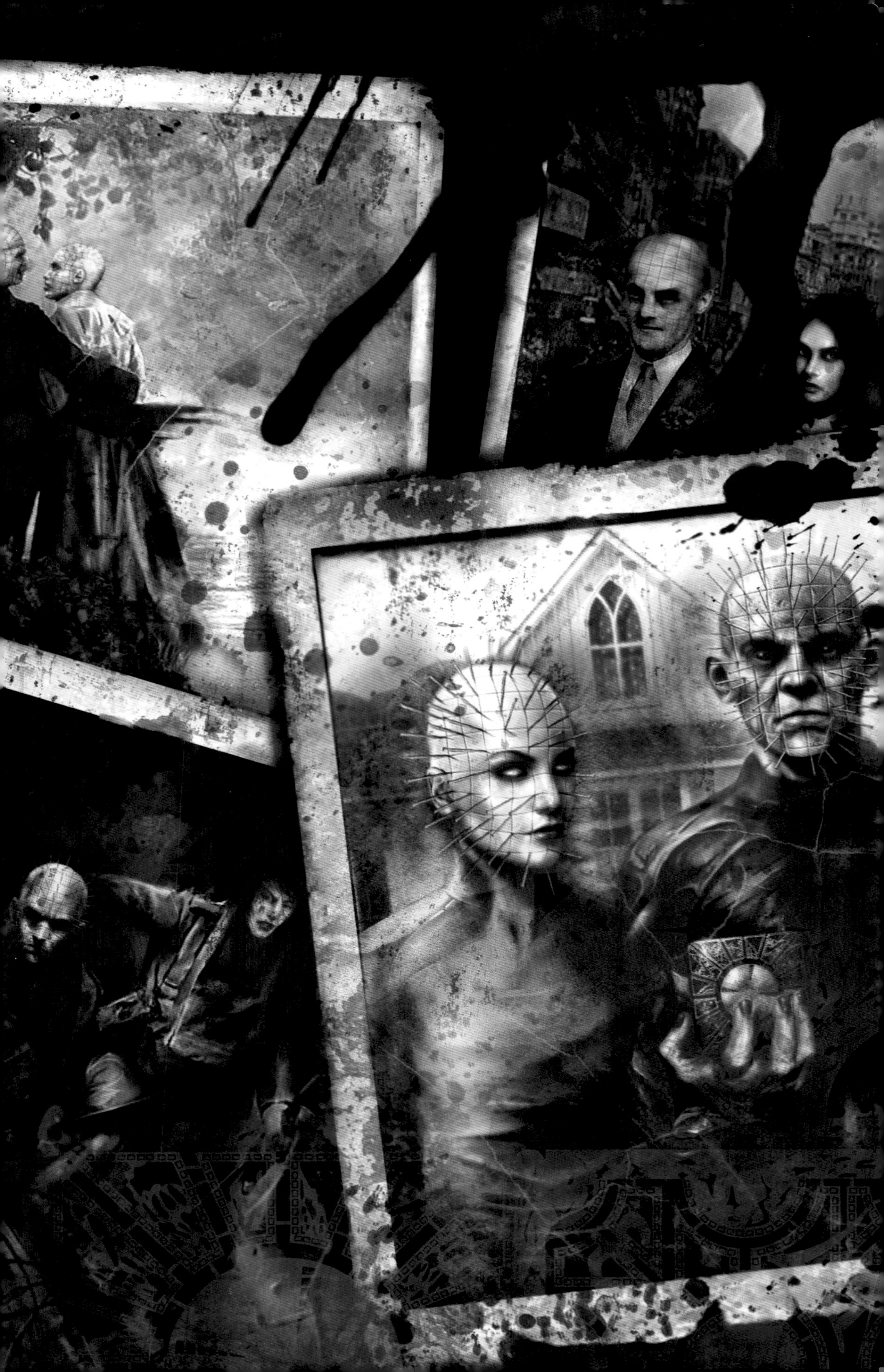

THE DARK WATCH
CHAPTER FIVE

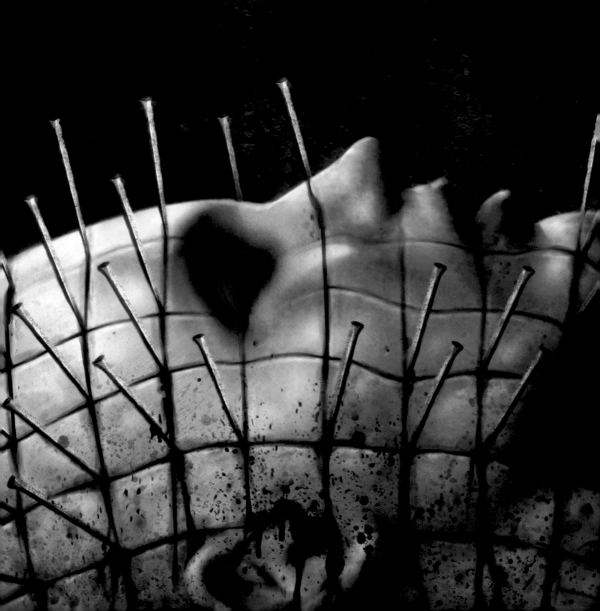

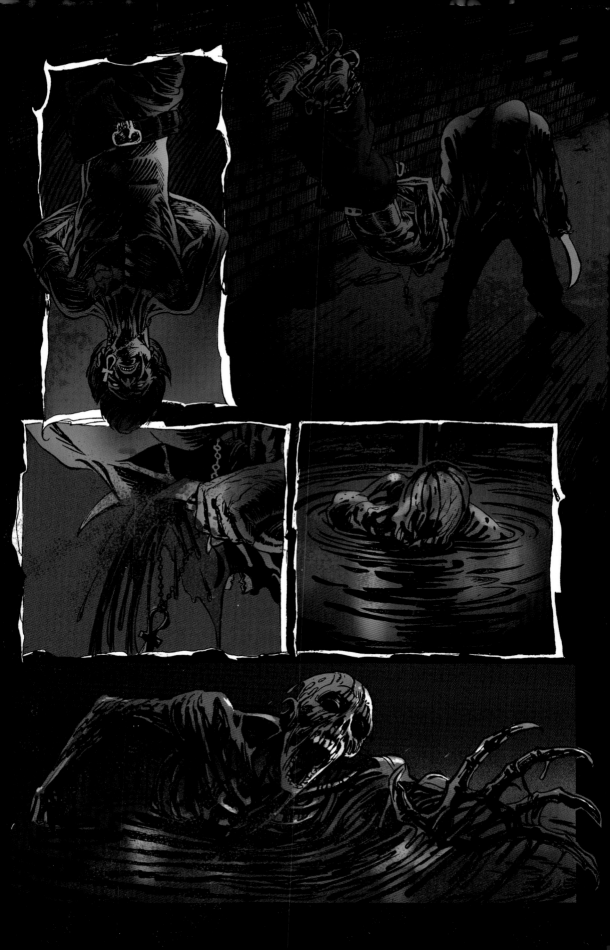

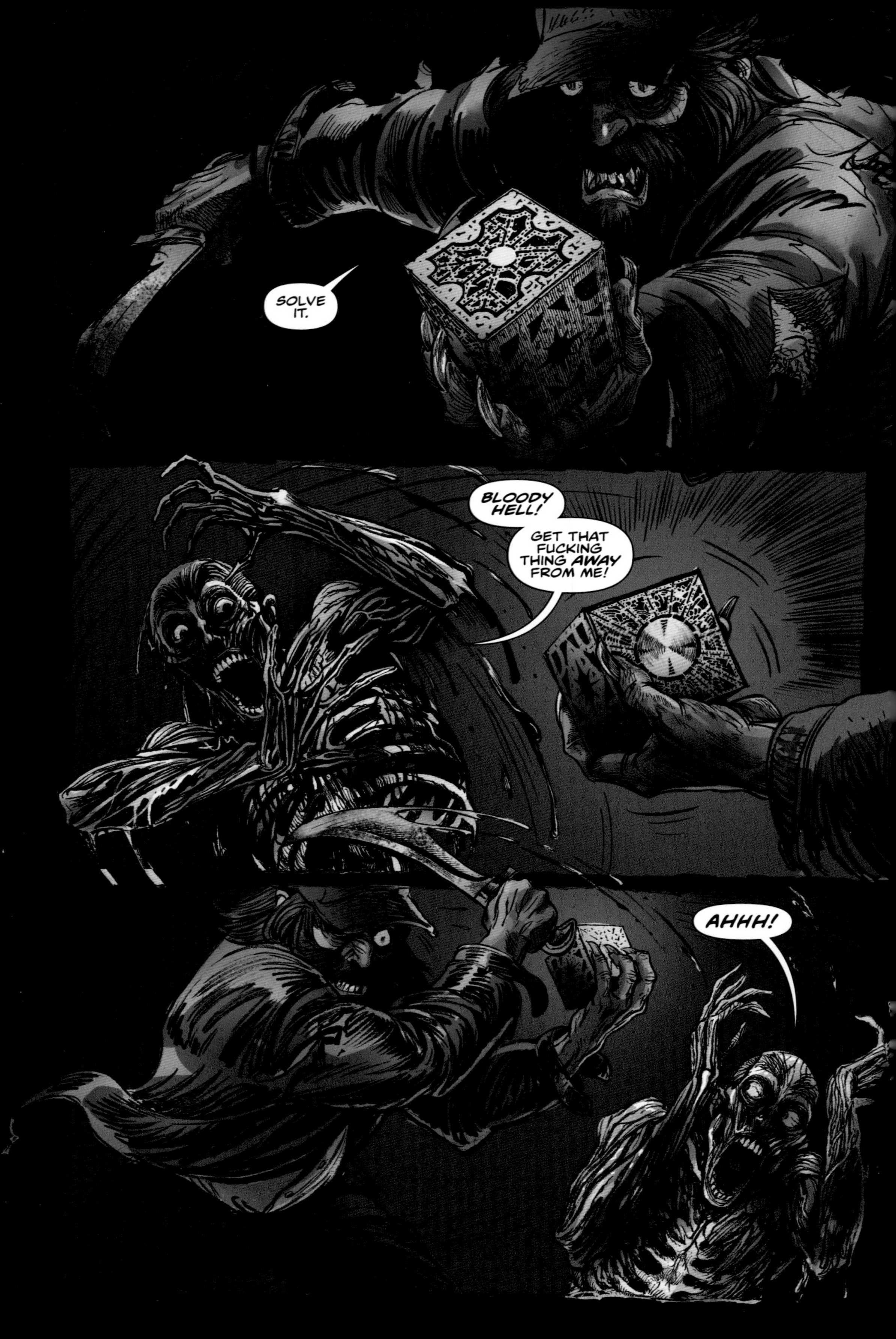
SOLVE IT.
BLOODY HELL!
GET THAT FUCKING THING AWAY FROM ME!
AHHH!

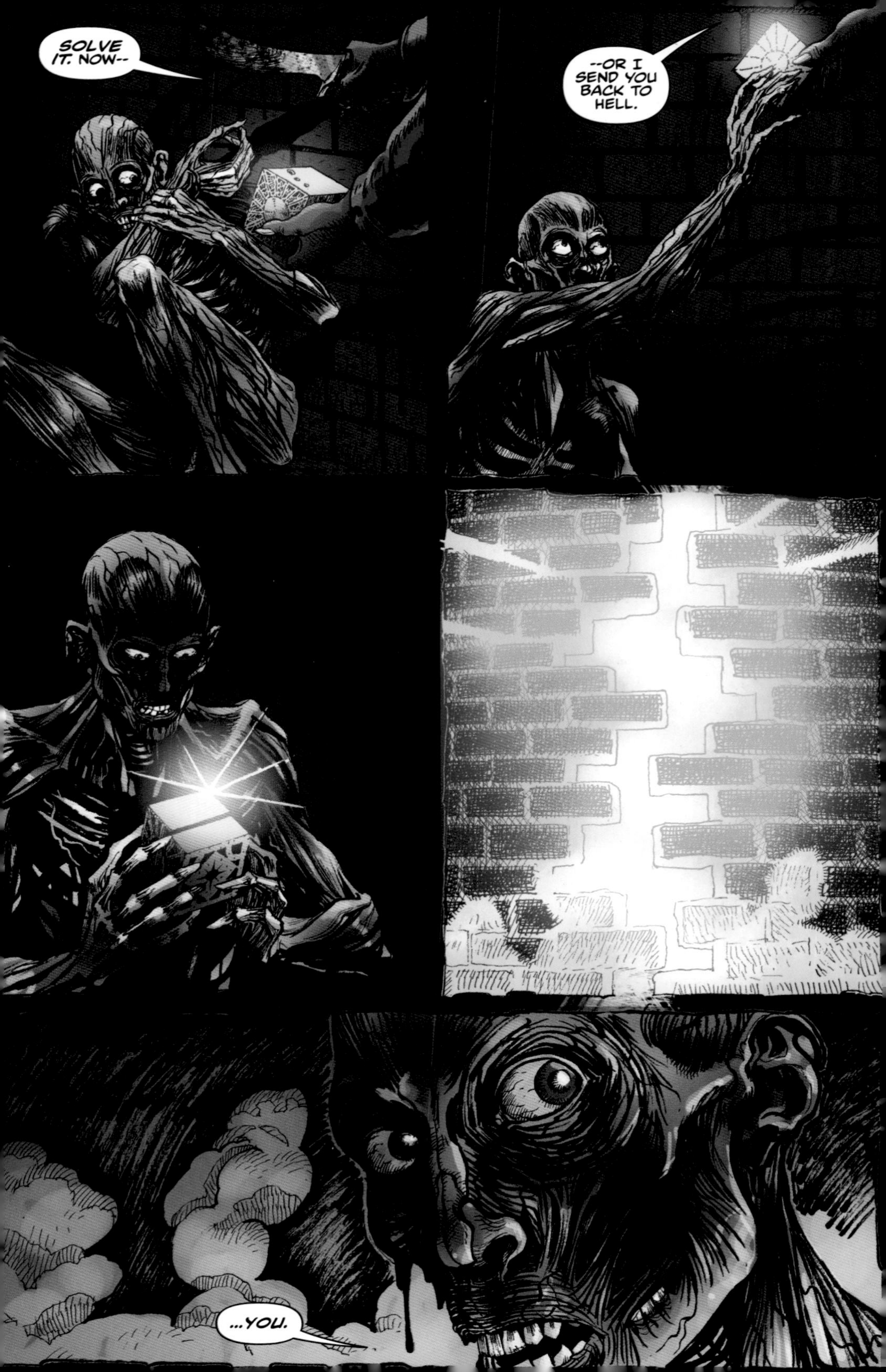
SOLVE IT. NOW--
--OR I SEND YOU BACK TO HELL.
...YOU.

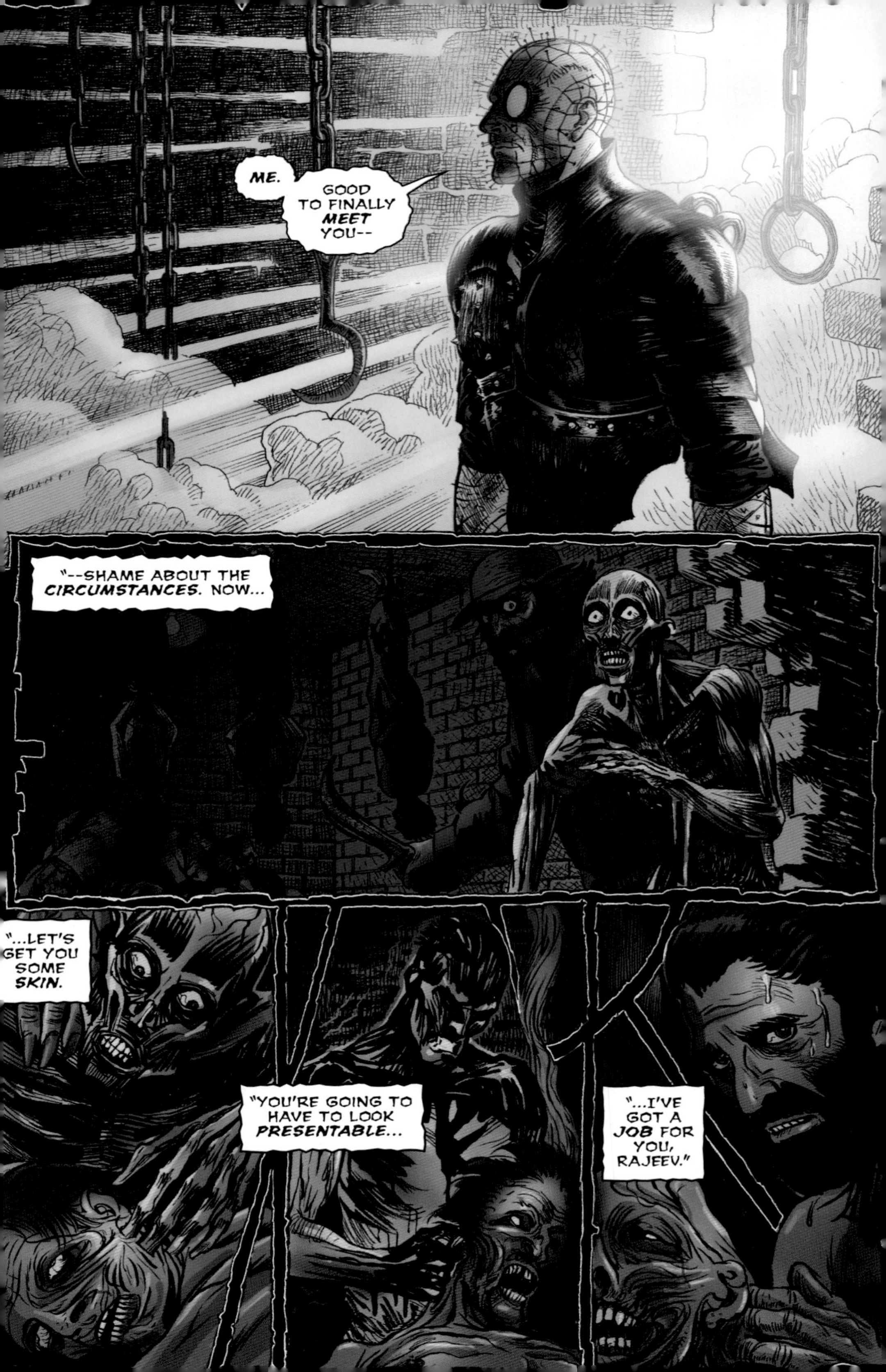

ME.
GOOD TO FINALLY MEET YOU--
"--SHAME ABOUT THE CIRCUMSTANCES. NOW...
"...LET'S GET YOU SOME SKIN.
"YOU'RE GOING TO HAVE TO LOOK PRESENTABLE...
"...I'VE GOT A JOB FOR YOU, RAJEEV."

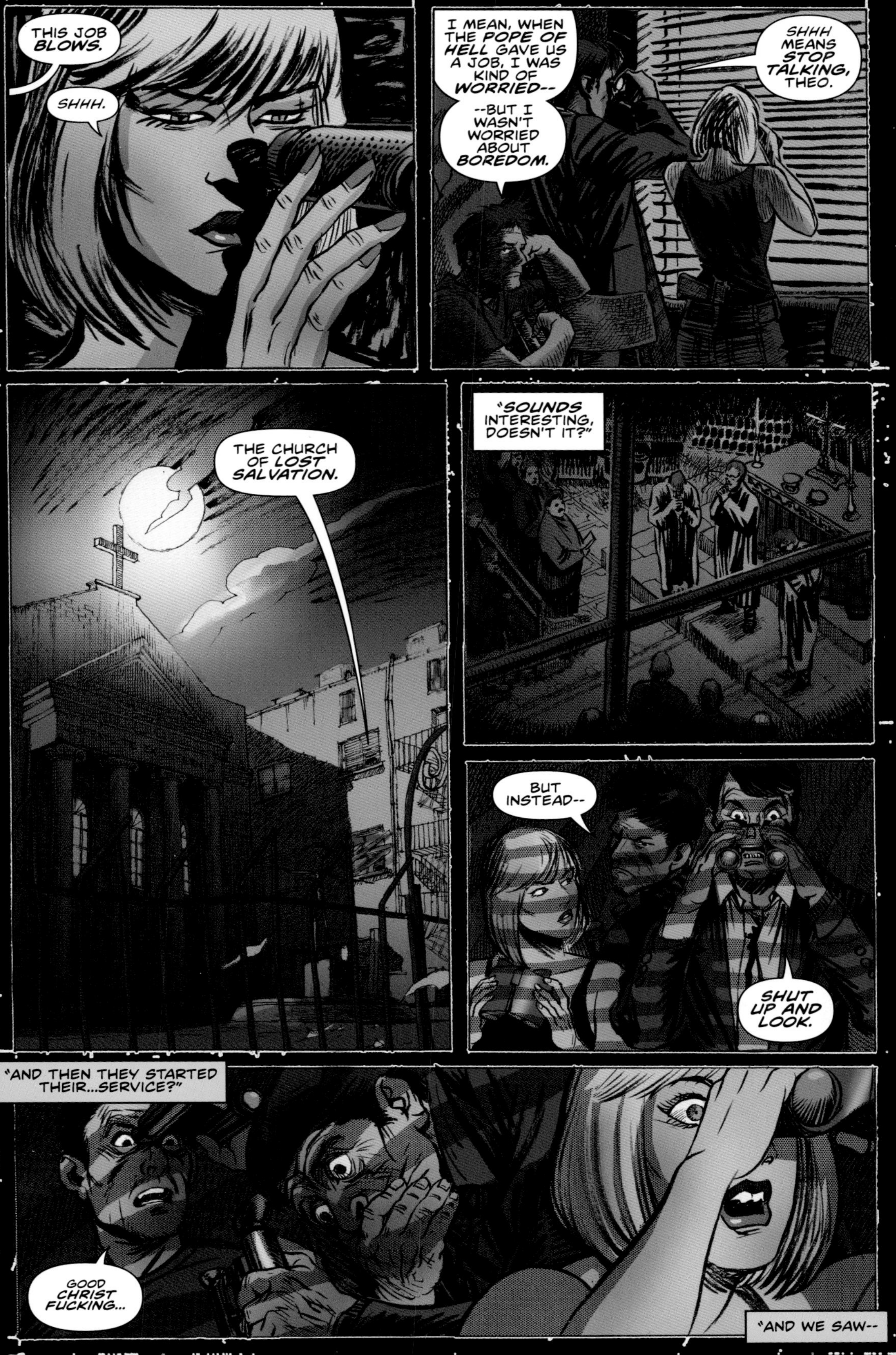

THIS JOB BLOWS.
SHHH.
I MEAN, WHEN THE POPE OF HELL GAVE US A JOB, I WAS KIND OF WORRIED--
--BUT I WASN'T WORRIED ABOUT BOREDOM.
SHHH MEANS STOP TALKING, THEO.
THE CHURCH OF LOST SALVATION.
"SOUNDS INTERESTING, DOESN'T IT?"
BUT INSTEAD--
SHUT UP AND LOOK.
"AND THEN THEY STARTED THEIR...SERVICE?"
GOOD CHRIST FUCKING...
"AND WE SAW--

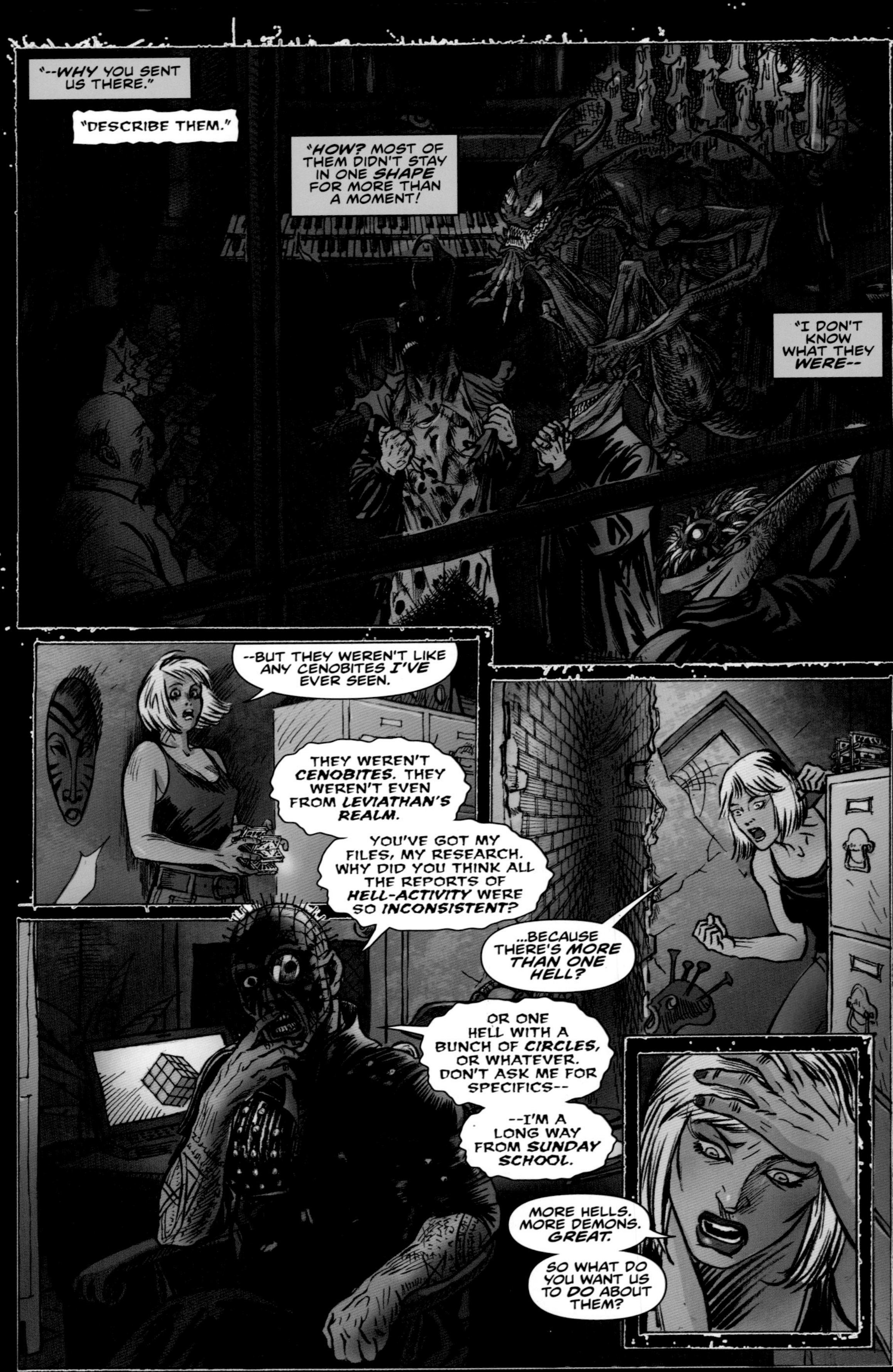
"--WHY YOU SENT US THERE."
"DESCRIBE THEM."
"HOW? MOST OF THEM DIDN'T STAY IN ONE SHAPE FOR MORE THAN A MOMENT!
"I DON'T KNOW WHAT THEY WERE--
--BUT THEY WEREN'T LIKE ANY CENOBITES I'VE EVER SEEN.
THEY WEREN'T CENOBITES. THEY WEREN'T EVEN FROM LEVIATHAN'S REALM.
YOU'VE GOT MY FILES, MY RESEARCH. WHY DID YOU THINK ALL THE REPORTS OF HELL-ACTIVITY WERE SO INCONSISTENT?
...BECAUSE THERE'S MORE THAN ONE HELL?
OR ONE HELL WITH A BUNCH OF CIRCLES, OR WHATEVER. DON'T ASK ME FOR SPECIFICS--
--I'M A LONG WAY FROM SUNDAY SCHOOL.
MORE HELLS. MORE DEMONS. GREAT.
SO WHAT DO YOU WANT US TO DO ABOUT THEM?

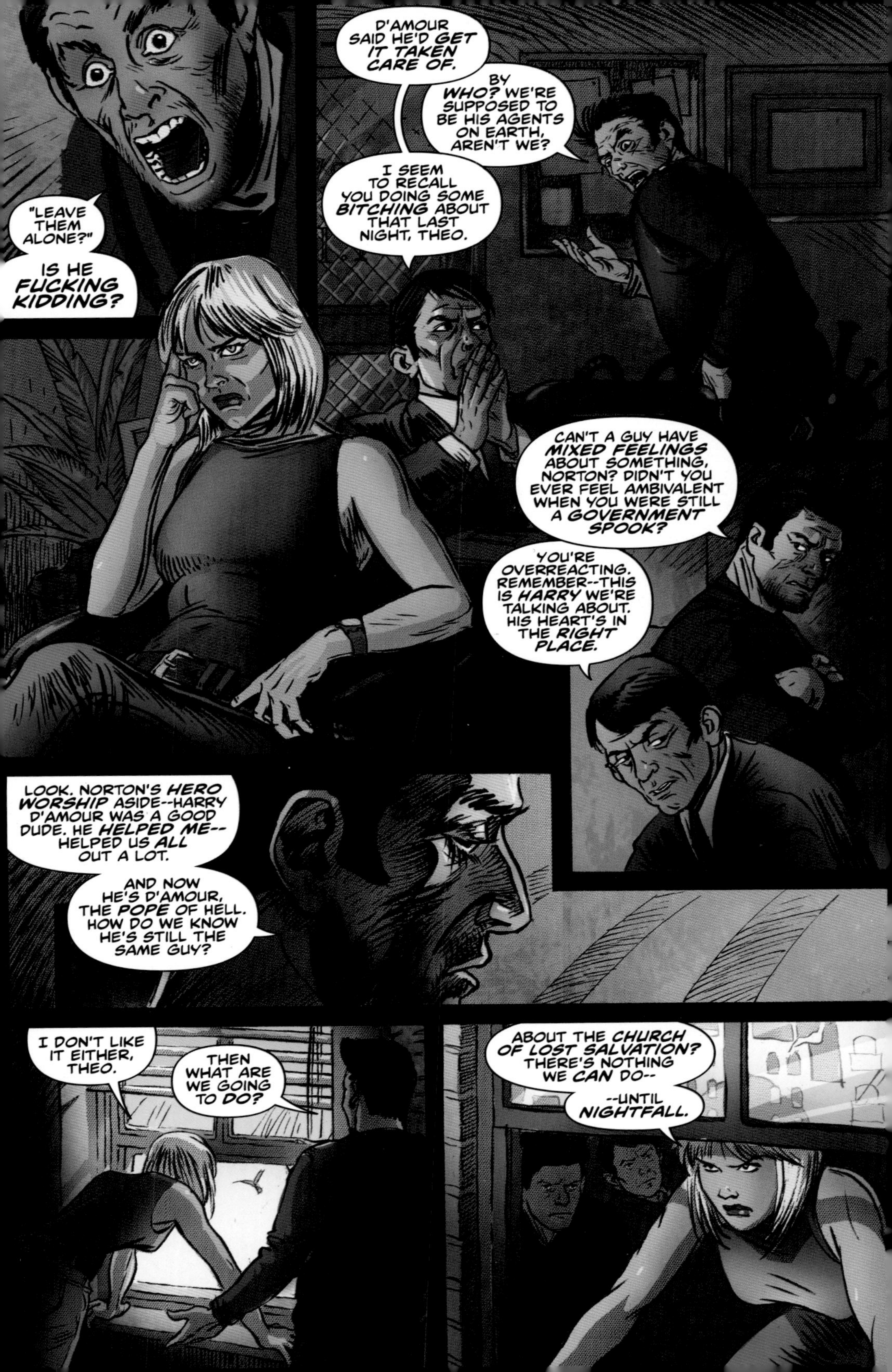
"LEAVE THEM ALONE?"
IS HE FUCKING KIDDING?
D'AMOUR SAID HE'D GET IT TAKEN CARE OF.
BY WHO? WE'RE SUPPOSED TO BE HIS AGENTS ON EARTH, AREN'T WE?
I SEEM TO RECALL YOU DOING SOME BITCHING ABOUT THAT LAST NIGHT, THEO.
CAN'T A GUY HAVE MIXED FEELINGS ABOUT SOMETHING, NORTON? DIDN'T YOU EVER FEEL AMBIVALENT WHEN YOU WERE STILL A GOVERNMENT SPOOK?
YOU'RE OVERREACTING. REMEMBER--THIS IS HARRY WE'RE TALKING ABOUT. HIS HEART'S IN THE RIGHT PLACE.
LOOK. NORTON'S HERO WORSHIP ASIDE--HARRY D'AMOUR WAS A GOOD DUDE. HE HELPED ME--HELPED US ALL OUT A LOT.
AND NOW HE'S D'AMOUR, THE POPE OF HELL. HOW DO WE KNOW HE'S STILL THE SAME GUY?
I DON'T LIKE IT EITHER, THEO.
THEN WHAT ARE WE GOING TO DO?
ABOUT THE CHURCH OF LOST SALVATION? THERE'S NOTHING WE CAN DO--
--UNTIL NIGHTFALL.

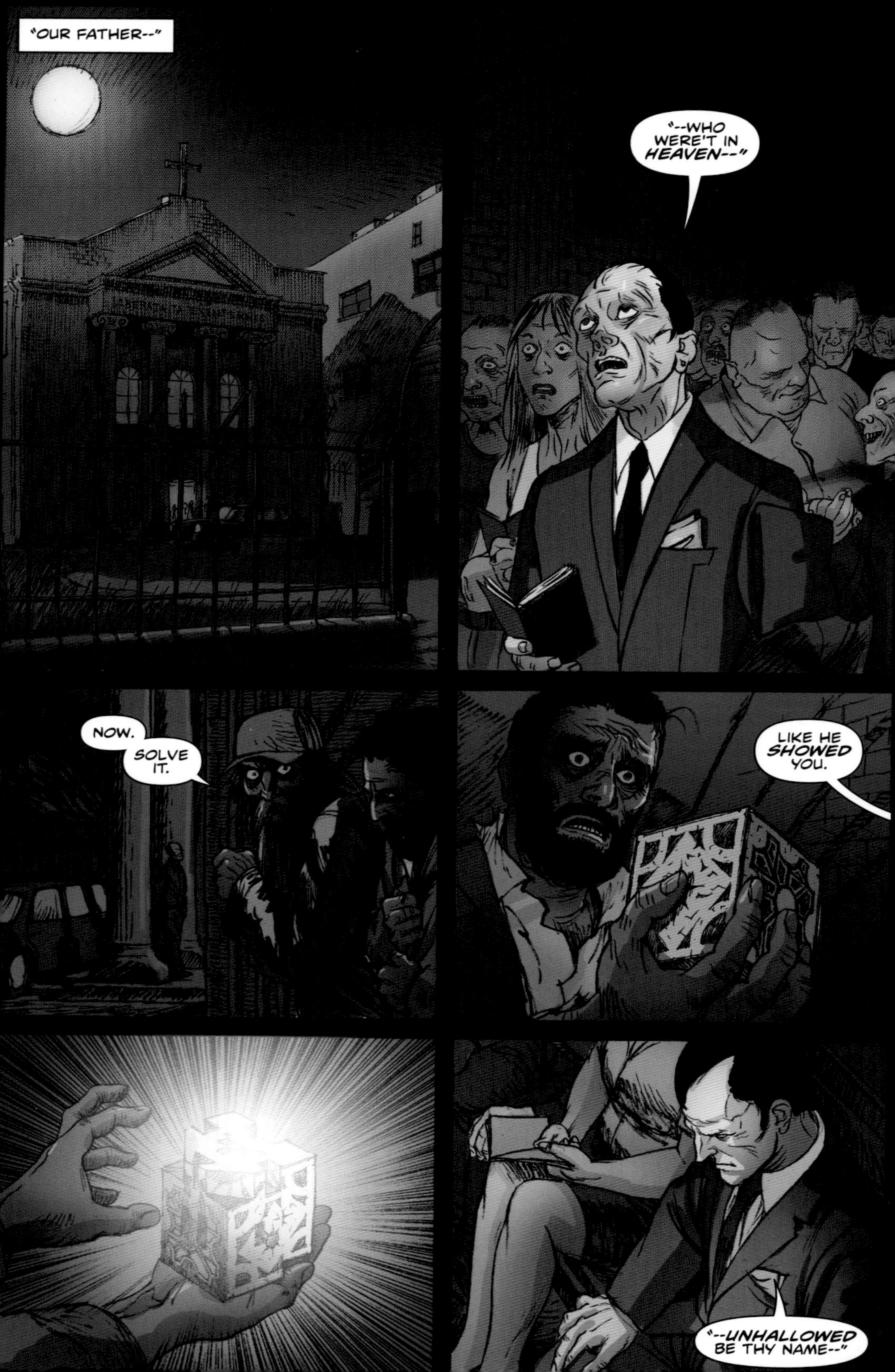
"OUR FATHER--"
"--WHO WERE'T IN HEAVEN--"
NOW. SOLVE IT.
LIKE HE SHOWED YOU.
"--UNHALLOWED BE THY NAME--"

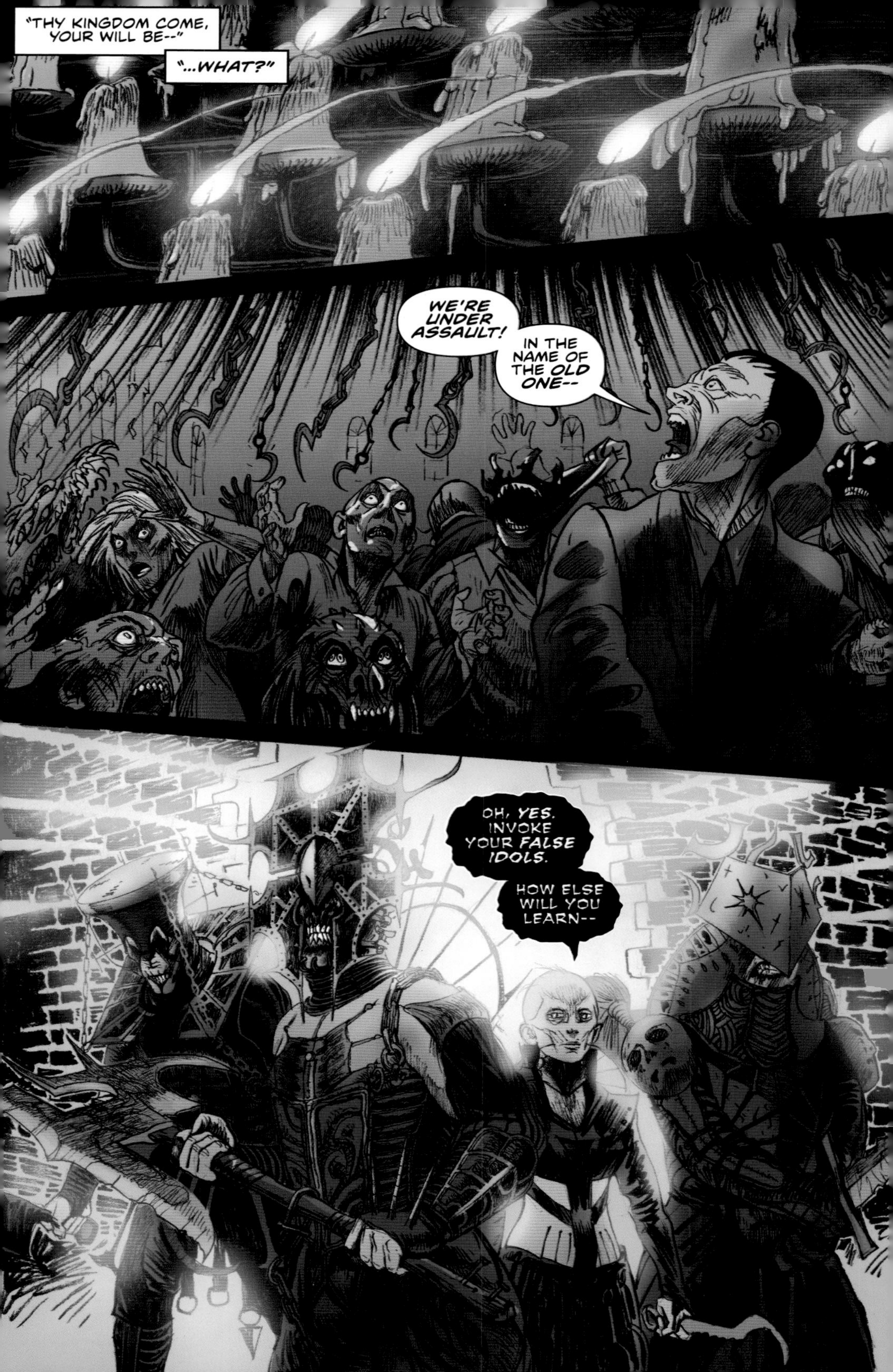
"THY KINGDOM COME, YOUR WILL BE--"
"...WHAT?"
WE'RE UNDER ASSAULT!
IN THE NAME OF THE OLD ONE--
OH, YES. INVOKE YOUR FALSE IDOLS.
HOW ELSE WILL YOU LEARN--

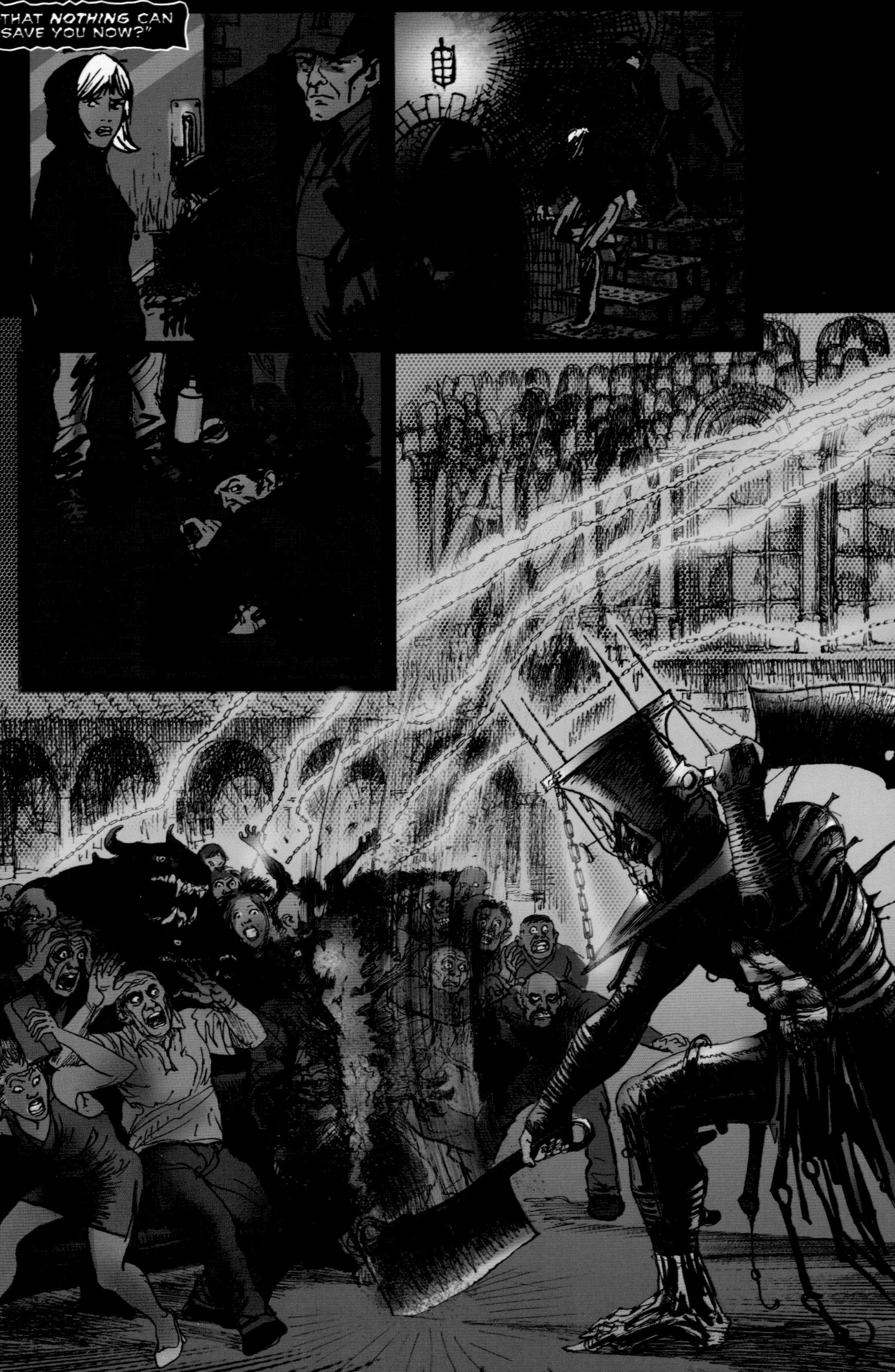
"THAT NOTHING CAN SAVE YOU NOW?"

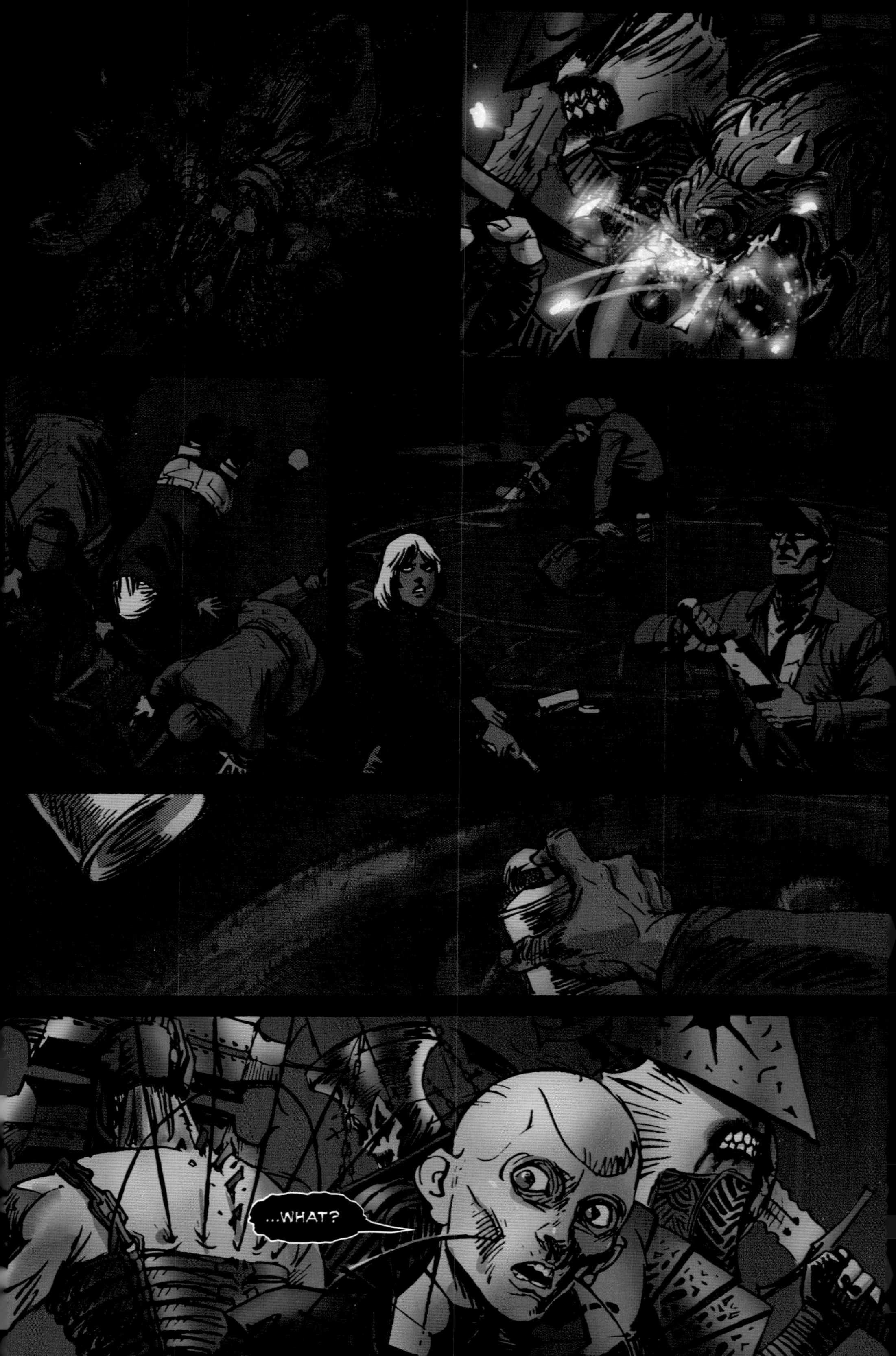
...WHAT?

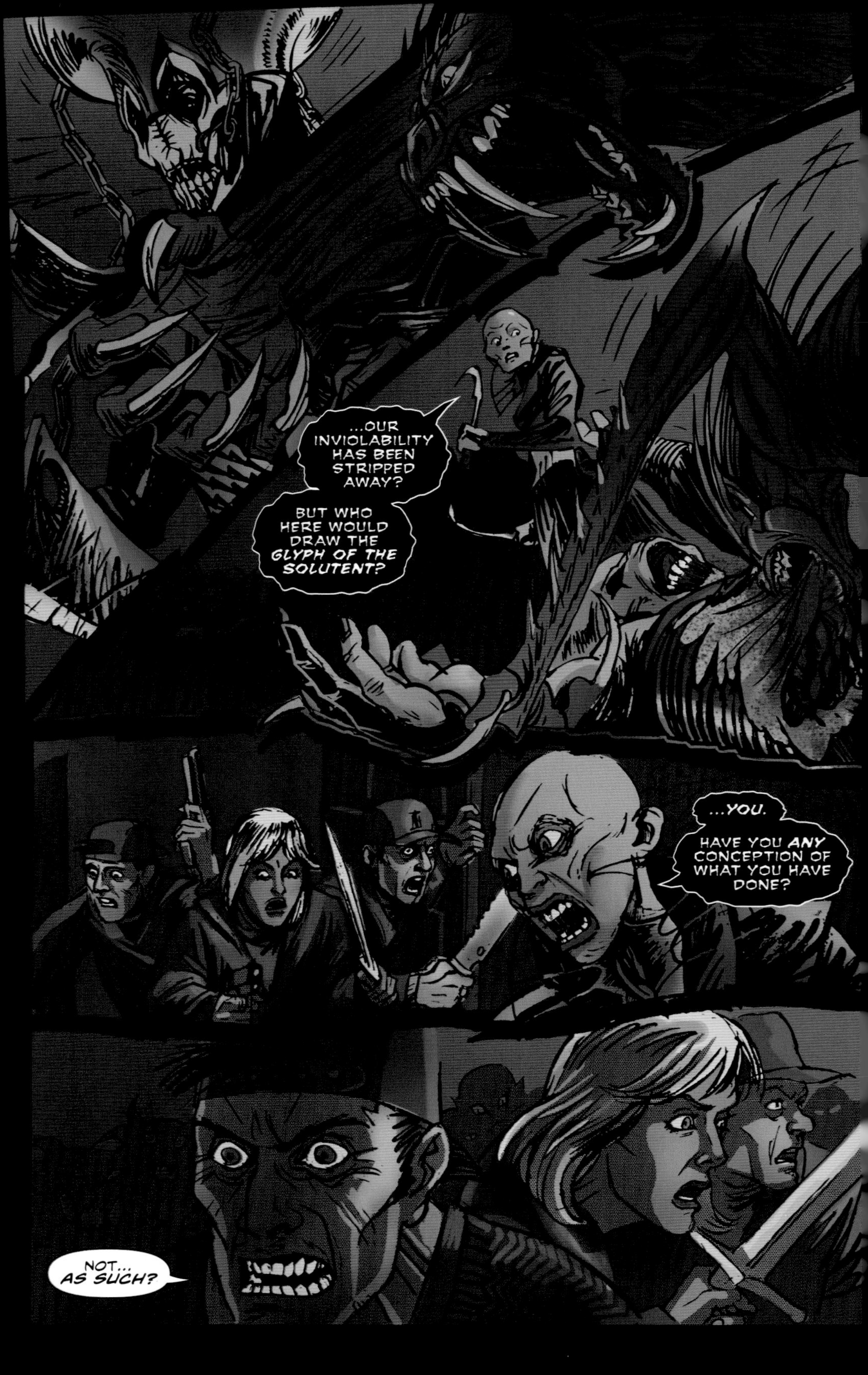
...OUR INVIOLABILITY HAS BEEN STRIPPED AWAY?
BUT WHO HERE WOULD DRAW THE *GLYPH OF THE SOLUTENT?*
...*YOU.*
HAVE YOU *ANY* CONCEPTION OF WHAT YOU HAVE DONE?
NOT... AS SUCH?

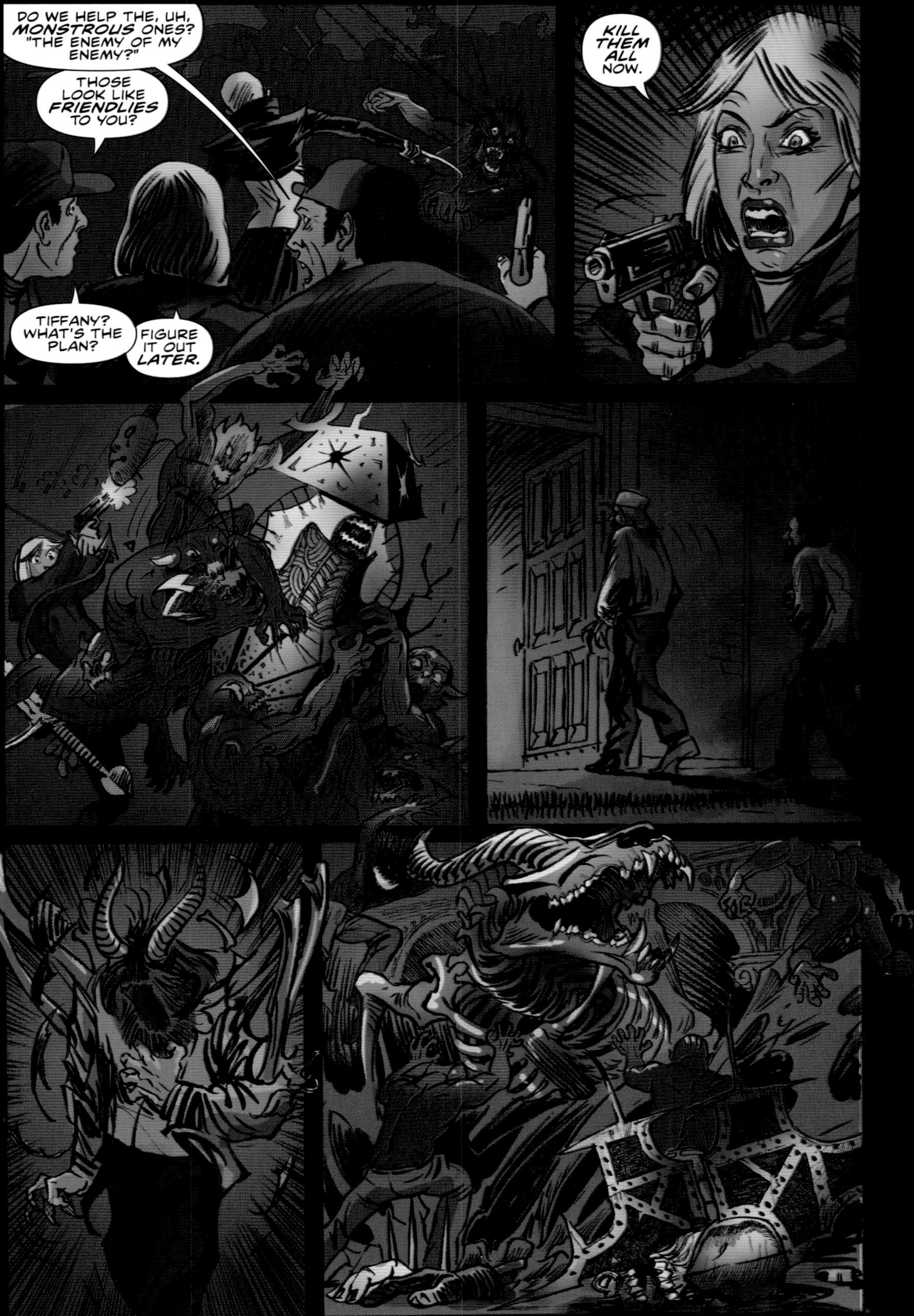
DO WE HELP THE, UH, MONSTROUS ONES? "THE ENEMY OF MY ENEMY?"
THOSE LOOK LIKE FRIENDLIES TO YOU?
TIFFANY? WHAT'S THE PLAN?
FIGURE IT OUT LATER.
KILL THEM ALL NOW.

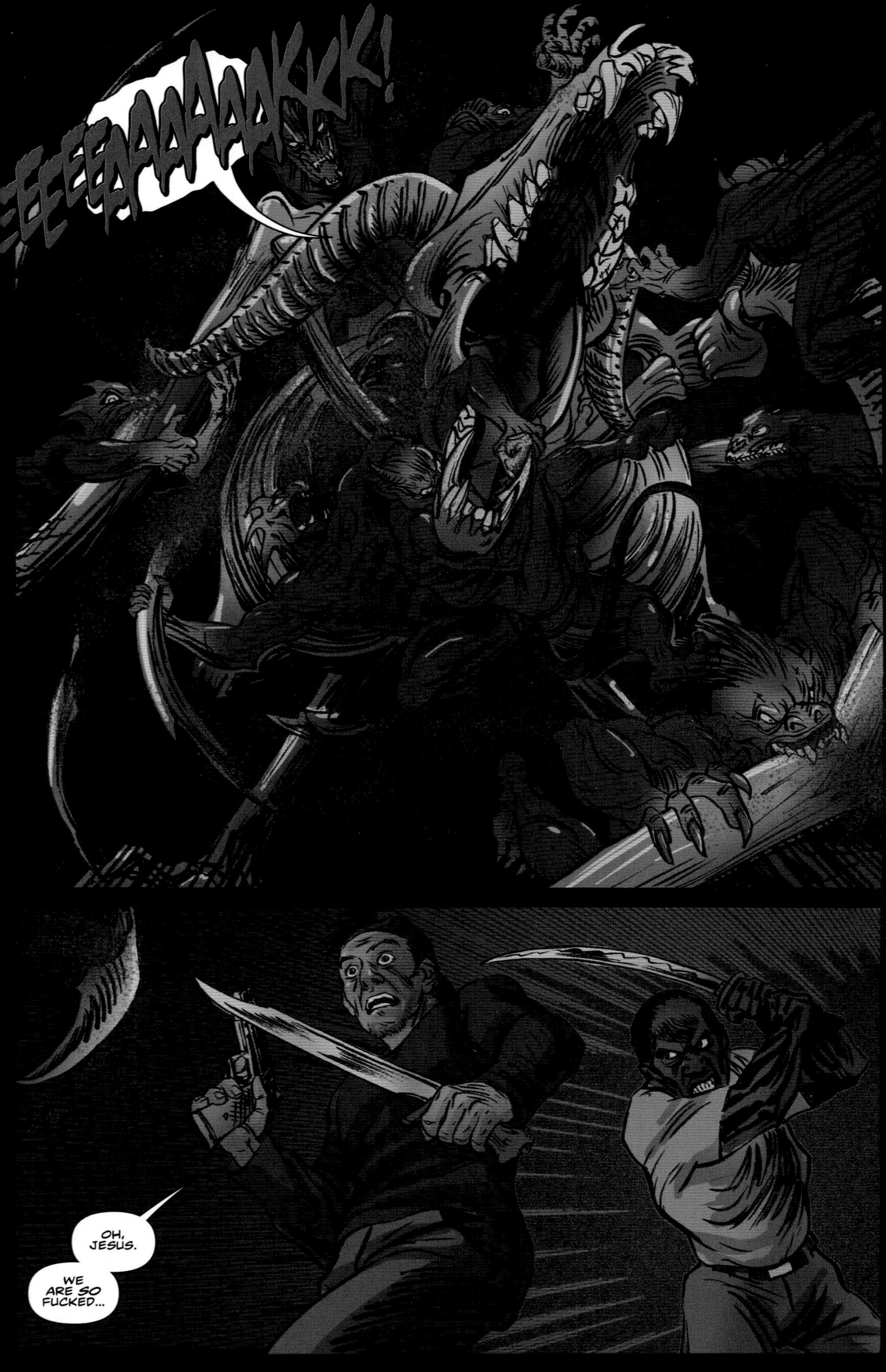
EEEEEAAAAAAKKK!
OH, JESUS.
WE ARE SO FUCKED...

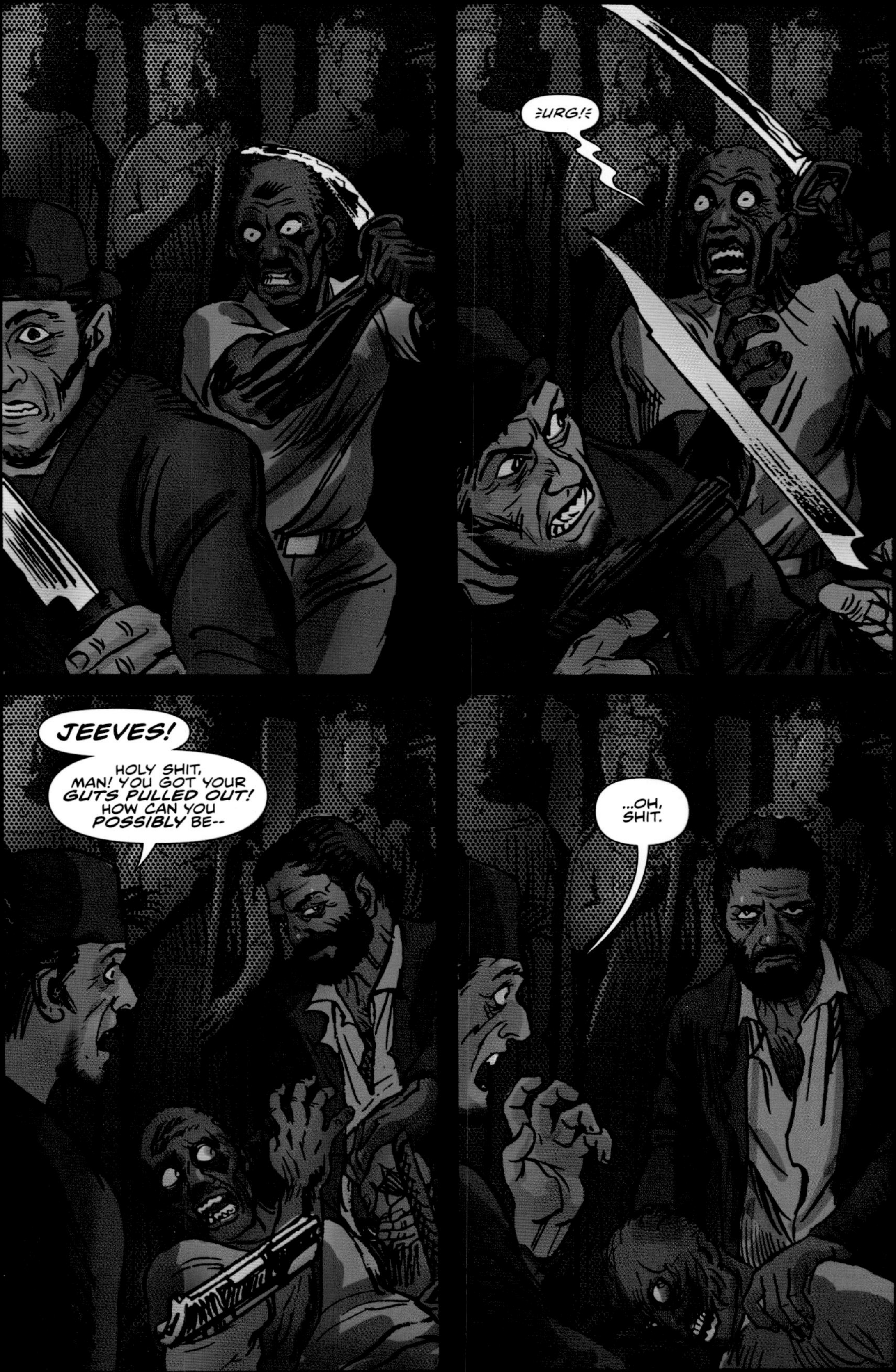
URG!
JEEVES!
HOLY SHIT, MAN! YOU GOT YOUR GUTS PULLED OUT! HOW CAN YOU POSSIBLY BE--
...OH, SHIT.

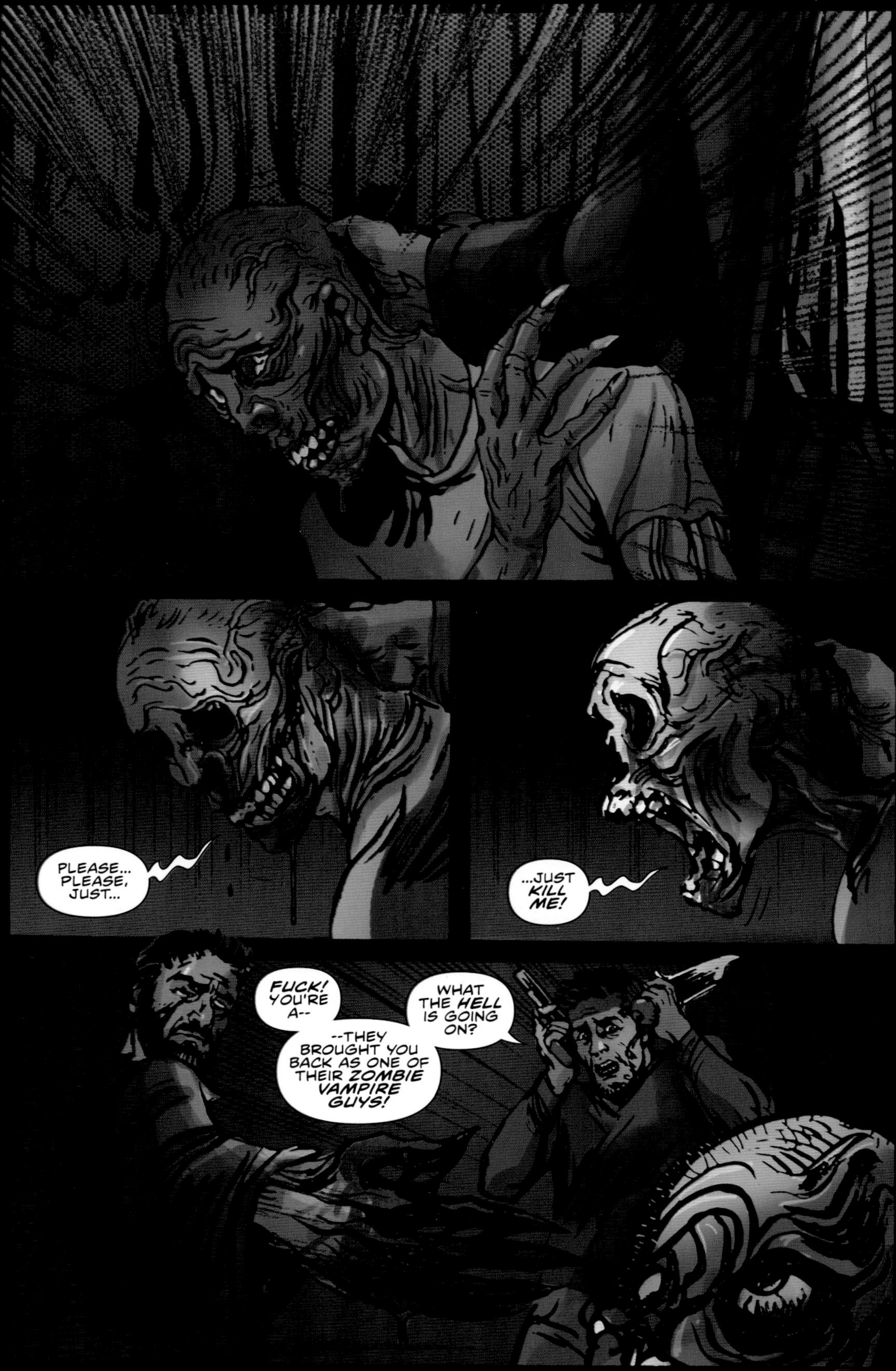
PLEASE... PLEASE, JUST...
...JUST KILL ME!
FUCK! YOU'RE A--
WHAT THE HELL IS GOING ON?
--THEY BROUGHT YOU BACK AS ONE OF THEIR ZOMBIE VAMPIRE GUYS!

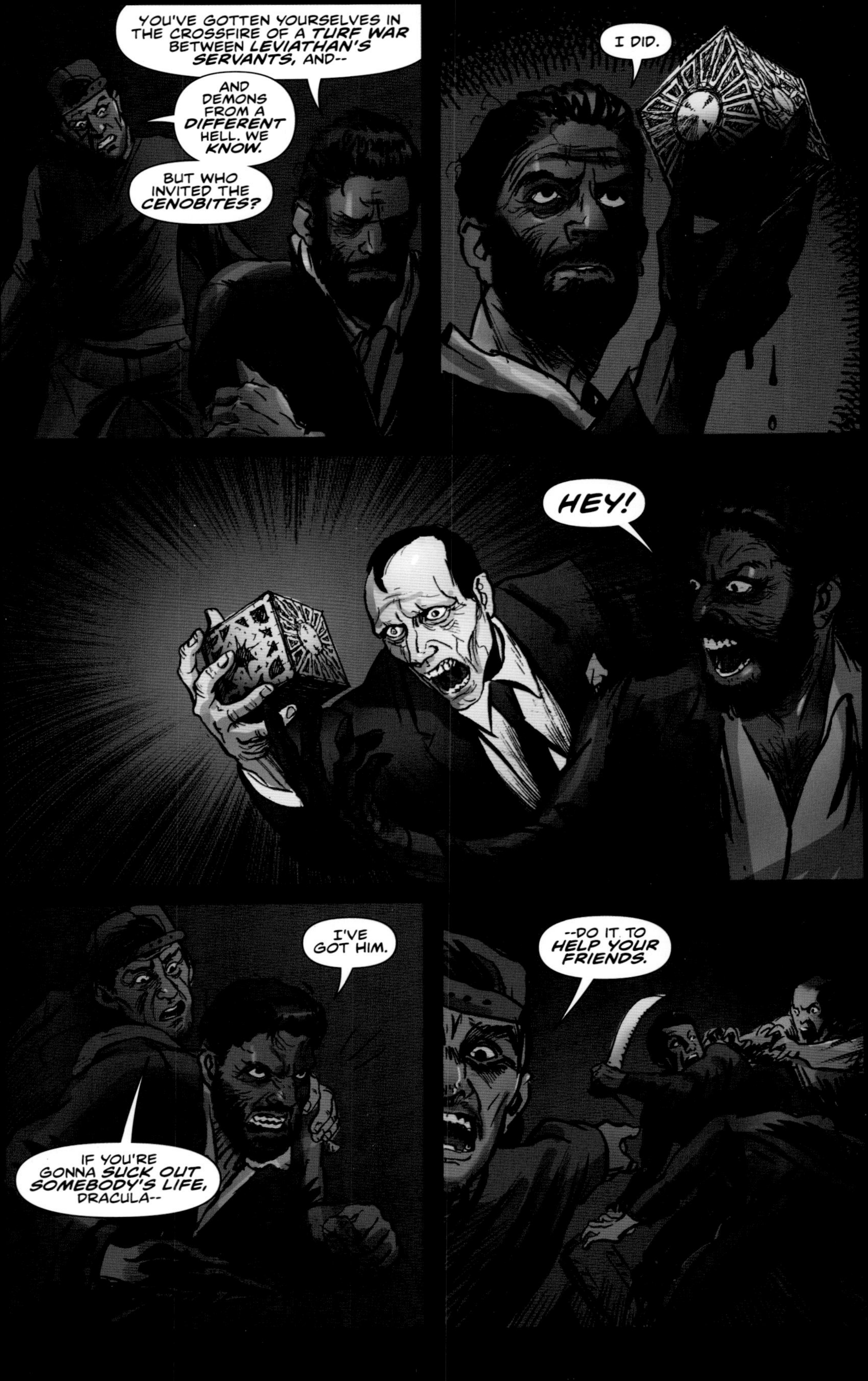
YOU'VE GOTTEN YOURSELVES IN THE CROSSFIRE OF A TURF WAR BETWEEN LEVIATHAN'S SERVANTS, AND--
AND DEMONS FROM A DIFFERENT HELL. WE KNOW.
BUT WHO INVITED THE CENOBITES?
I DID.
HEY!
I'VE GOT HIM.
IF YOU'RE GONNA SUCK OUT SOMEBODY'S LIFE, DRACULA--
--DO IT TO HELP YOUR FRIENDS.

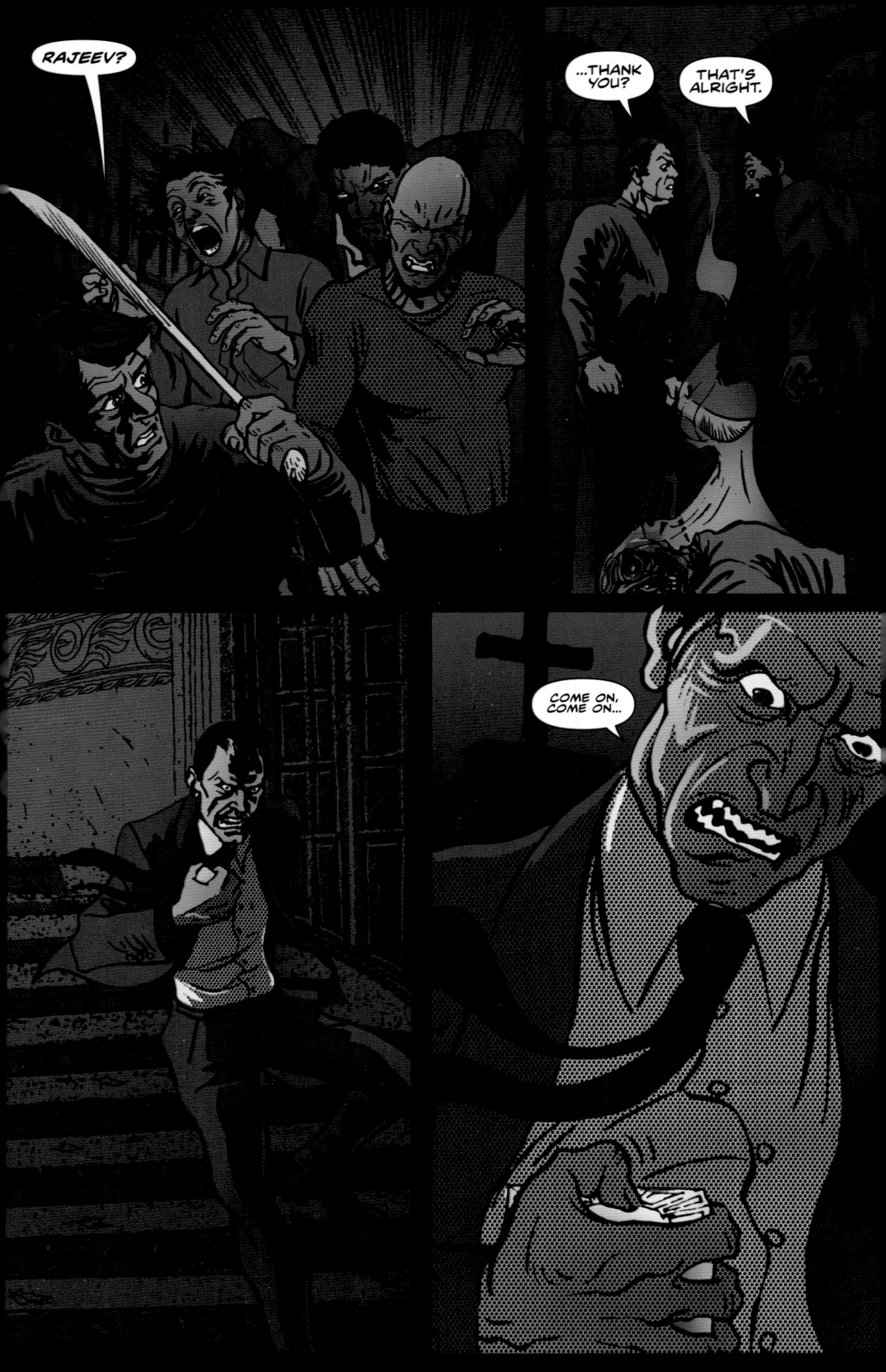
RAJEEV?
...THANK YOU?
THAT'S ALRIGHT.
COME ON, COME ON...

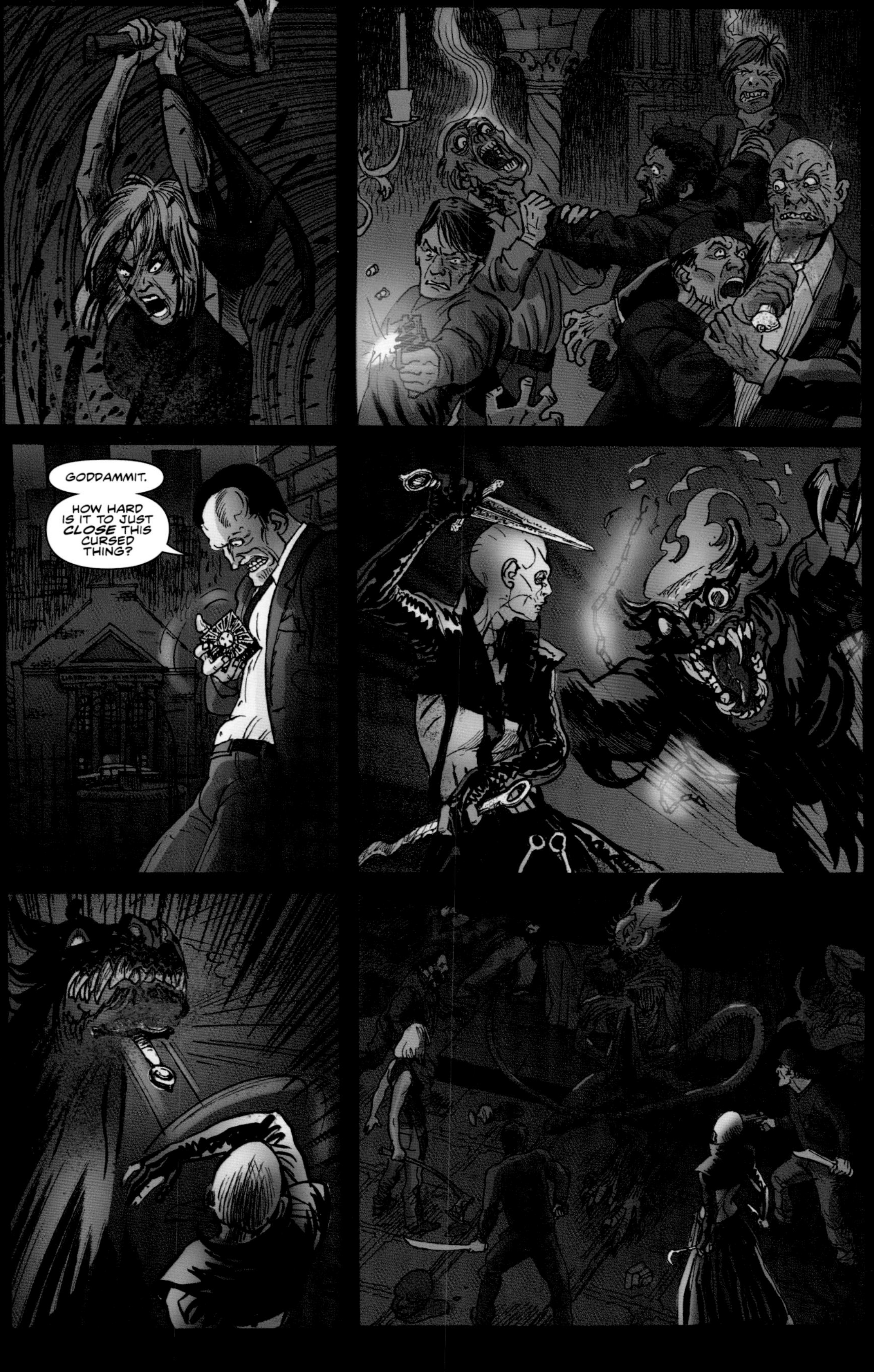
GODDAMMIT.
HOW HARD IS IT TO JUST CLOSE THIS CURSED THING?

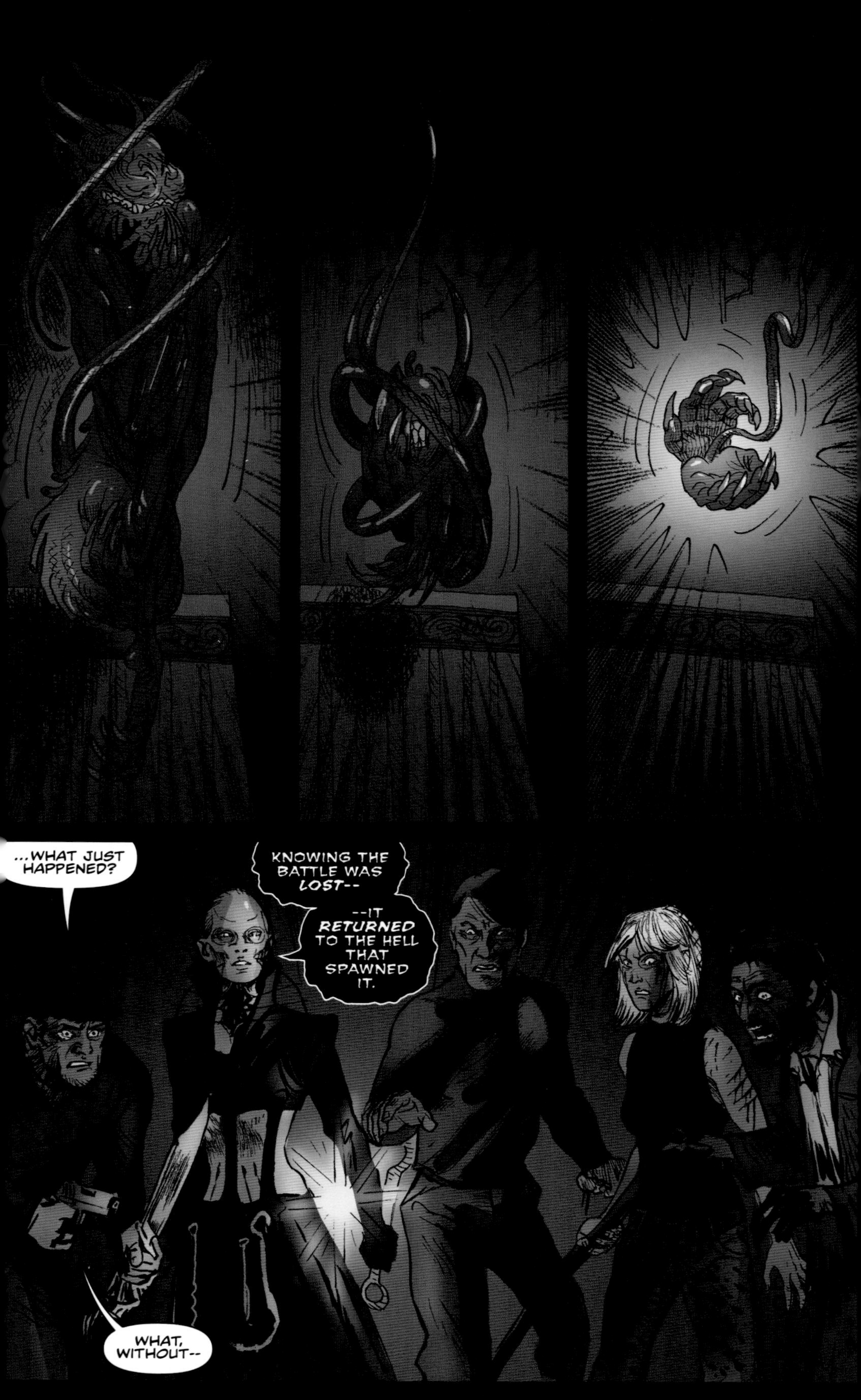
...WHAT JUST HAPPENED?
KNOWING THE BATTLE WAS LOST--
--IT RETURNED TO THE HELL THAT SPAWNED IT.
WHAT, WITHOUT--

"--A BOX?"

"I'VE NEVER HEARD OF A DEMON DOING *THAT!*"

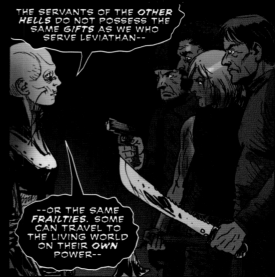

THE SERVANTS OF THE *OTHER HELLS* DO NOT POSSESS THE SAME *GIFTS* AS WE WHO SERVE LEVIATHAN--

--OR THE SAME *FRAILTIES.* SOME CAN TRAVEL TO THE LIVING WORLD ON THEIR *OWN* POWER--

"--AND TRAVEL *BACK* AS WELL."

...WAIT!

WHERE'D SHE GO?

ONE OF THE CULTISTS GOT THE *PUZZLE* FROM ME. HE MUST HAVE *CLOSED THE GATE.*

RAJEEV... *HOW ARE YOU ALIVE?*

D'AMOUR. D'AMOUR BROUGHT ME BACK. HE GAVE ME A *PUZZLE* TO SOLVE AT SPECIFIC TIMES AND PLACES--

--TO GIVE THE CENOBITES *ACCESS* TO EARTH.

JESUS, THAT'S *FUCKED!*

THAT'S... THAT'S *IT.* HE'S GONE TOO *FAR.*

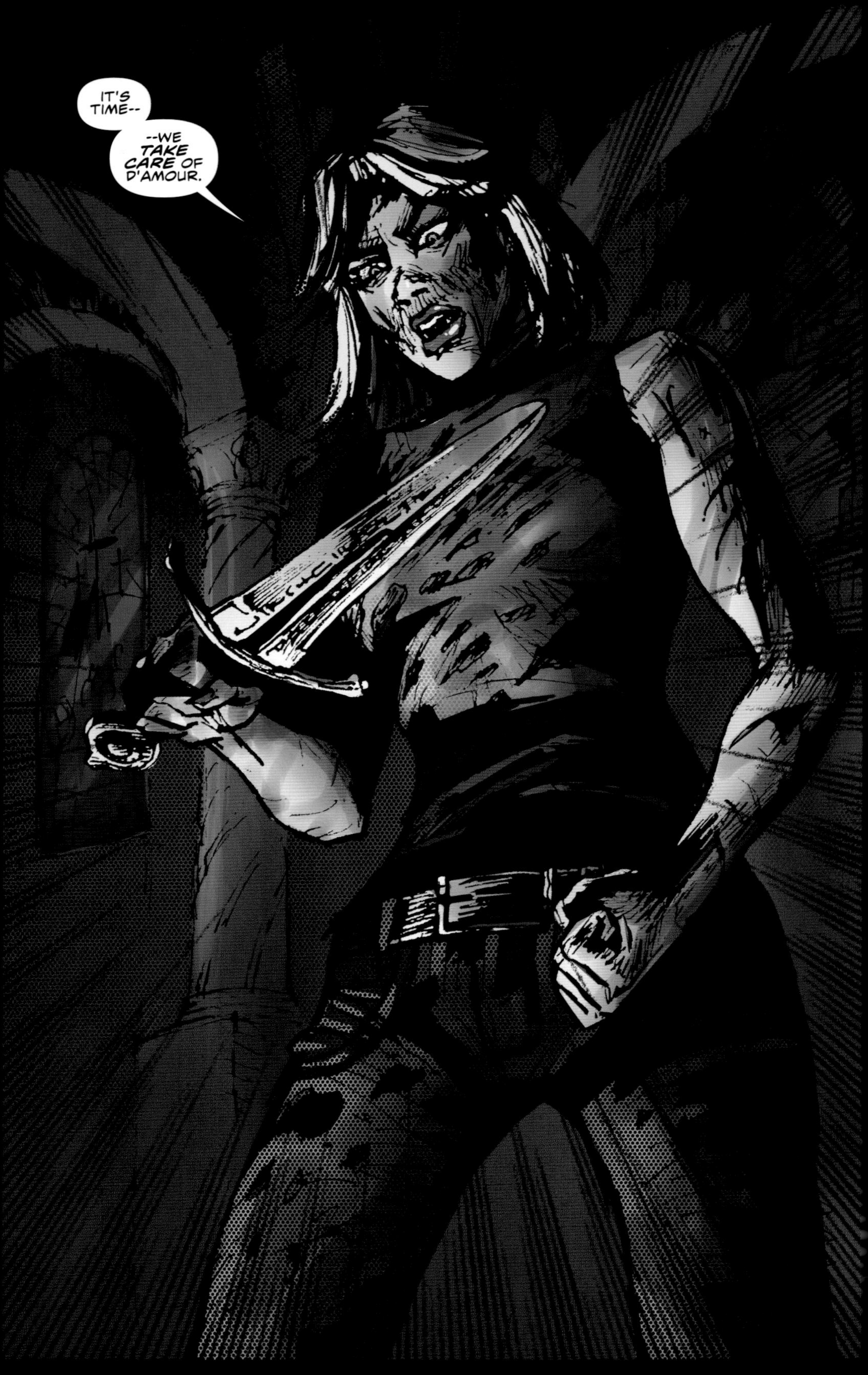
IT'S TIME--
--WE TAKE CARE OF D'AMOUR.

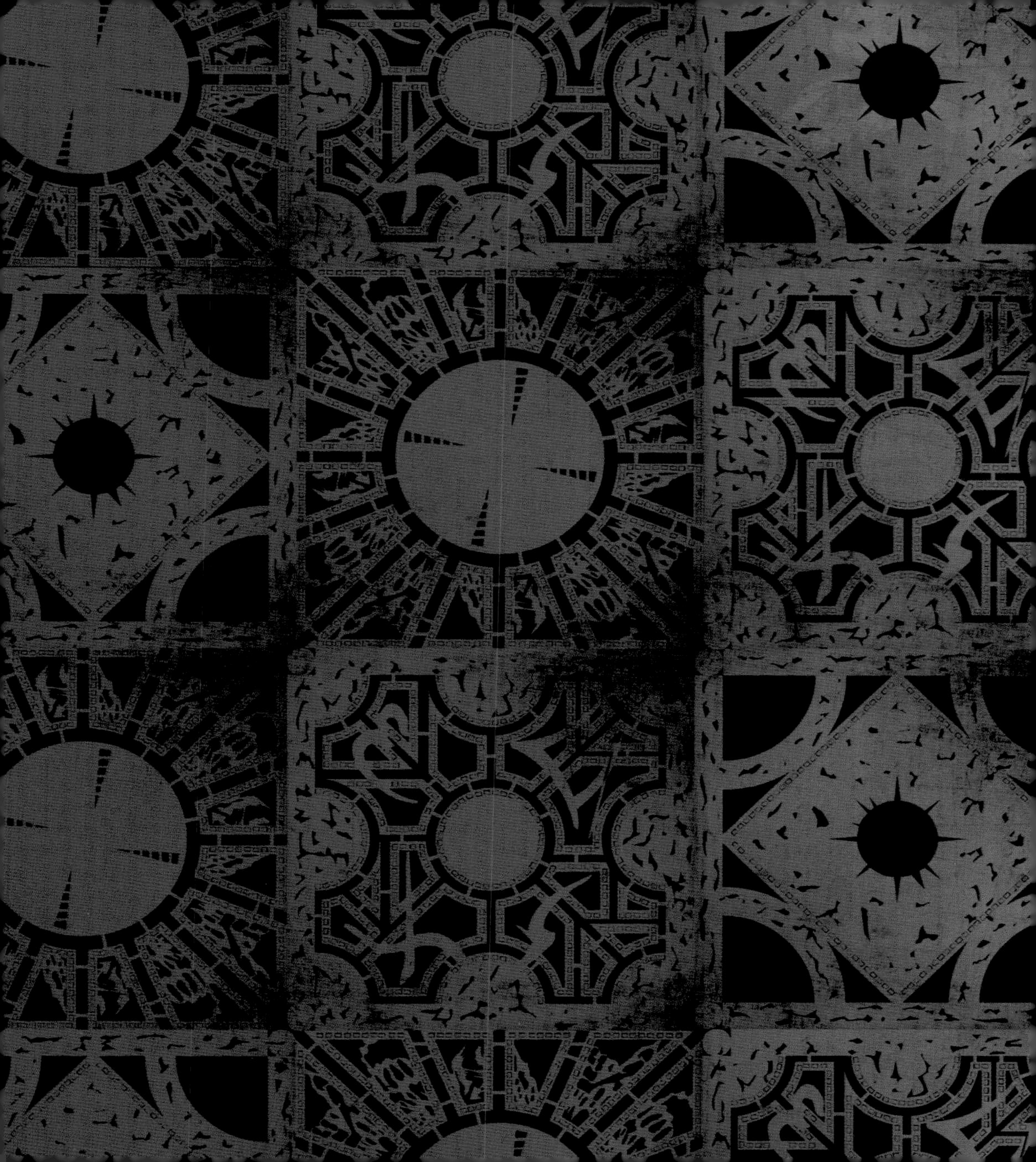

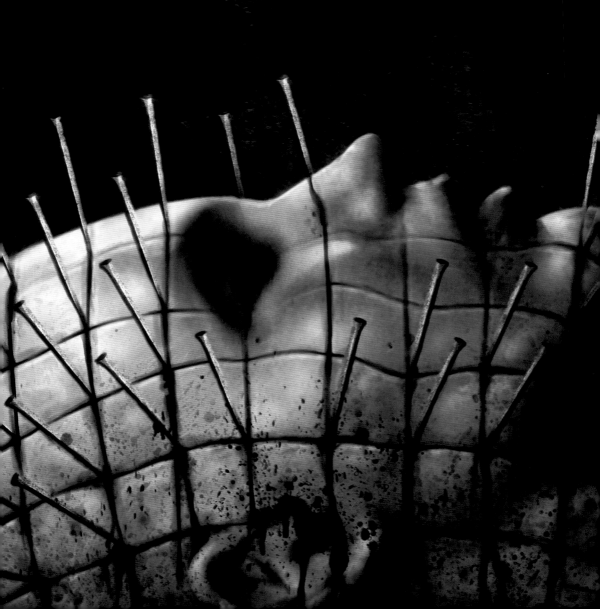

CHAPTER SIX

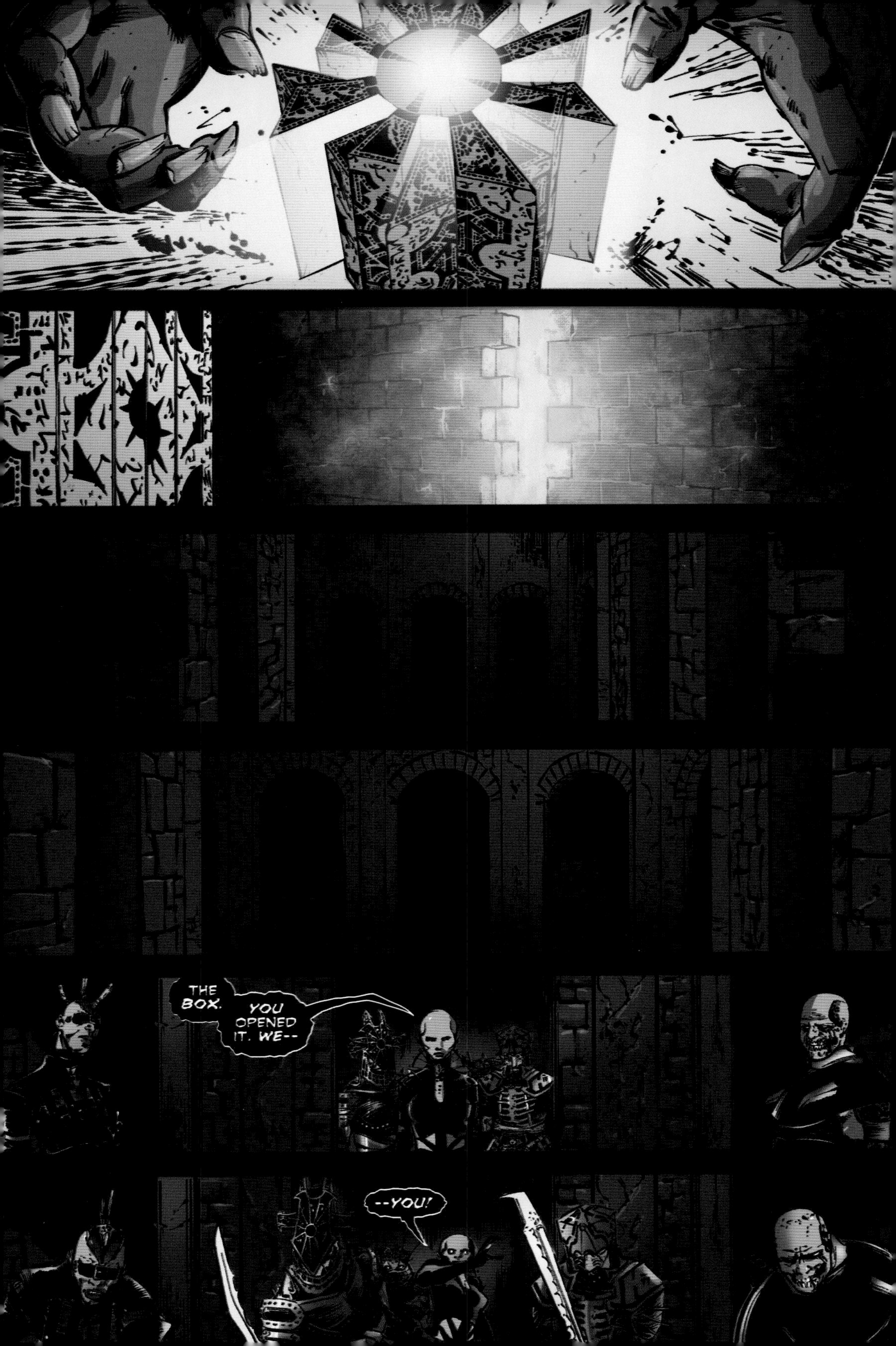
THE BOX.
YOU OPENED IT. WE--
--YOU!

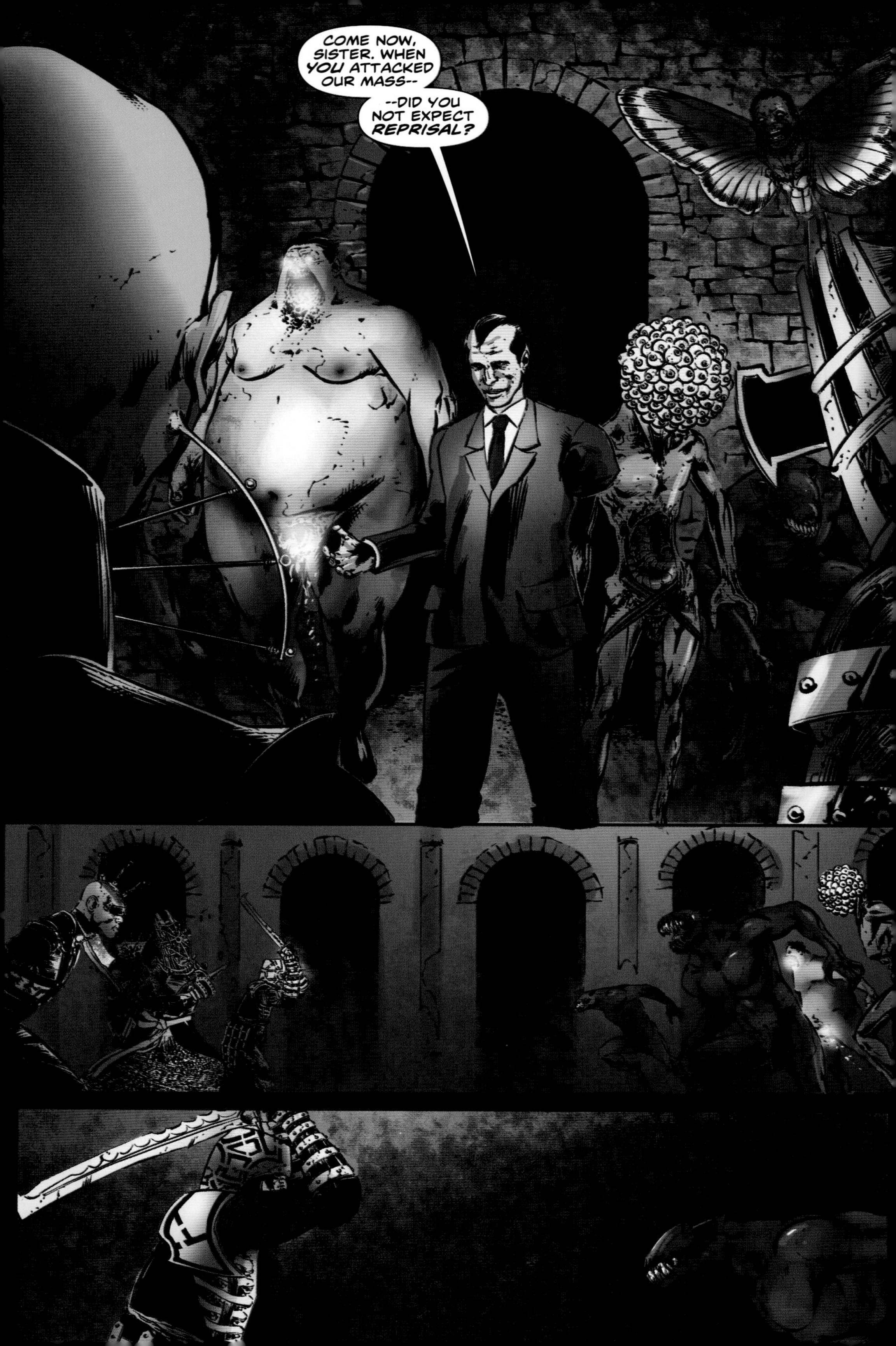
COME NOW, SISTER. WHEN YOU ATTACKED OUR MASS--
--DID YOU NOT EXPECT REPRISAL?

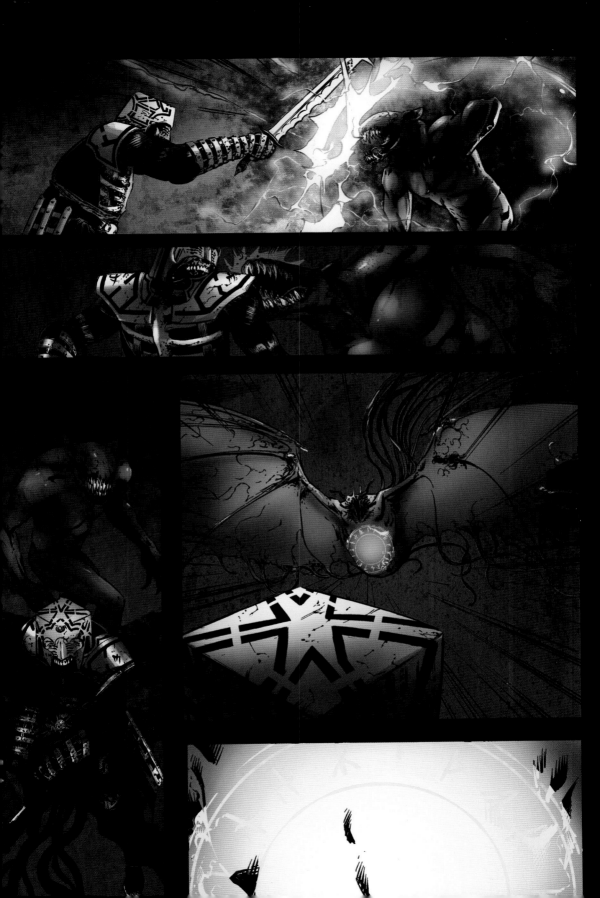

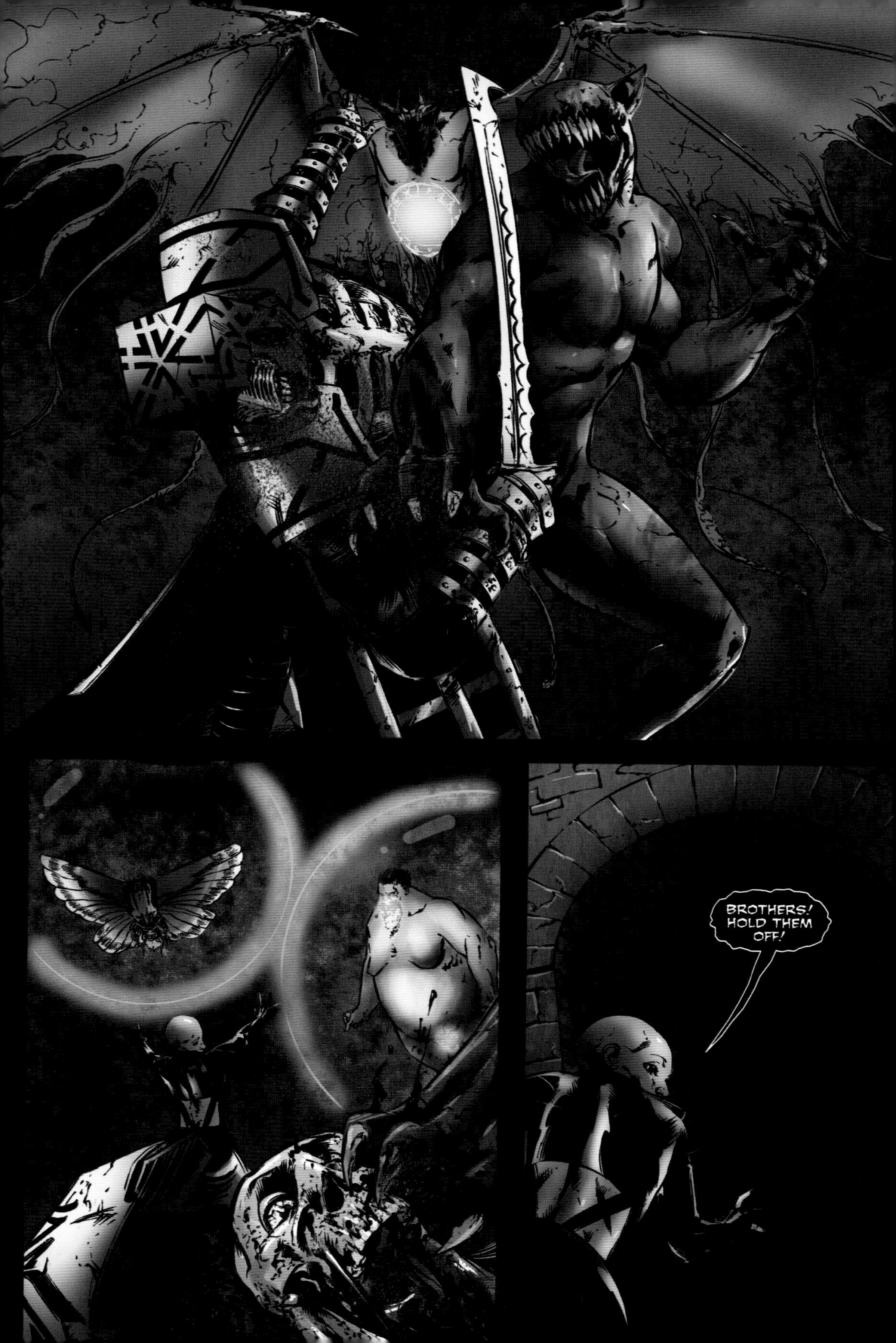
BROTHERS! HOLD THEM OFF!

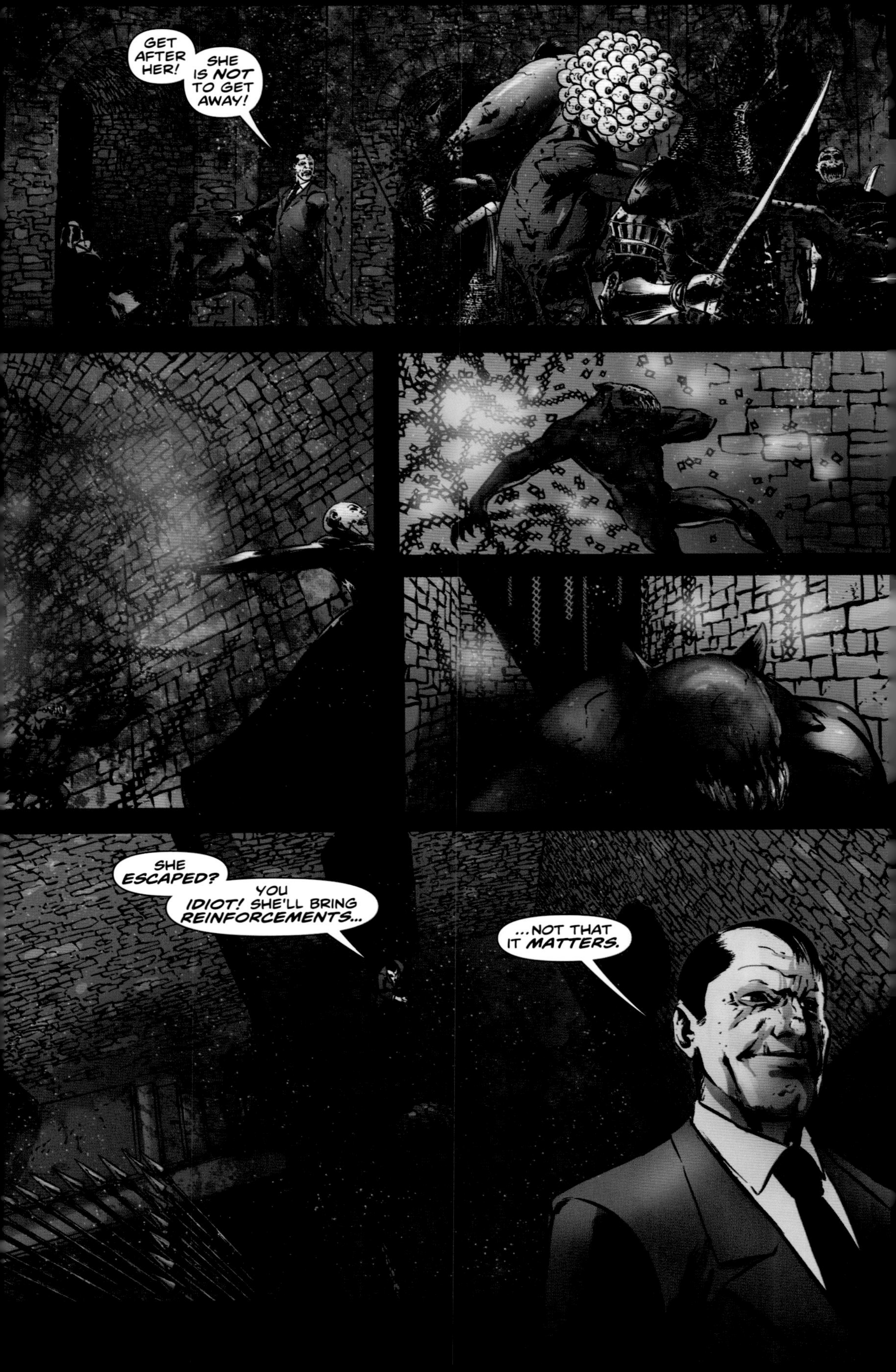
GET AFTER HER!
SHE IS NOT TO GET AWAY!
SHE ESCAPED?
YOU IDIOT! SHE'LL BRING REINFORCEMENTS...
...NOT THAT IT MATTERS.

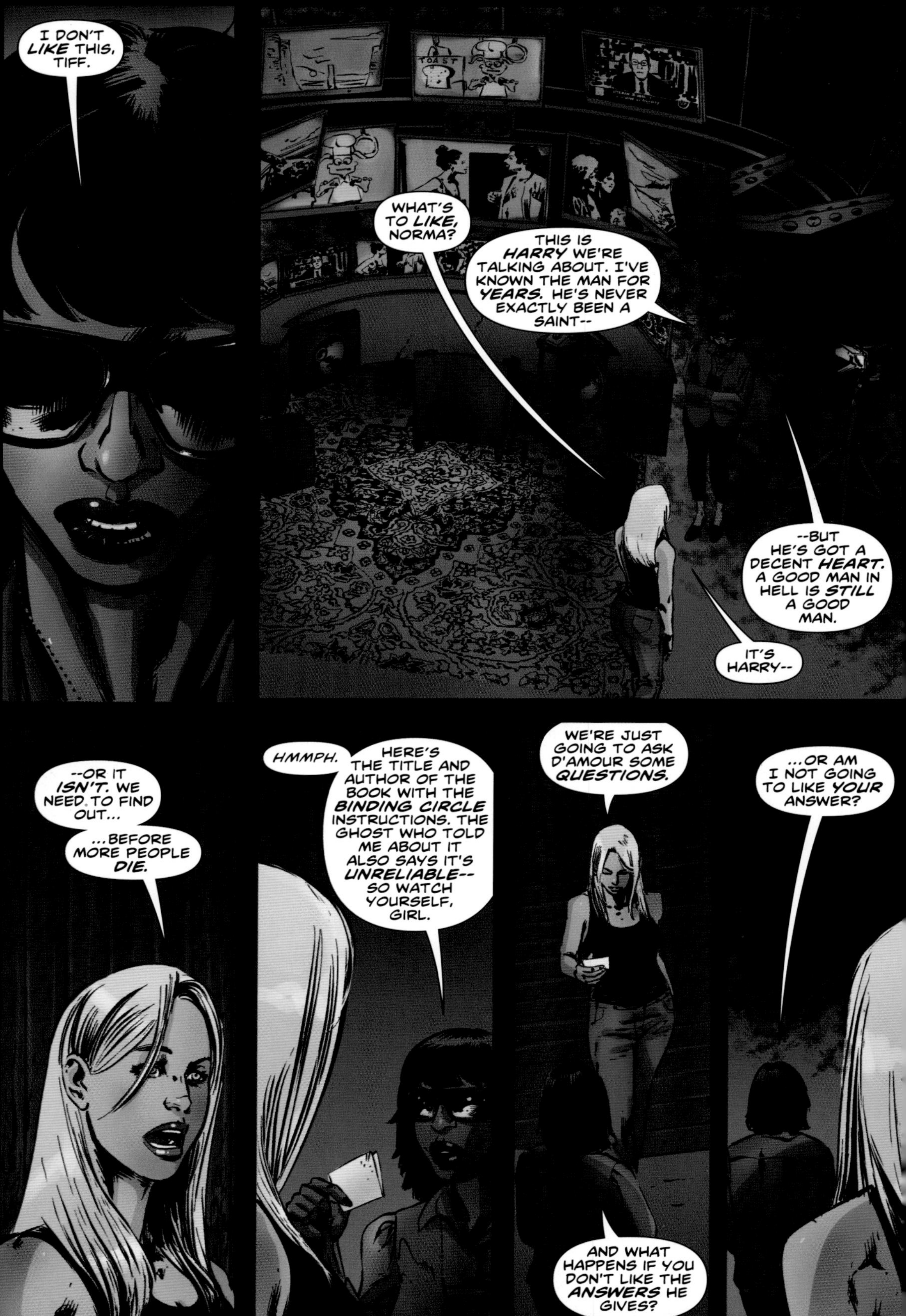

I DON'T LIKE THIS, TIFF.
WHAT'S TO LIKE, NORMA?
THIS IS HARRY WE'RE TALKING ABOUT. I'VE KNOWN THE MAN FOR YEARS. HE'S NEVER EXACTLY BEEN A SAINT--
--BUT HE'S GOT A DECENT HEART. A GOOD MAN IN HELL IS STILL A GOOD MAN.
IT'S HARRY--
--OR IT ISN'T. WE NEED TO FIND OUT...
...BEFORE MORE PEOPLE DIE.
HMMPH.
HERE'S THE TITLE AND AUTHOR OF THE BOOK WITH THE BINDING CIRCLE INSTRUCTIONS. THE GHOST WHO TOLD ME ABOUT IT ALSO SAYS IT'S UNRELIABLE-- SO WATCH YOURSELF, GIRL.
WE'RE JUST GOING TO ASK D'AMOUR SOME QUESTIONS.
AND WHAT HAPPENS IF YOU DON'T LIKE THE ANSWERS HE GIVES?
...OR AM I NOT GOING TO LIKE YOUR ANSWER?

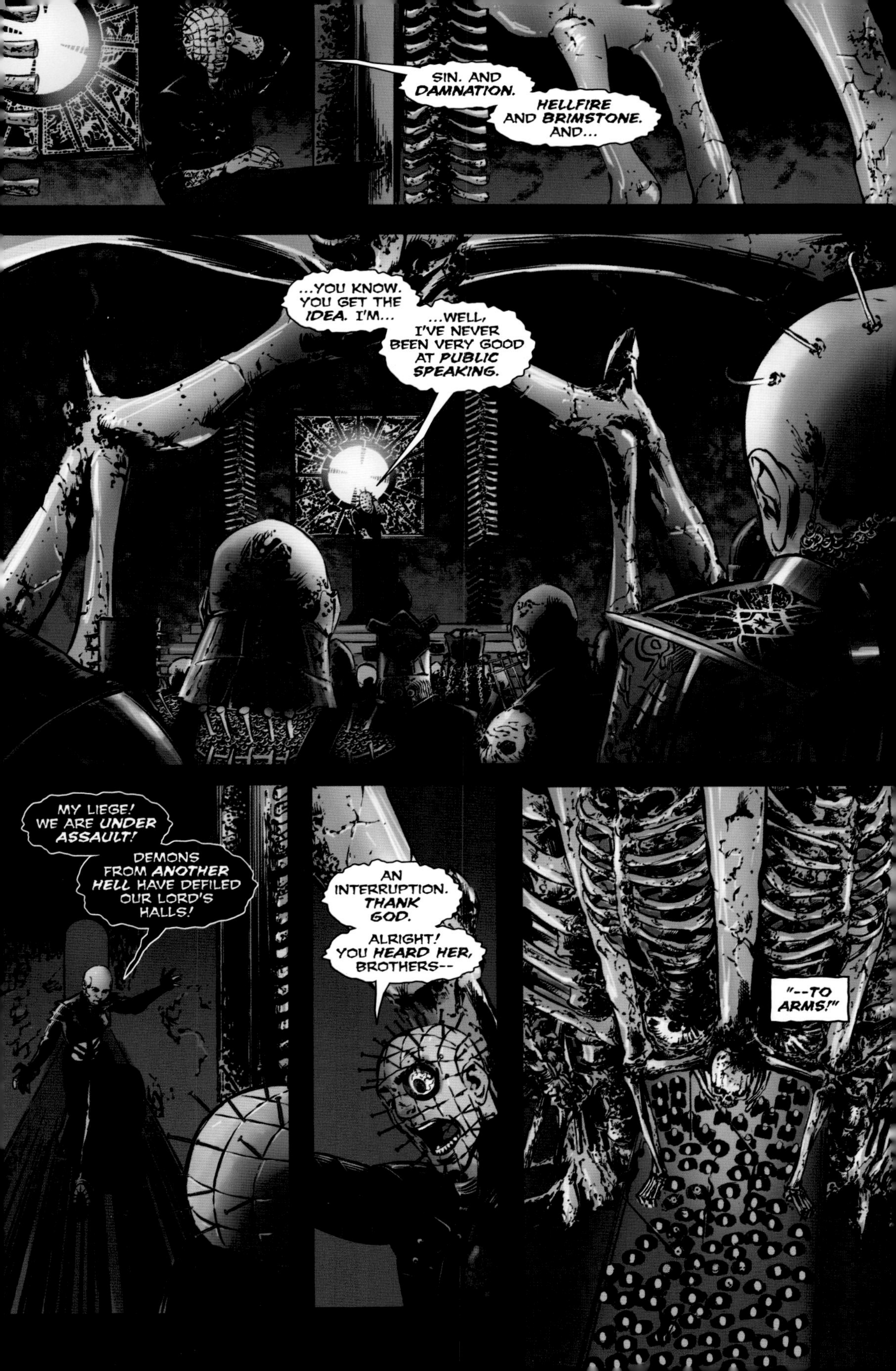
SIN. AND DAMNATION.
HELLFIRE AND BRIMSTONE. AND...
...YOU KNOW. YOU GET THE IDEA. I'M...
...WELL, I'VE NEVER BEEN VERY GOOD AT PUBLIC SPEAKING.
MY LIEGE! WE ARE UNDER ASSAULT!
DEMONS FROM ANOTHER HELL HAVE DEFILED OUR LORD'S HALLS!
AN INTERRUPTION. THANK GOD.
ALRIGHT! YOU HEARD HER, BROTHERS--
"--TO ARMS!"

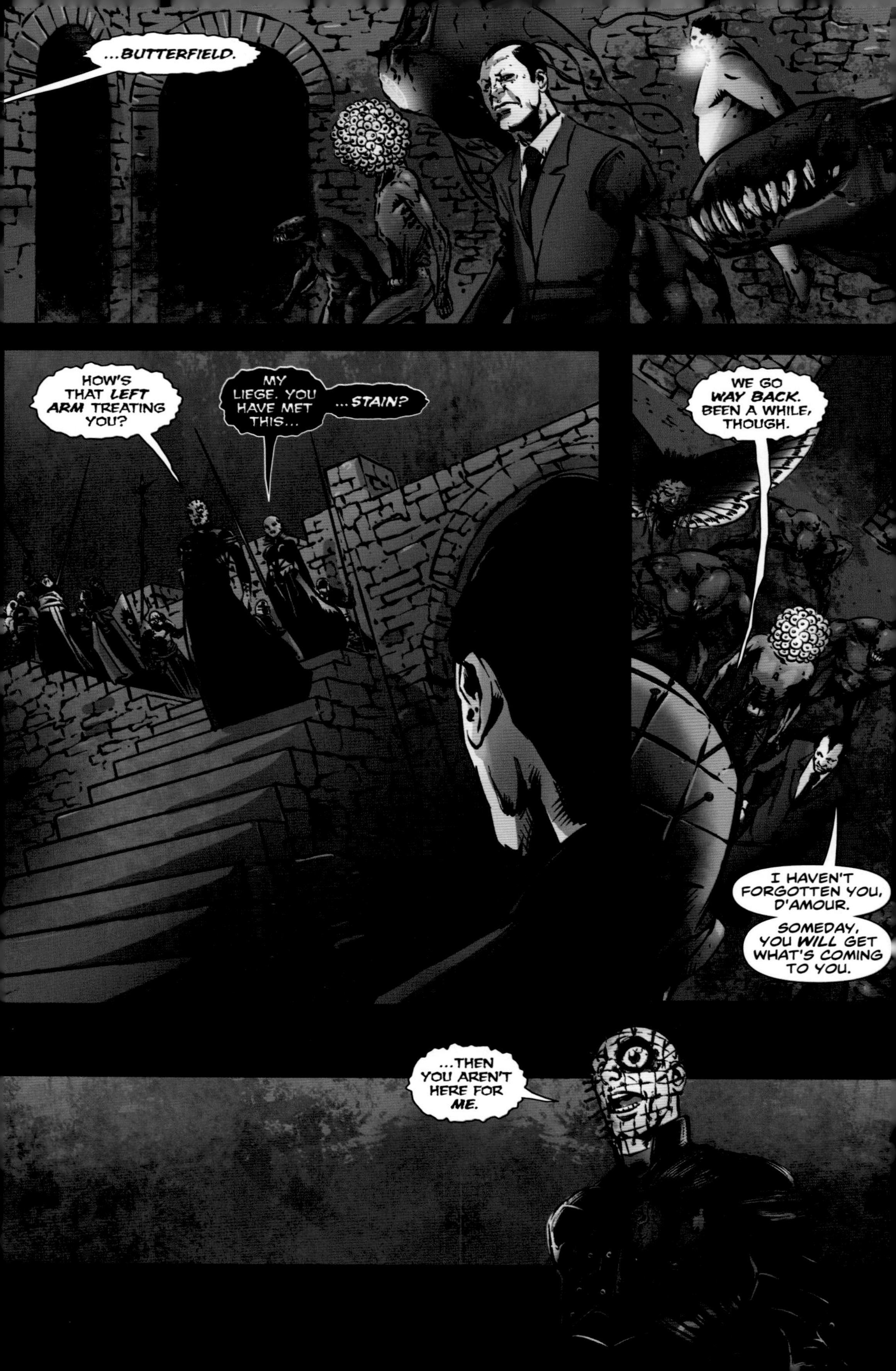
...BUTTERFIELD.
HOW'S THAT LEFT ARM TREATING YOU?
MY LIEGE. YOU HAVE MET THIS...
...STAIN?
WE GO WAY BACK. BEEN A WHILE, THOUGH.
I HAVEN'T FORGOTTEN YOU, D'AMOUR.
SOMEDAY, YOU WILL GET WHAT'S COMING TO YOU.
...THEN YOU AREN'T HERE FOR ME.

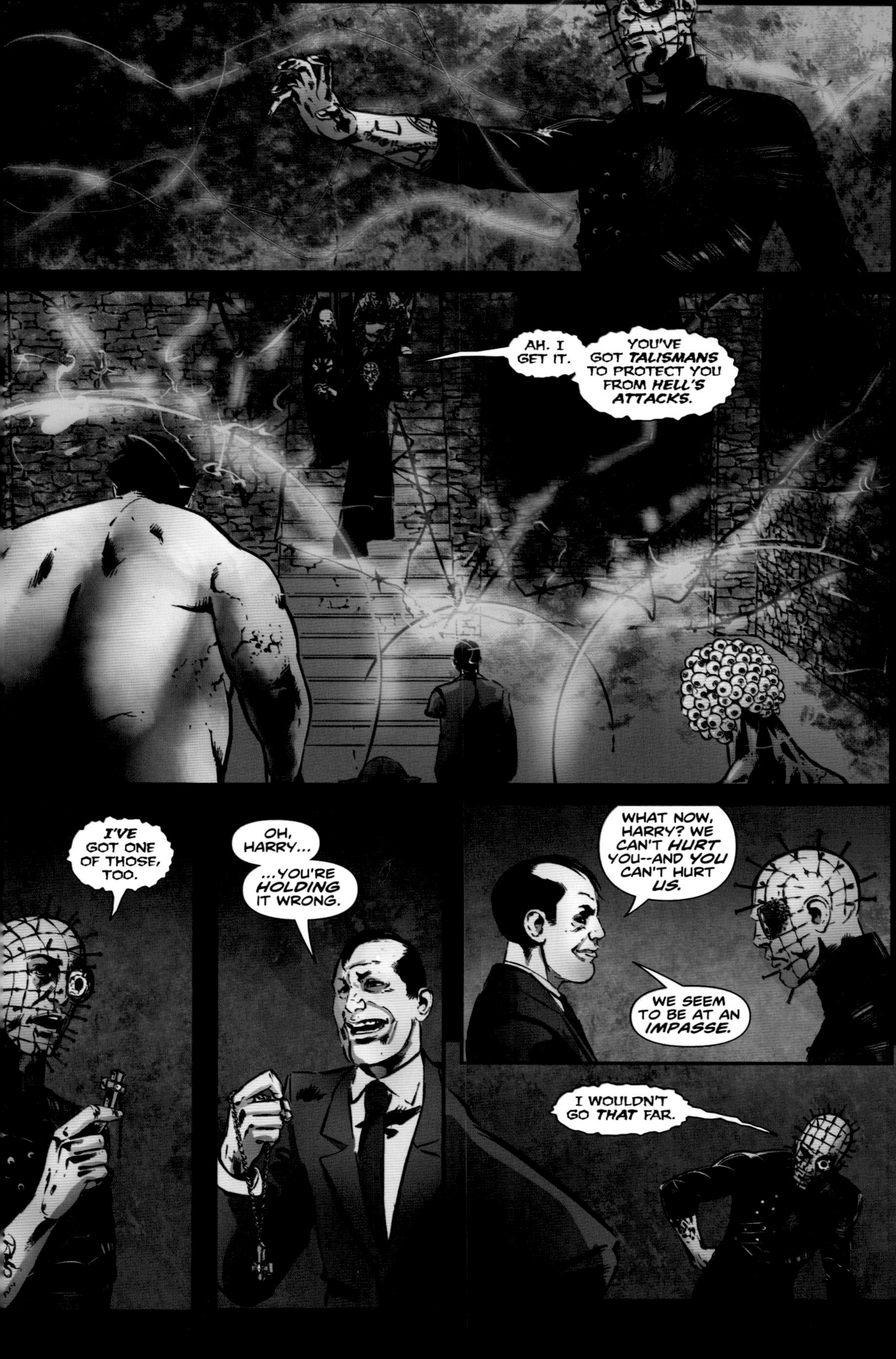
AH. I GET IT.
YOU'VE GOT TALISMANS TO PROTECT YOU FROM HELL'S ATTACKS.
I'VE GOT ONE OF THOSE, TOO.
OH, HARRY...
...YOU'RE HOLDING IT WRONG.
WHAT NOW, HARRY? WE CAN'T HURT YOU--AND YOU CAN'T HURT US.
WE SEEM TO BE AT AN IMPASSE.
I WOULDN'T GO THAT FAR.

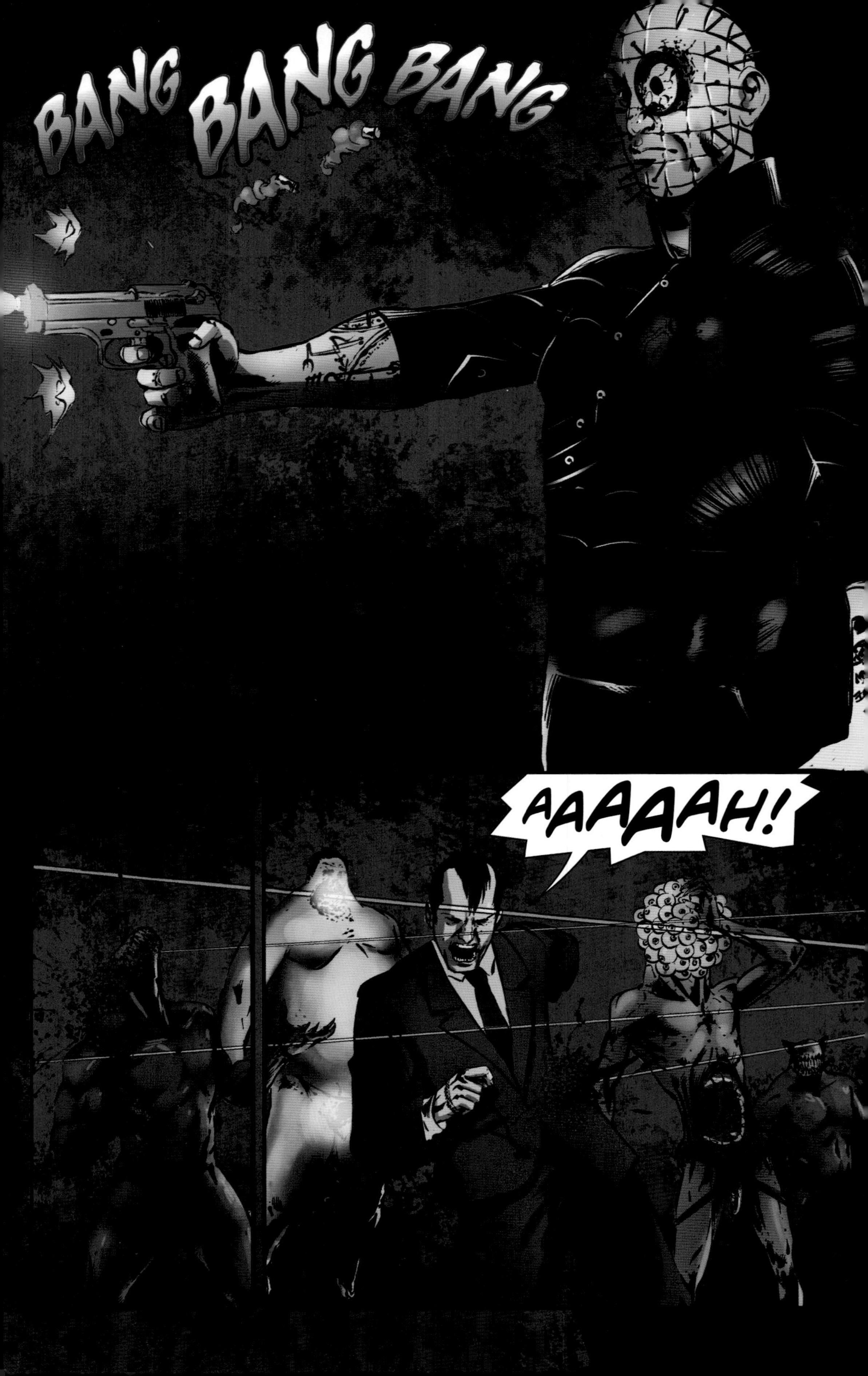
BANG BANG BANG
AAAAAH!

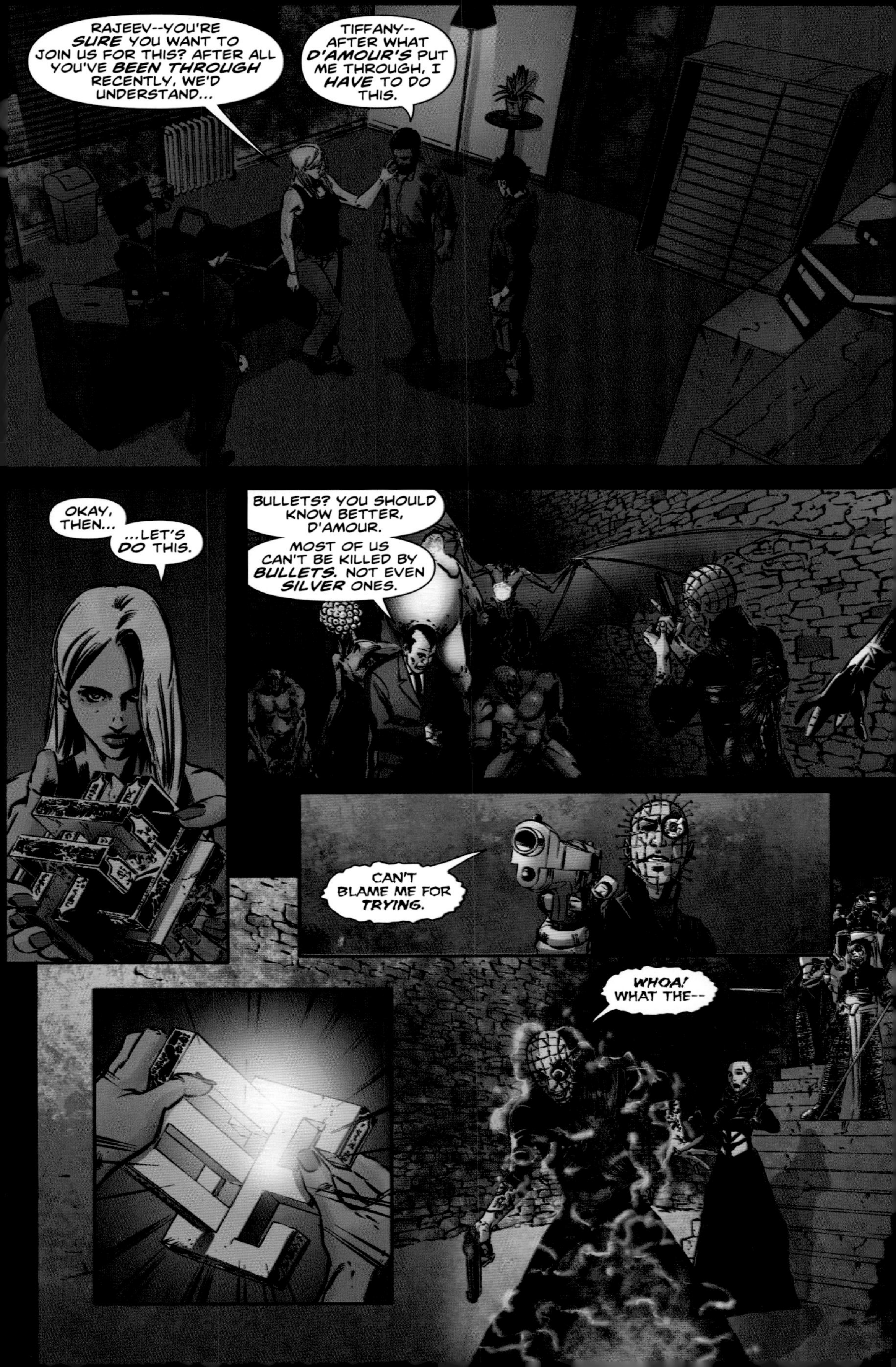
RAJEEV--YOU'RE SURE YOU WANT TO JOIN US FOR THIS? AFTER ALL YOU'VE BEEN THROUGH RECENTLY, WE'D UNDERSTAND...
TIFFANY--AFTER WHAT D'AMOUR'S PUT ME THROUGH, I HAVE TO DO THIS.
OKAY, THEN...
...LET'S DO THIS.
BULLETS? YOU SHOULD KNOW BETTER, D'AMOUR.
MOST OF US CAN'T BE KILLED BY BULLETS. NOT EVEN SILVER ONES.
CAN'T BLAME ME FOR TRYING.
WHOA! WHAT THE--

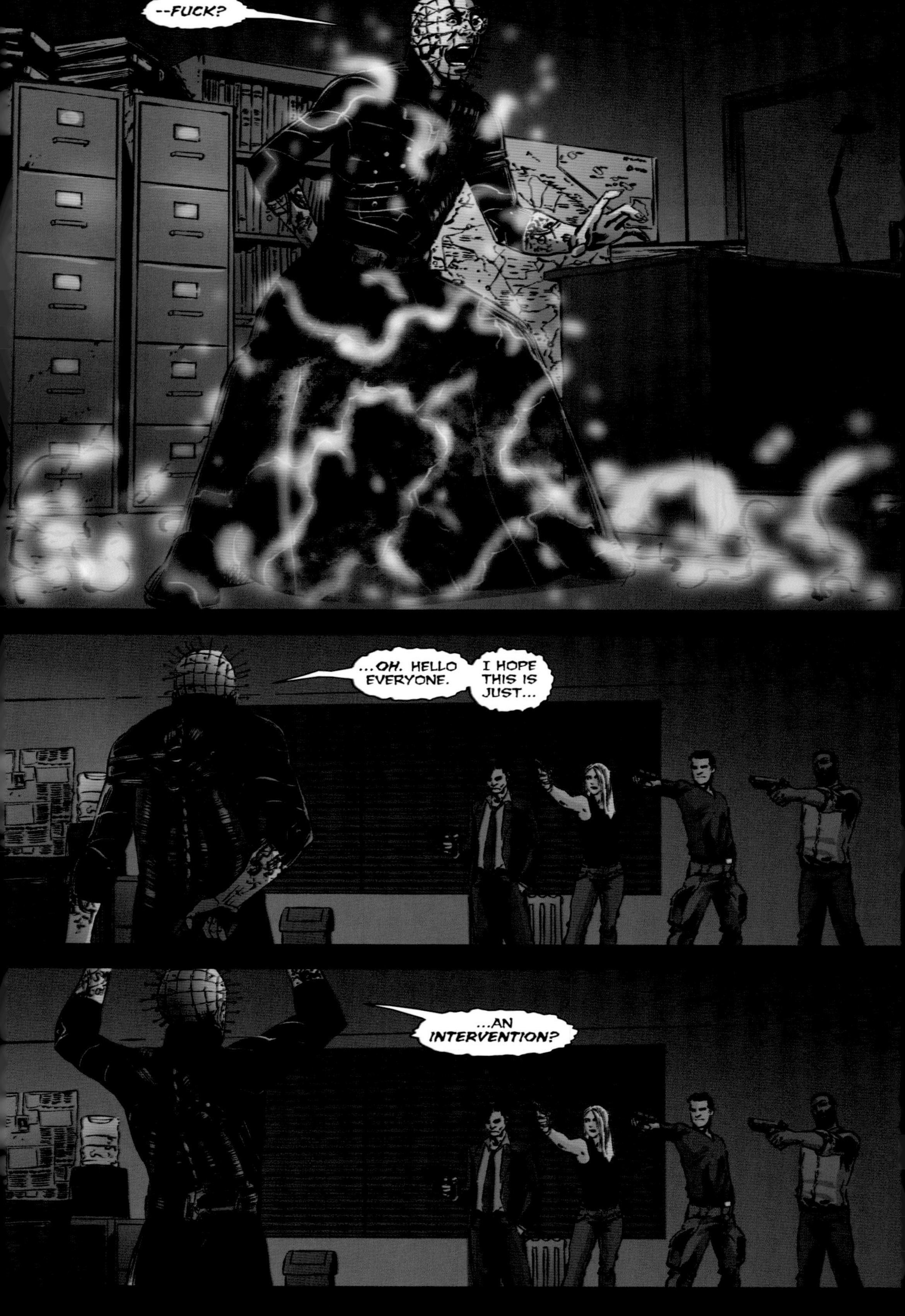
--FUCK?
...OH. HELLO EVERYONE.
I HOPE THIS IS JUST...
...AN INTERVENTION?

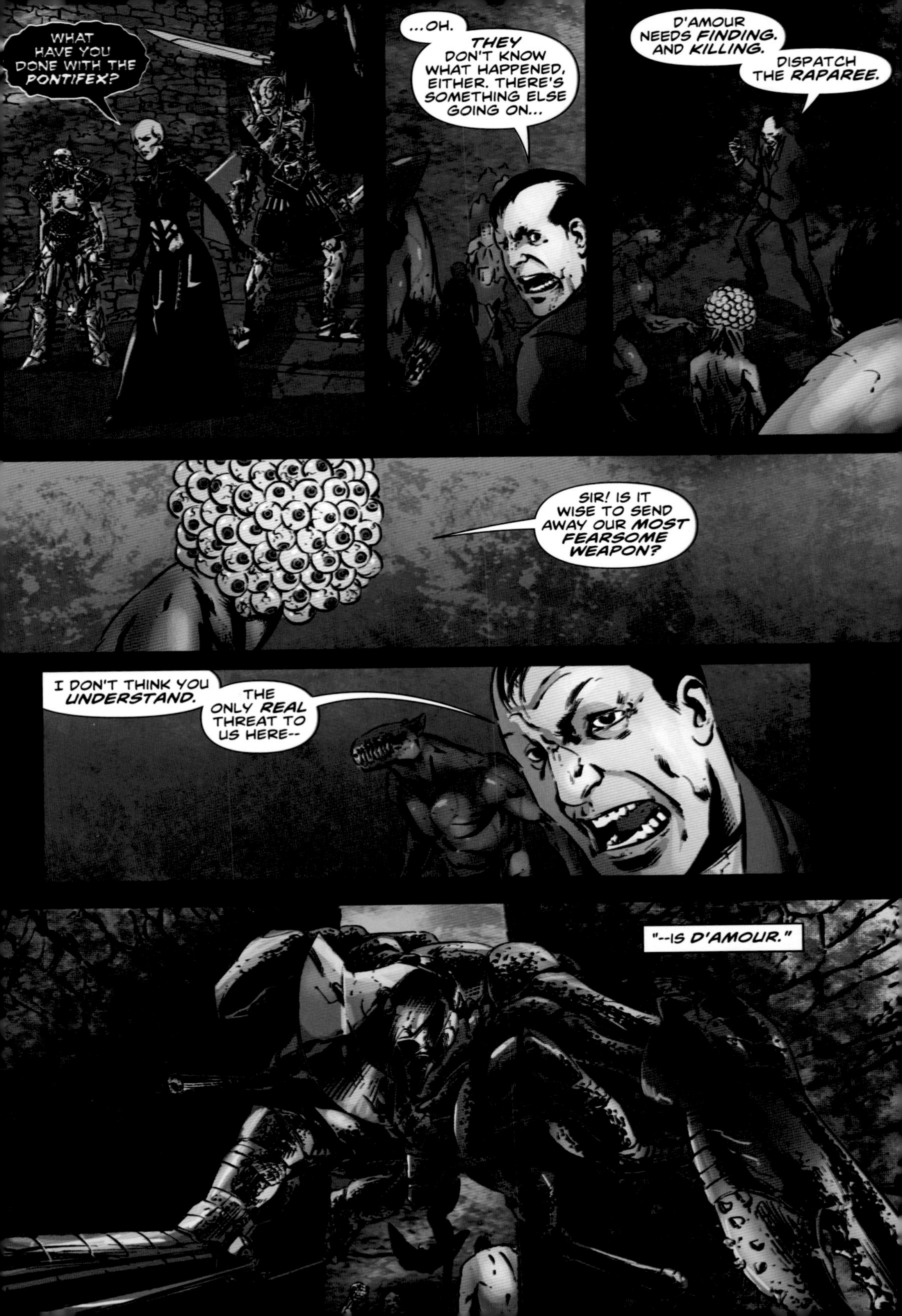

WHAT HAVE YOU DONE WITH THE PONTIFEX?
...OH.
THEY DON'T KNOW WHAT HAPPENED, EITHER. THERE'S SOMETHING ELSE GOING ON...
D'AMOUR NEEDS FINDING. AND KILLING.
DISPATCH THE RAPAREE.
SIR! IS IT WISE TO SEND AWAY OUR MOST FEARSOME WEAPON?
I DON'T THINK YOU UNDERSTAND.
THE ONLY REAL THREAT TO US HERE--
"--IS D'AMOUR."

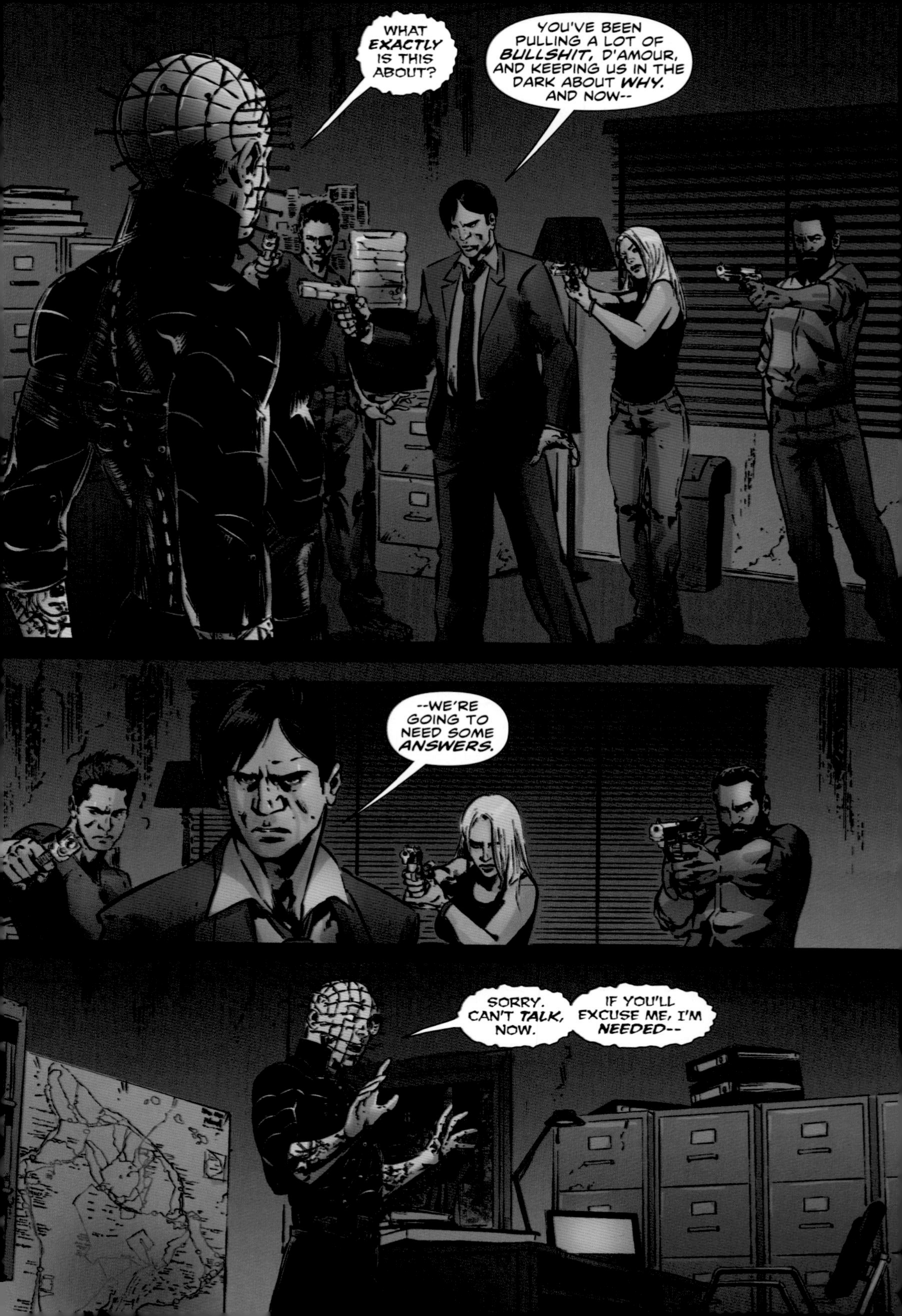
WHAT EXACTLY IS THIS ABOUT?
YOU'VE BEEN PULLING A LOT OF BULLSHIT, D'AMOUR, AND KEEPING US IN THE DARK ABOUT WHY. AND NOW--
--WE'RE GOING TO NEED SOME ANSWERS.
SORRY. CAN'T TALK, NOW.
IF YOU'LL EXCUSE ME, I'M NEEDED--

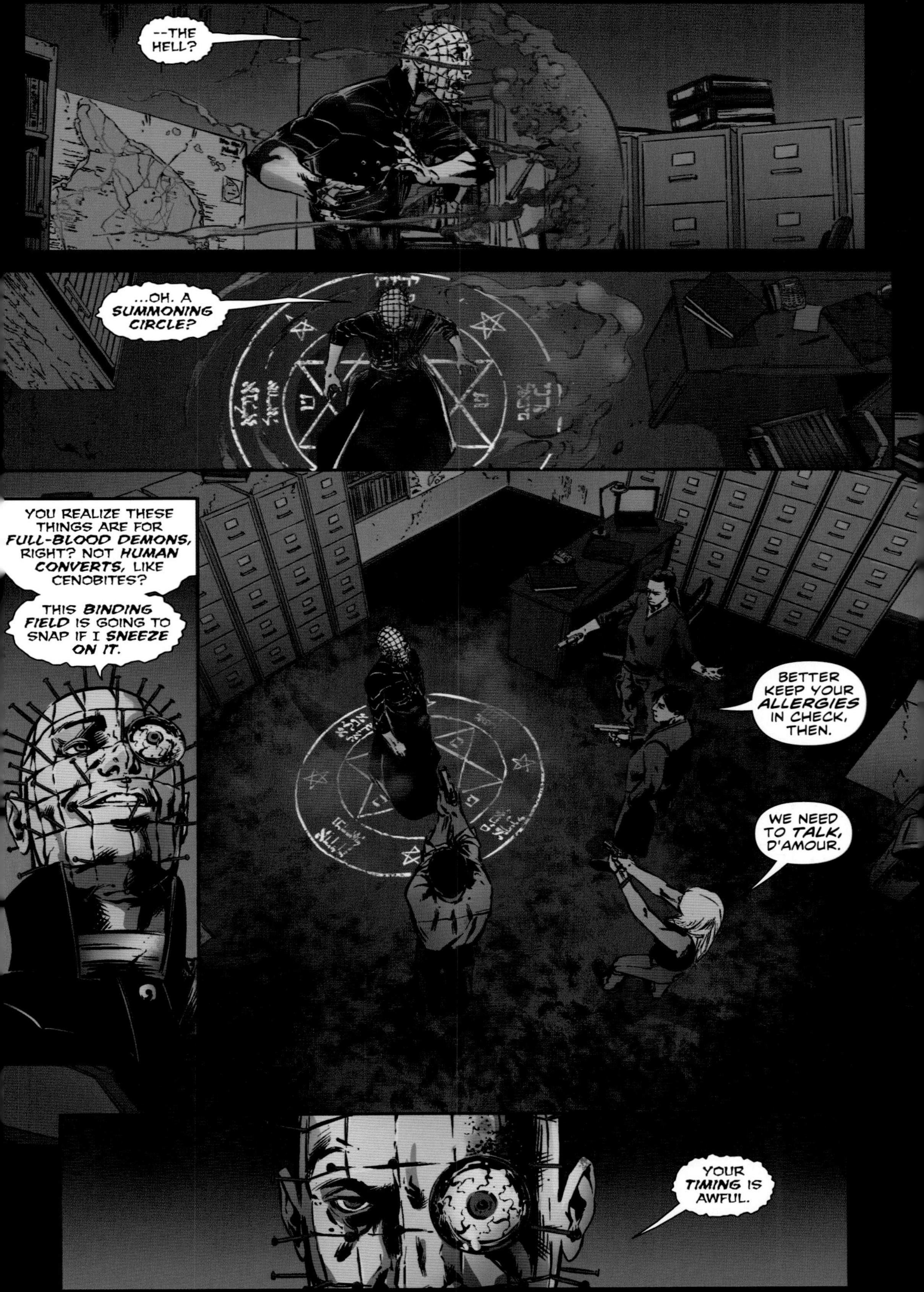
--THE HELL?
...OH. A SUMMONING CIRCLE?
YOU REALIZE THESE THINGS ARE FOR FULL-BLOOD DEMONS, RIGHT? NOT HUMAN CONVERTS, LIKE CENOBITES?
THIS BINDING FIELD IS GOING TO SNAP IF I SNEEZE ON IT.
BETTER KEEP YOUR ALLERGIES IN CHECK, THEN.
WE NEED TO TALK, D'AMOUR.
YOUR TIMING IS AWFUL.

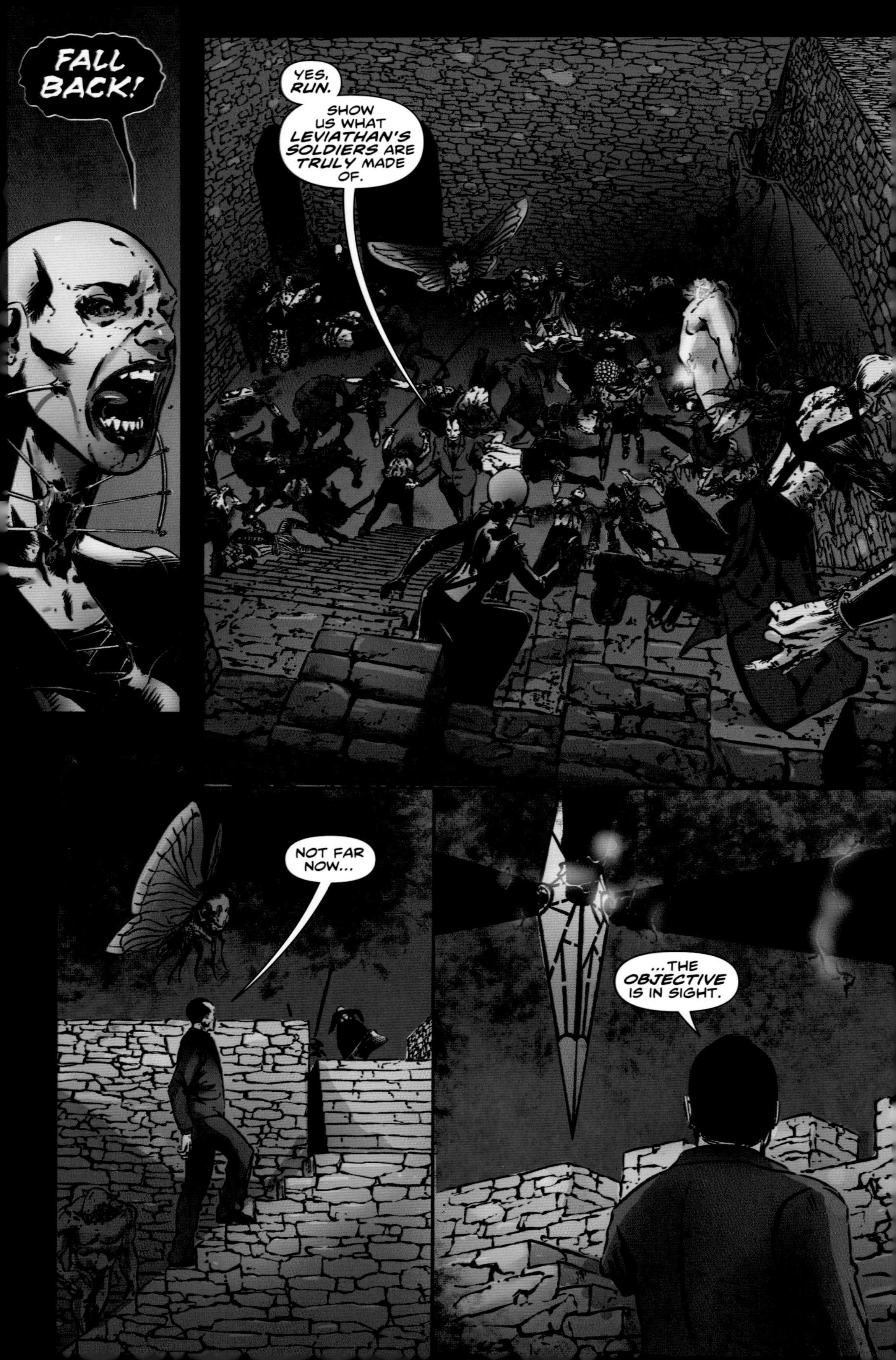
FALL BACK!
YES, RUN.
SHOW US WHAT LEVIATHAN'S SOLDIERS ARE TRULY MADE OF.
NOT FAR NOW...
...THE OBJECTIVE IS IN SIGHT.

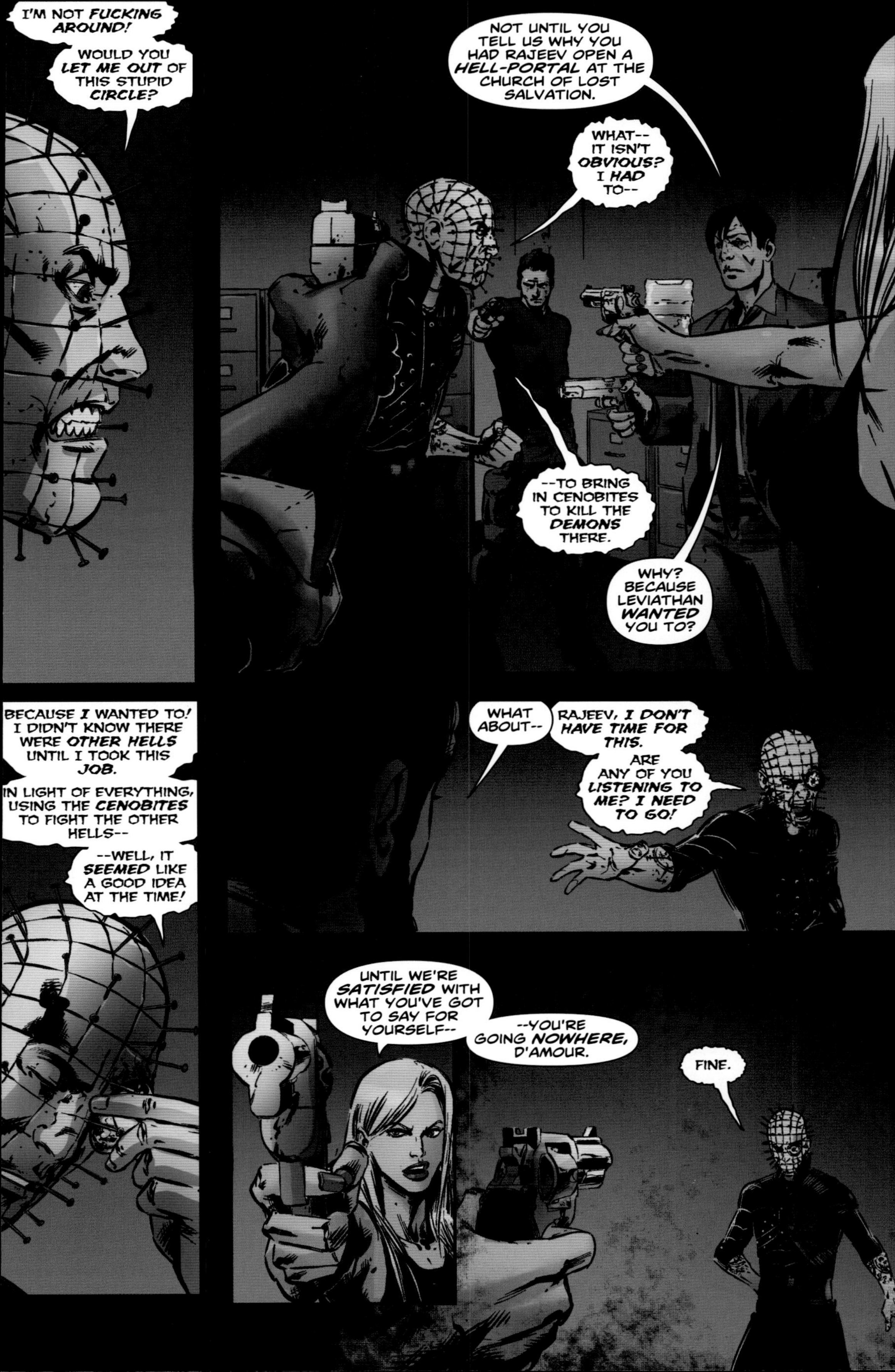

I'M NOT *FUCKING AROUND!*
WOULD YOU *LET ME OUT* OF THIS STUPID *CIRCLE?*
NOT UNTIL YOU TELL US WHY YOU HAD RAJEEV OPEN A *HELL-PORTAL* AT THE CHURCH OF LOST SALVATION.
WHAT-- IT ISN'T *OBVIOUS?* I *HAD* TO--
--TO BRING IN CENOBITES TO KILL THE *DEMONS* THERE.
WHY? BECAUSE LEVIATHAN *WANTED* YOU TO?
BECAUSE *I* WANTED TO! I DIDN'T KNOW THERE WERE *OTHER HELLS* UNTIL I TOOK THIS *JOB.*
IN LIGHT OF EVERYTHING, USING THE *CENOBITES* TO FIGHT THE OTHER HELLS--
--WELL, IT *SEEMED* LIKE A GOOD IDEA AT THE TIME!
WHAT ABOUT--
RAJEEV, *I DON'T HAVE TIME FOR THIS.*
ARE ANY OF YOU *LISTENING TO ME? I NEED TO GO!*
UNTIL WE'RE *SATISFIED* WITH WHAT YOU'VE GOT TO SAY FOR YOURSELF--
--YOU'RE GOING *NOWHERE,* D'AMOUR.
FINE.

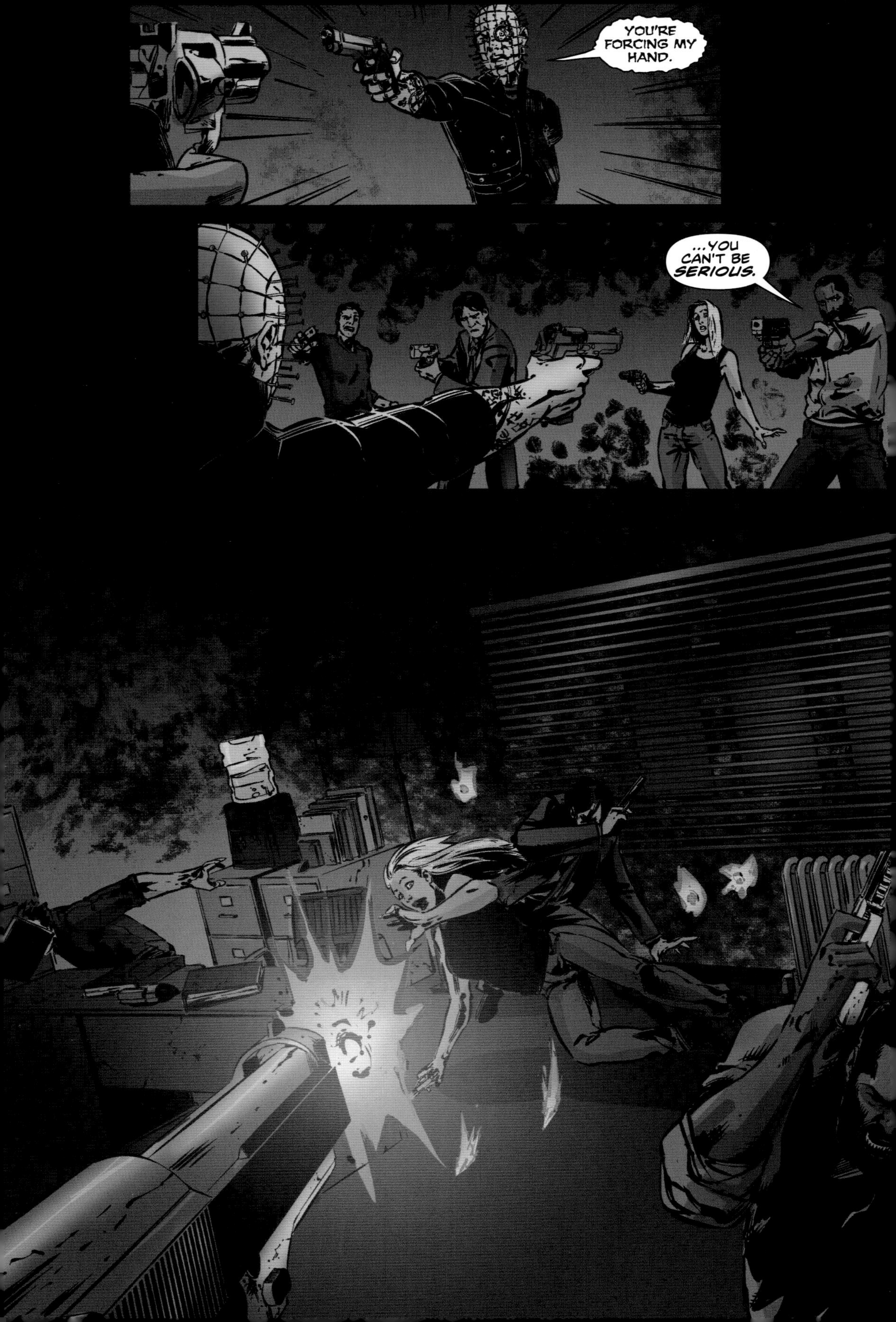
YOU'RE FORCING MY HAND.
...YOU CAN'T BE SERIOUS.

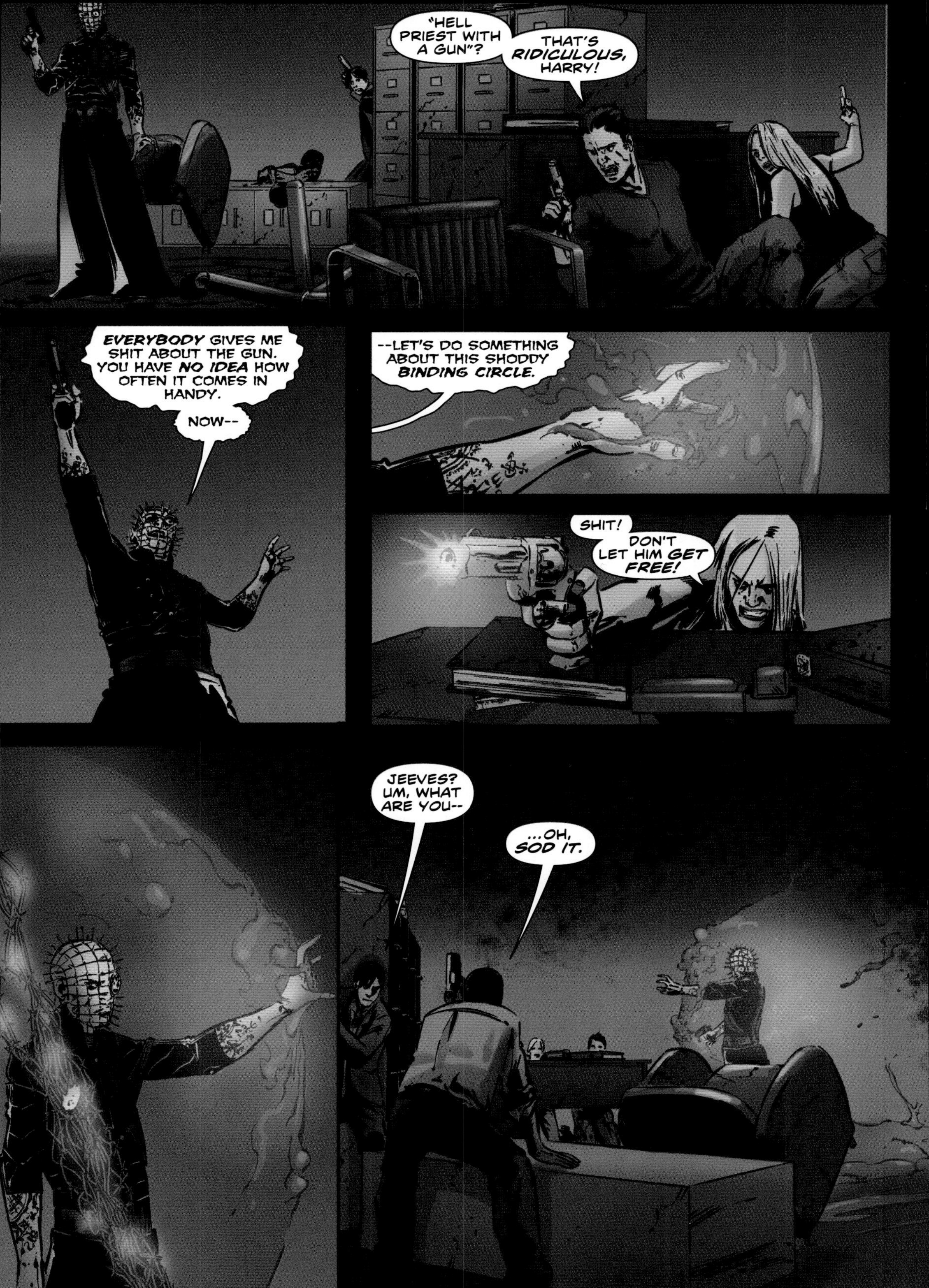
"HELL PRIEST WITH A GUN"?
THAT'S RIDICULOUS, HARRY!
EVERYBODY GIVES ME SHIT ABOUT THE GUN. YOU HAVE NO IDEA HOW OFTEN IT COMES IN HANDY.
NOW--
--LET'S DO SOMETHING ABOUT THIS SHODDY BINDING CIRCLE.
SHIT!
DON'T LET HIM GET FREE!
JEEVES? UM, WHAT ARE YOU--
...OH, SOD IT.

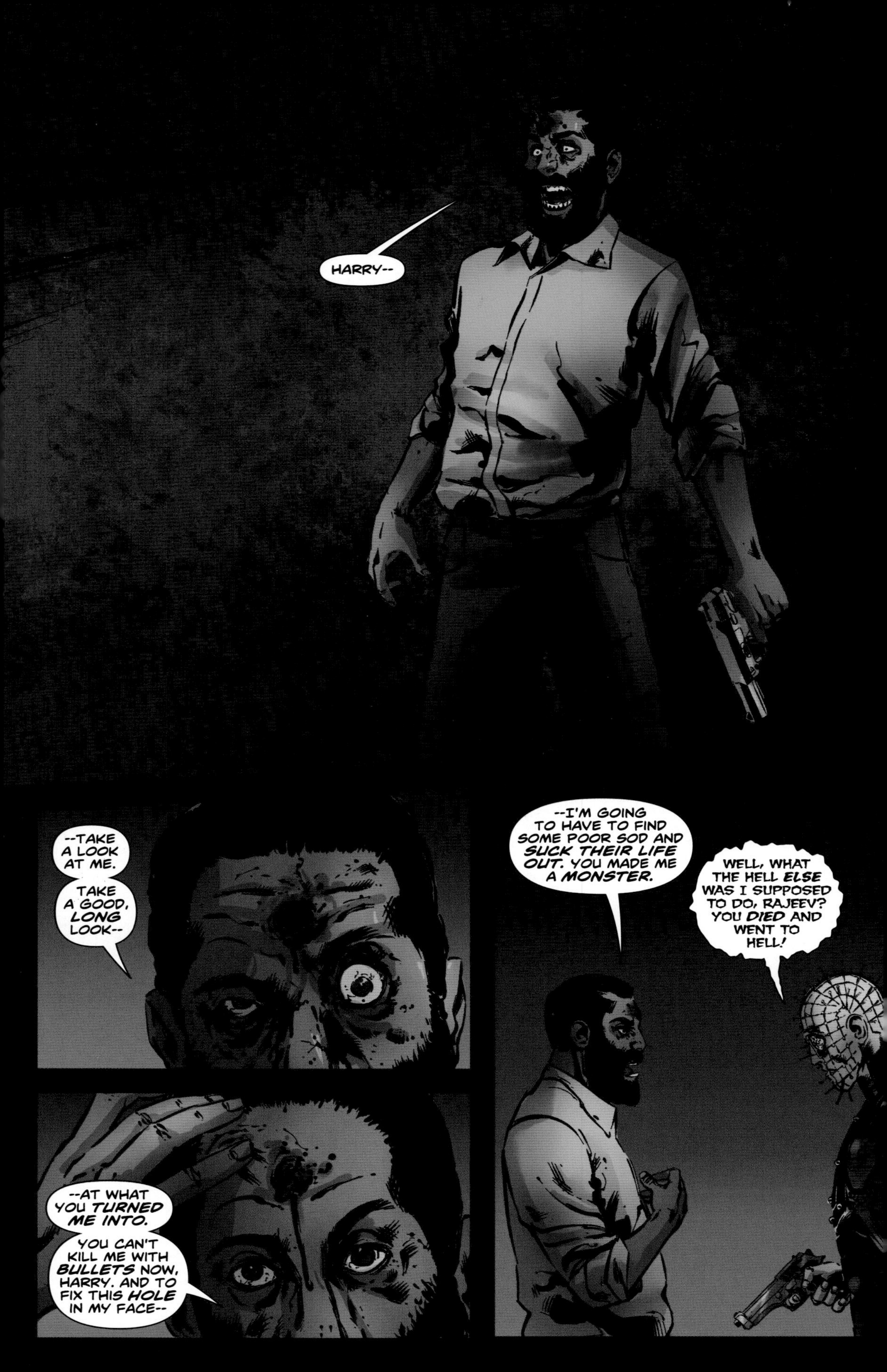
HARRY--
--TAKE A LOOK AT ME.
TAKE A GOOD, LONG LOOK--
--AT WHAT YOU TURNED ME INTO.
YOU CAN'T KILL ME WITH BULLETS NOW, HARRY. AND TO FIX THIS HOLE IN MY FACE--
--I'M GOING TO HAVE TO FIND SOME POOR SOD AND SUCK THEIR LIFE OUT. YOU MADE ME A MONSTER.
WELL, WHAT THE HELL ELSE WAS I SUPPOSED TO DO, RAJEEV? YOU DIED AND WENT TO HELL!

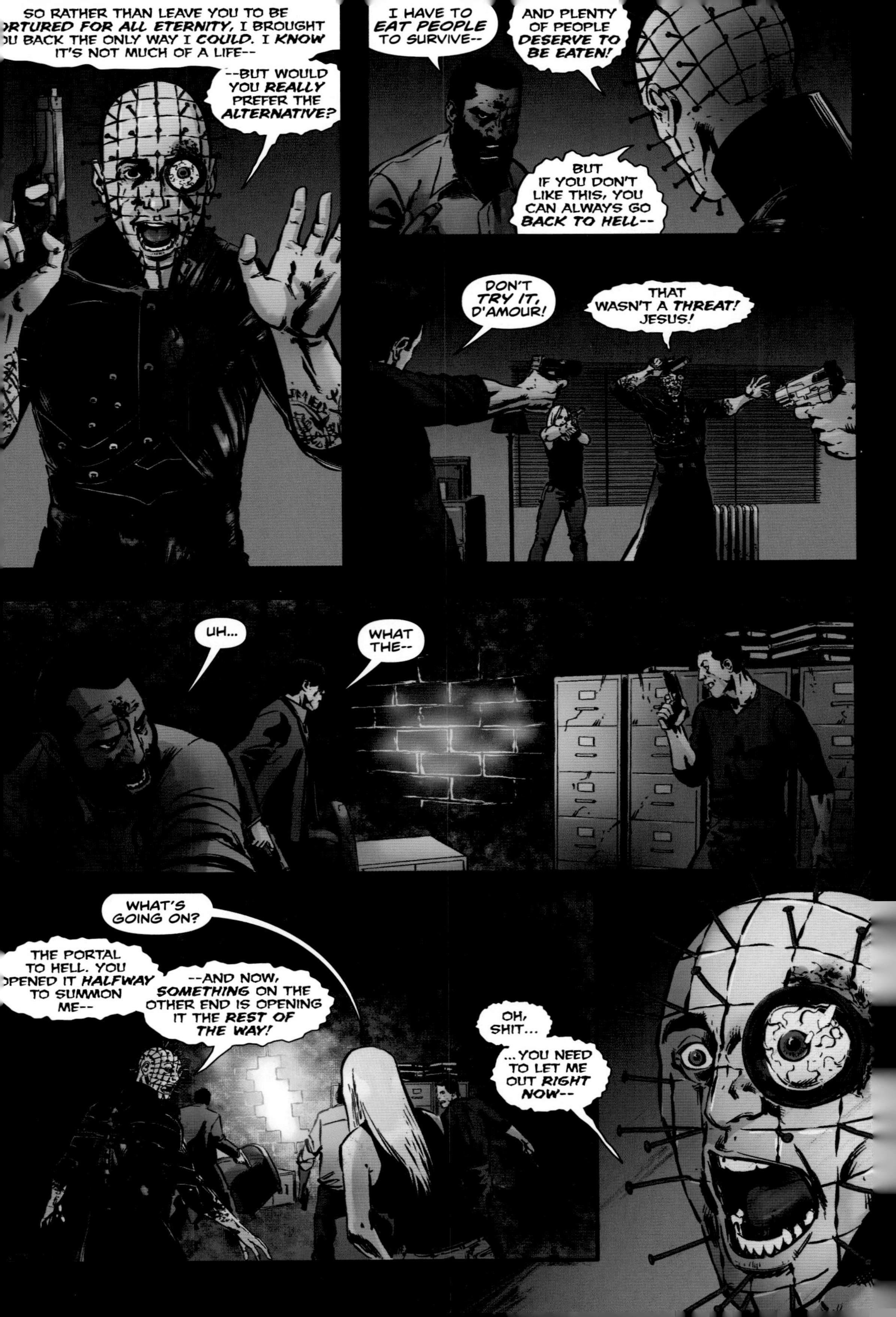
SO RATHER THAN LEAVE YOU TO BE
ORTURED FOR ALL ETERNITY, I BROUGHT
U BACK THE ONLY WAY I COULD. I KNOW
IT'S NOT MUCH OF A LIFE--
--BUT WOULD YOU REALLY PREFER THE ALTERNATIVE?
I HAVE TO EAT PEOPLE TO SURVIVE--
AND PLENTY OF PEOPLE DESERVE TO BE EATEN!
BUT IF YOU DON'T LIKE THIS, YOU CAN ALWAYS GO BACK TO HELL--
DON'T TRY IT, D'AMOUR!
THAT WASN'T A THREAT! JESUS!
UH...
WHAT THE--
WHAT'S GOING ON?
THE PORTAL TO HELL. YOU
PENED IT HALFWAY TO SUMMON ME--
--AND NOW, SOMETHING ON THE OTHER END IS OPENING IT THE REST OF THE WAY!
OH, SHIT...
...YOU NEED TO LET ME OUT RIGHT NOW--

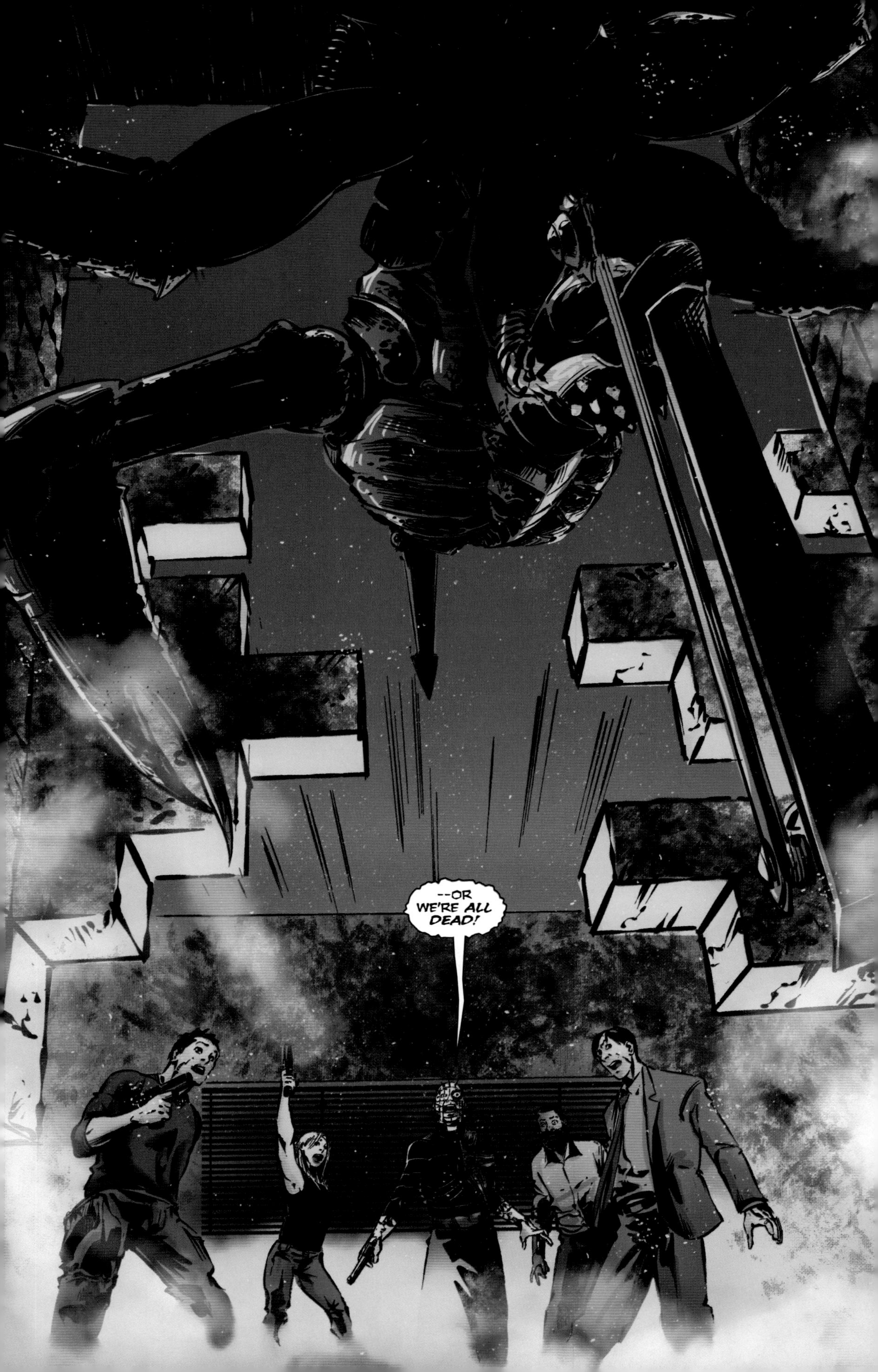
--OR WE'RE ALL DEAD!

CHAPTER SEVEN

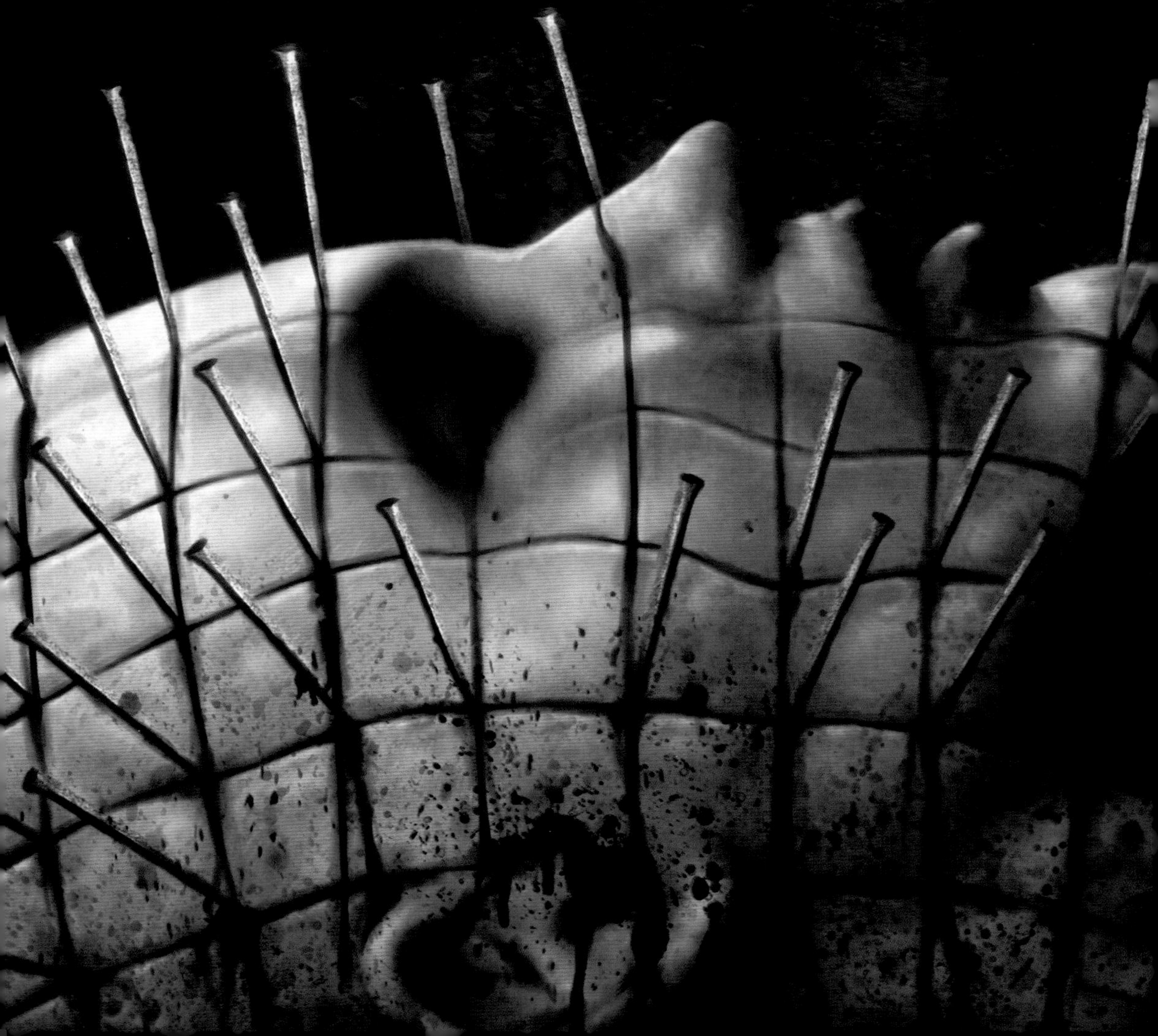

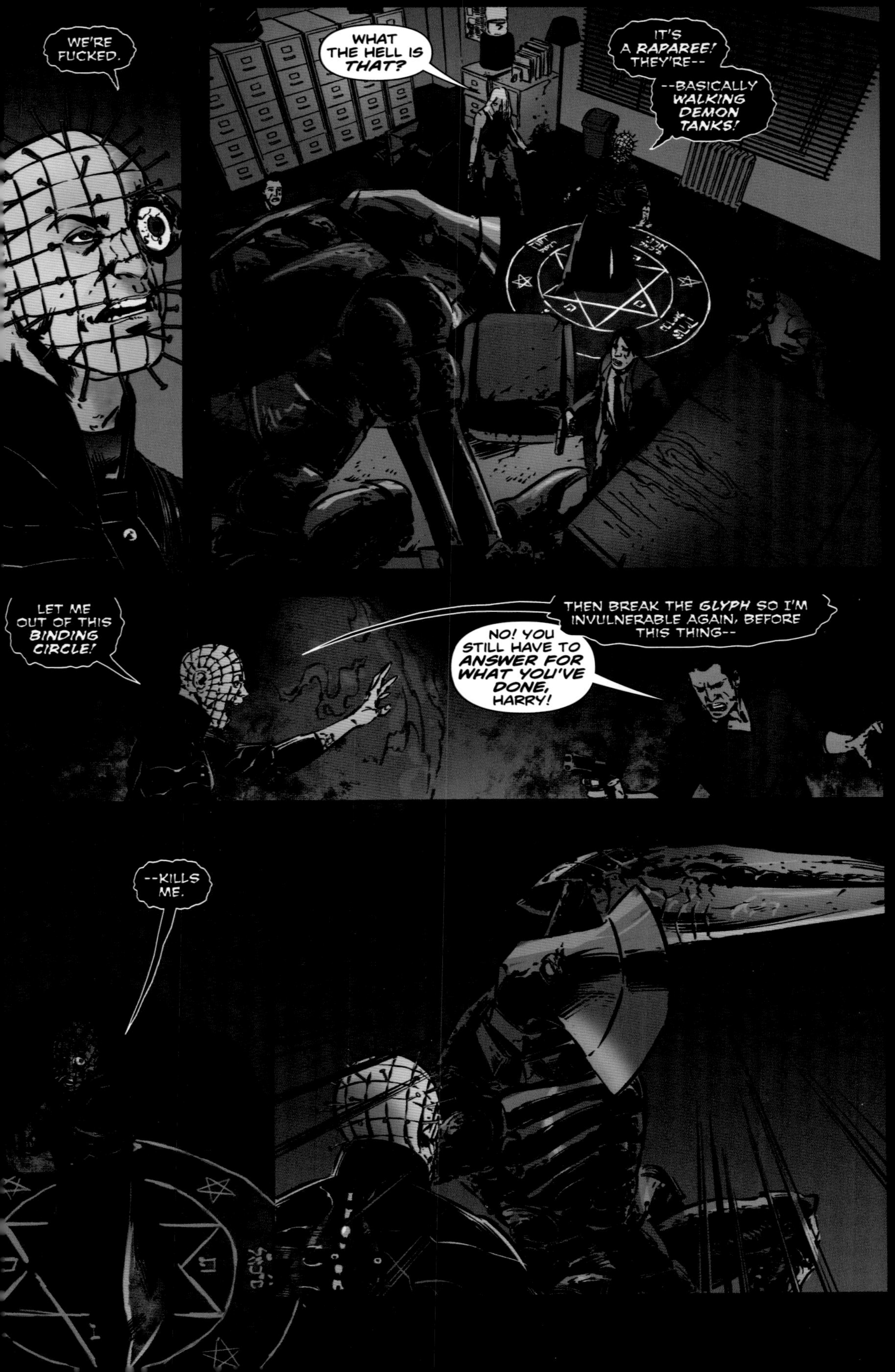
WE'RE FUCKED.
WHAT THE HELL IS THAT?
IT'S A RAPAREE! THEY'RE--
--BASICALLY WALKING DEMON TANKS!
LET ME OUT OF THIS BINDING CIRCLE!
THEN BREAK THE GLYPH SO I'M INVULNERABLE AGAIN, BEFORE THIS THING--
NO! YOU STILL HAVE TO ANSWER FOR WHAT YOU'VE DONE, HARRY!
--KILLS ME.

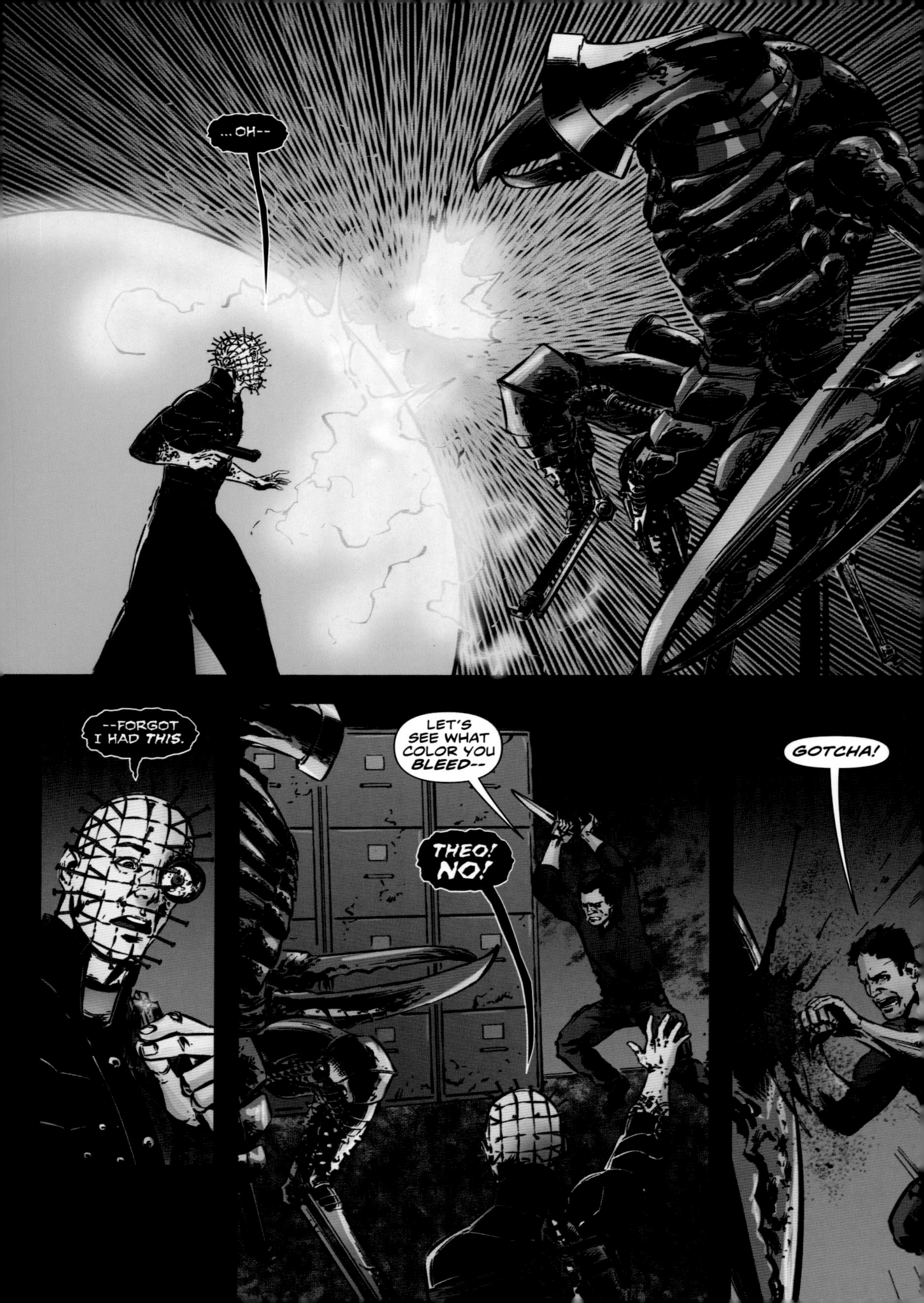
...OH--
--FORGOT I HAD THIS.
LET'S SEE WHAT COLOR YOU BLEED--
THEO! NO!
GOTCHA!

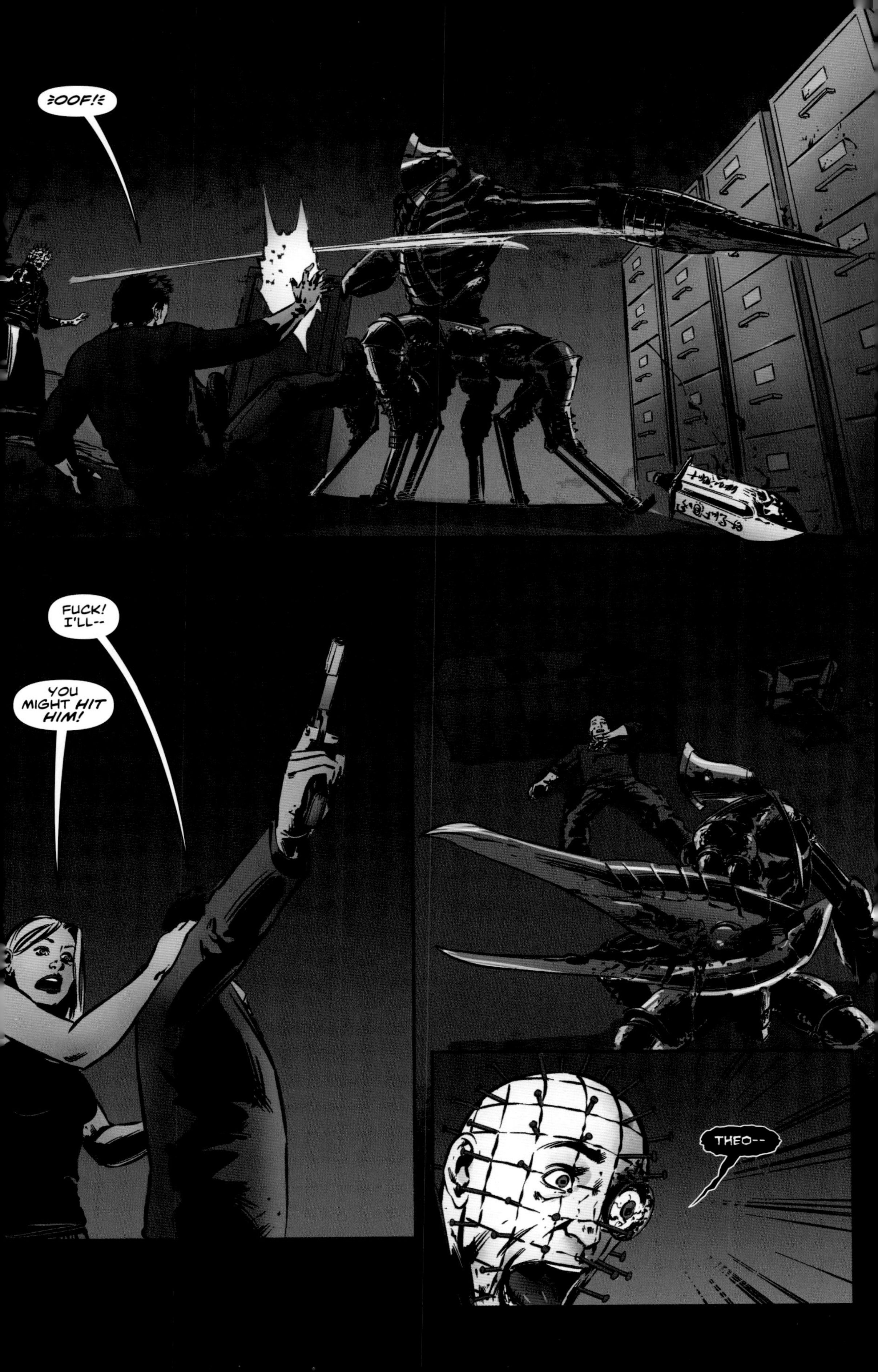
OOF!
FUCK! I'LL--
YOU MIGHT HIT HIM!
THEO--

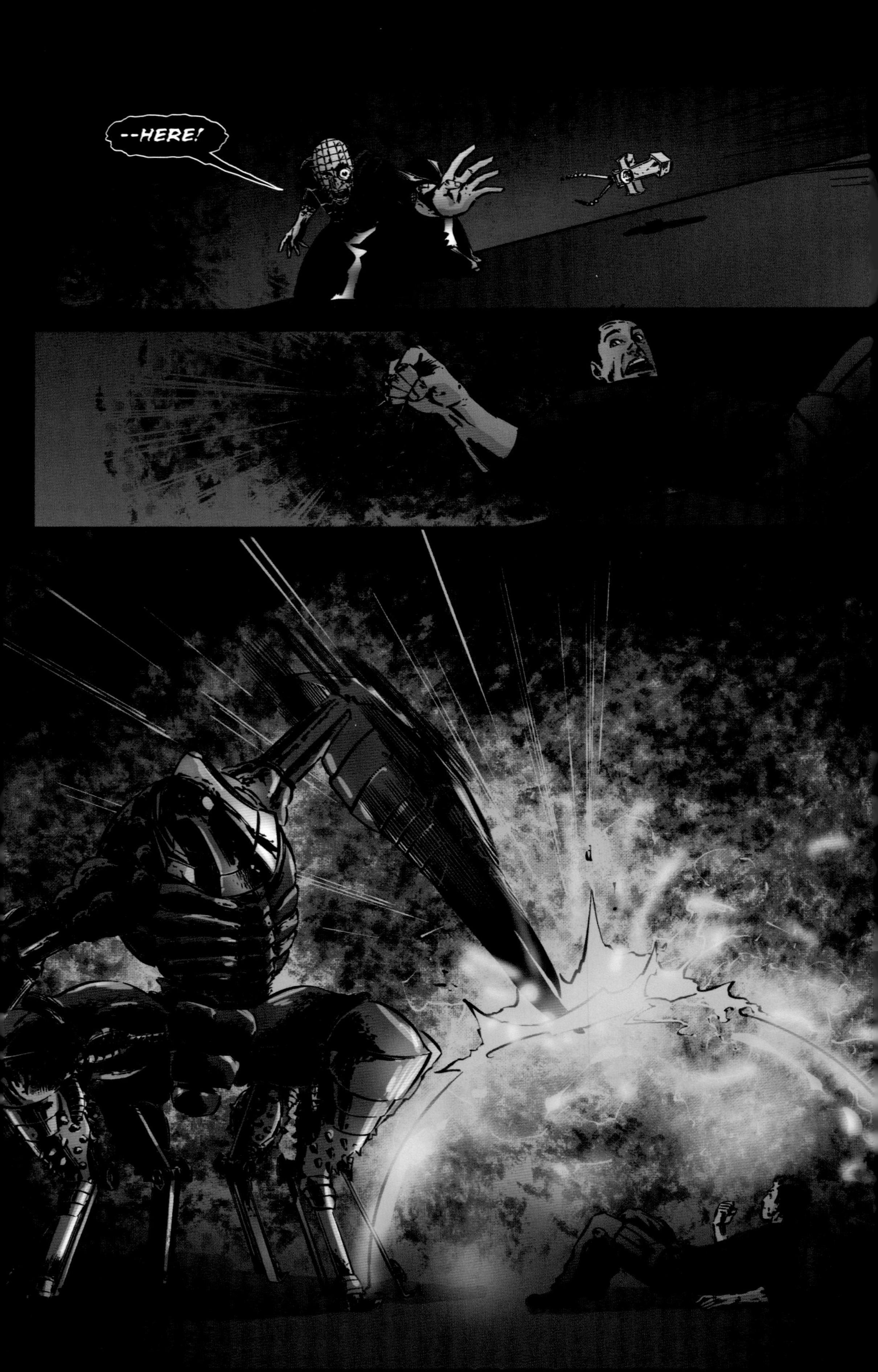
--HERE!

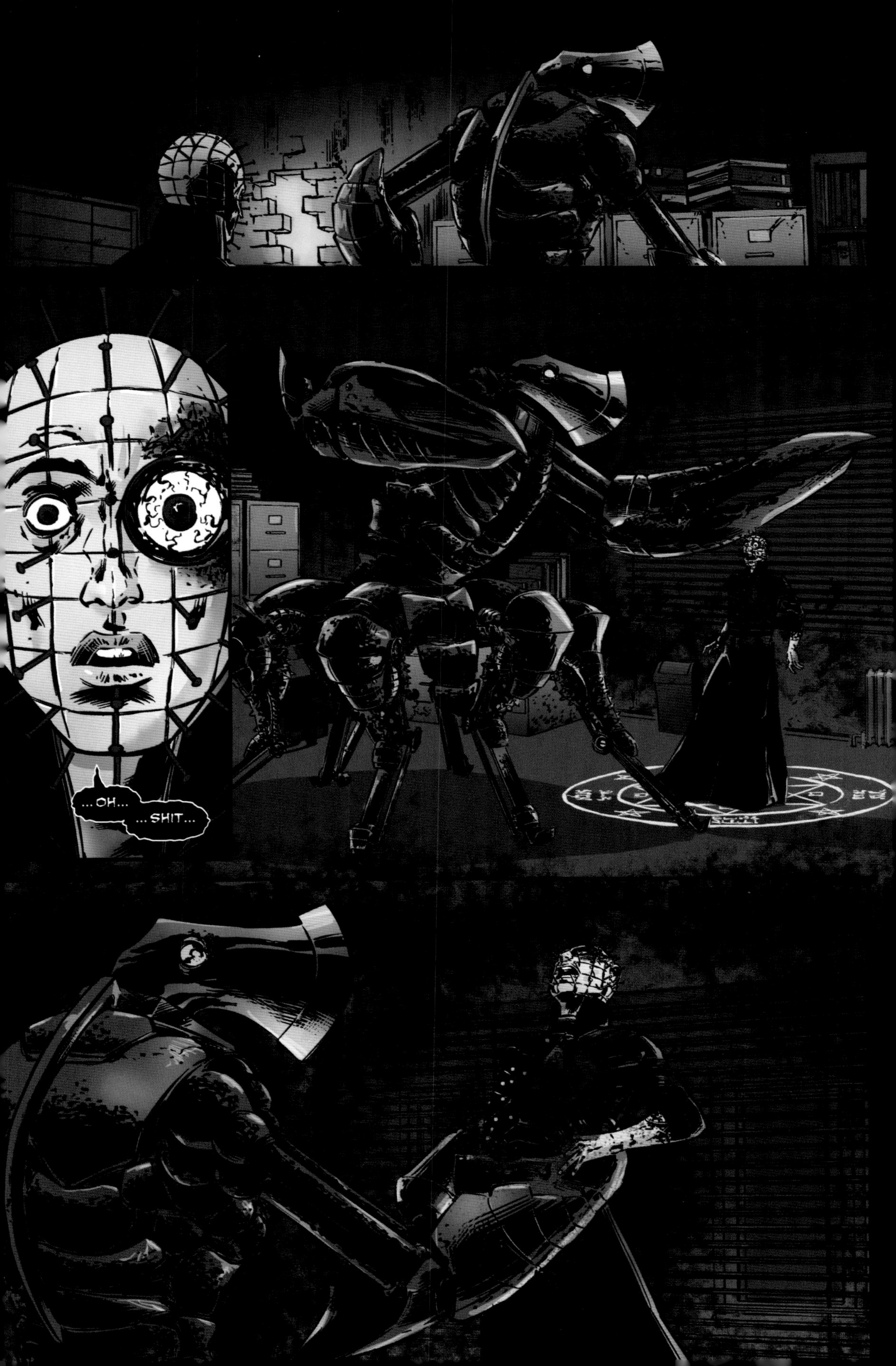
...OH...
...SHIT...

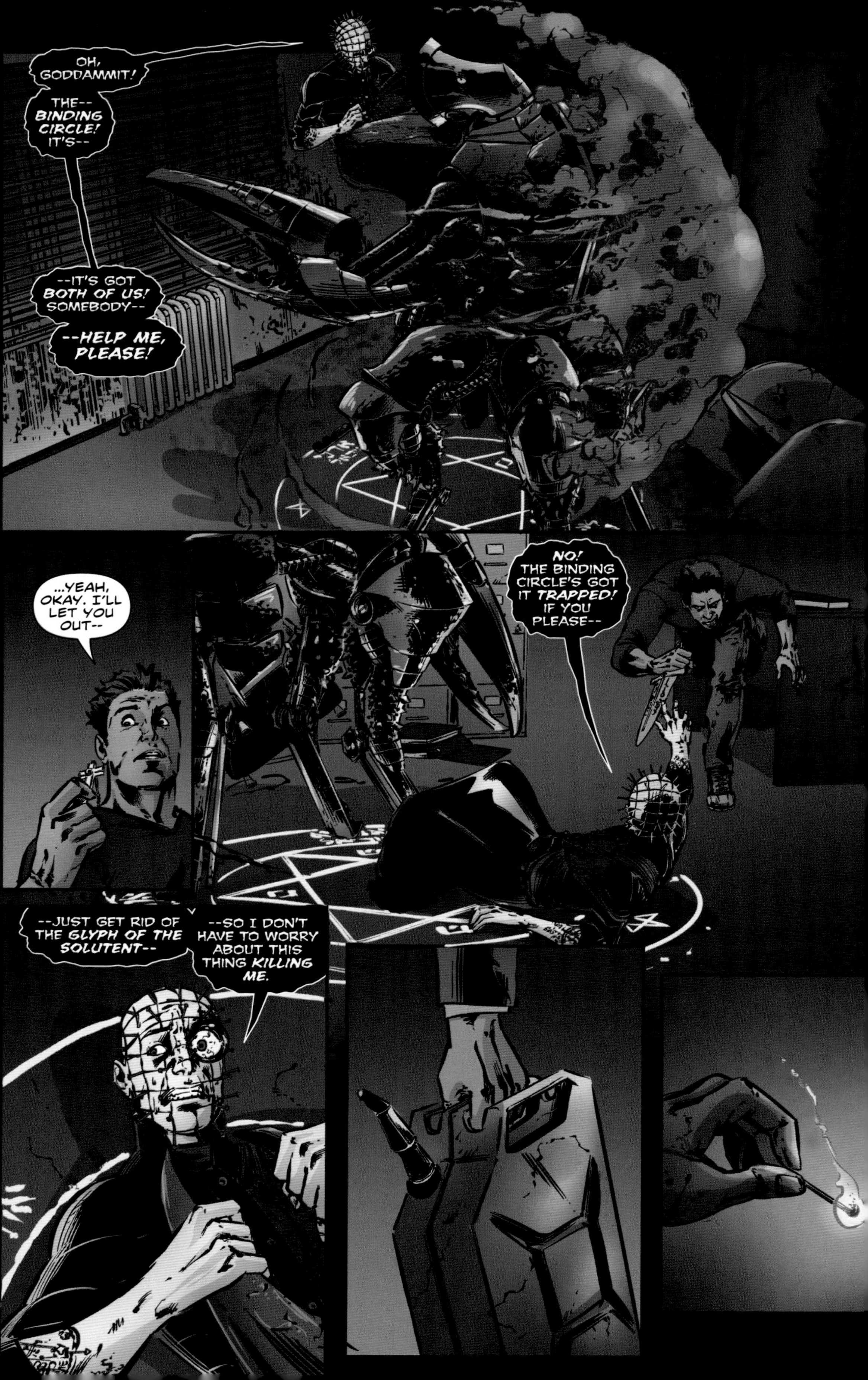
OH, GODDAMMIT!
THE-- BINDING CIRCLE! IT'S--
--IT'S GOT BOTH OF US! SOMEBODY--
--HELP ME, PLEASE!
...YEAH, OKAY. I'LL LET YOU OUT--
NO! THE BINDING CIRCLE'S GOT IT TRAPPED! IF YOU PLEASE--
--JUST GET RID OF THE GLYPH OF THE SOLUTENT--
--SO I DON'T HAVE TO WORRY ABOUT THIS THING KILLING ME.

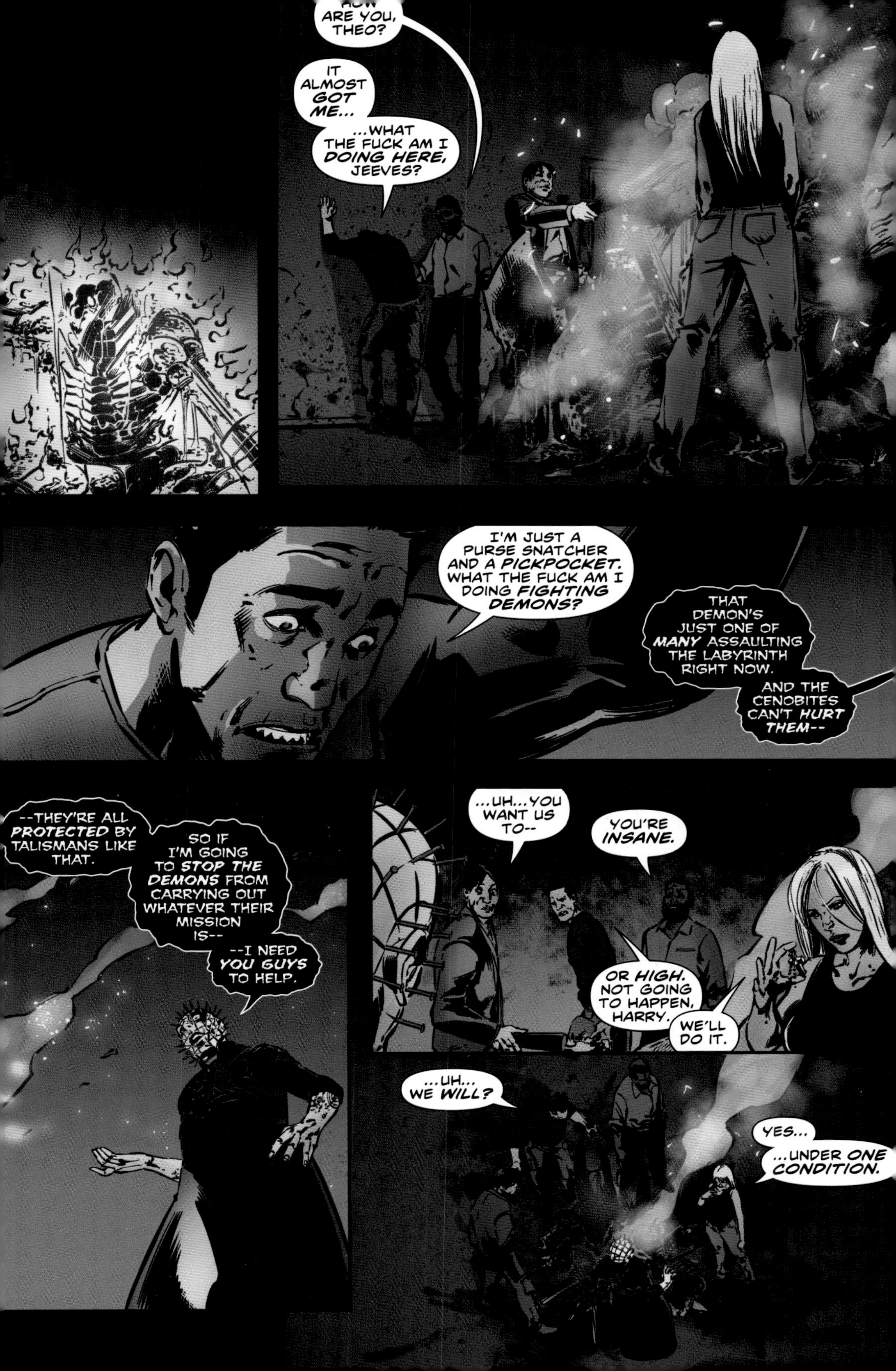
HOW ARE YOU, THEO?
IT ALMOST GOT ME...
...WHAT THE FUCK AM I DOING HERE, JEEVES?
I'M JUST A PURSE SNATCHER AND A PICKPOCKET. WHAT THE FUCK AM I DOING FIGHTING DEMONS?
THAT DEMON'S JUST ONE OF MANY ASSAULTING THE LABYRINTH RIGHT NOW.
AND THE CENOBITES CAN'T HURT THEM--
--THEY'RE ALL PROTECTED BY TALISMANS LIKE THAT.
SO IF I'M GOING TO STOP THE DEMONS FROM CARRYING OUT WHATEVER THEIR MISSION IS--
--I NEED YOU GUYS TO HELP.
...UH...YOU WANT US TO--
YOU'RE INSANE.
OR HIGH. NOT GOING TO HAPPEN, HARRY.
WE'LL DO IT.
...UH... WE WILL?
YES...
...UNDER ONE CONDITION.

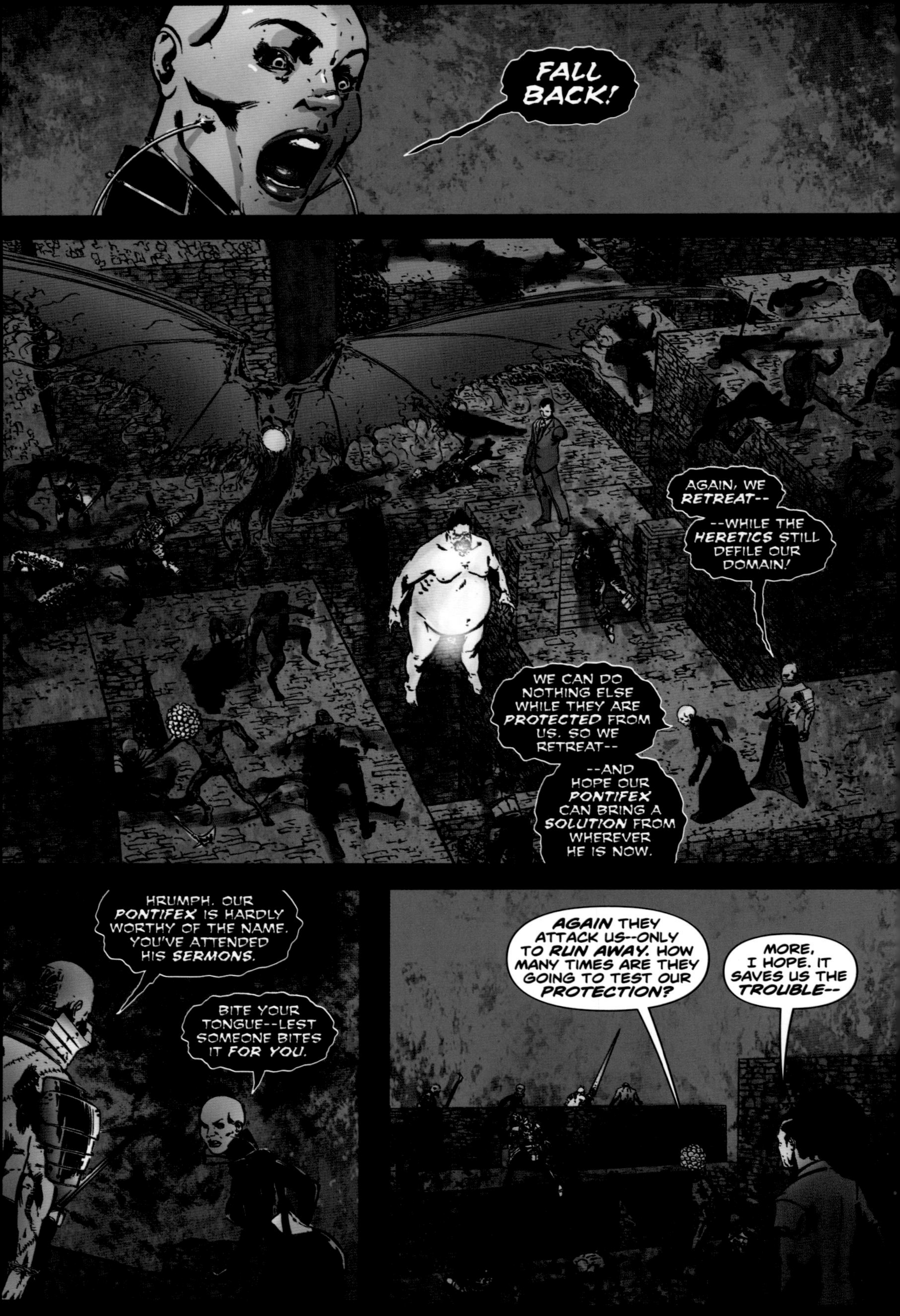
FALL BACK!
AGAIN, WE RETREAT--
--WHILE THE HERETICS STILL DEFILE OUR DOMAIN!
WE CAN DO NOTHING ELSE WHILE THEY ARE PROTECTED FROM US. SO WE RETREAT--
--AND HOPE OUR PONTIFEX CAN BRING A SOLUTION FROM WHEREVER HE IS NOW.
HRUMPH. OUR PONTIFEX IS HARDLY WORTHY OF THE NAME. YOU'VE ATTENDED HIS SERMONS.
BITE YOUR TONGUE--LEST SOMEONE BITES IT FOR YOU.
AGAIN THEY ATTACK US--ONLY TO RUN AWAY. HOW MANY TIMES ARE THEY GOING TO TEST OUR PROTECTION?
MORE, I HOPE. IT SAVES US THE TROUBLE--

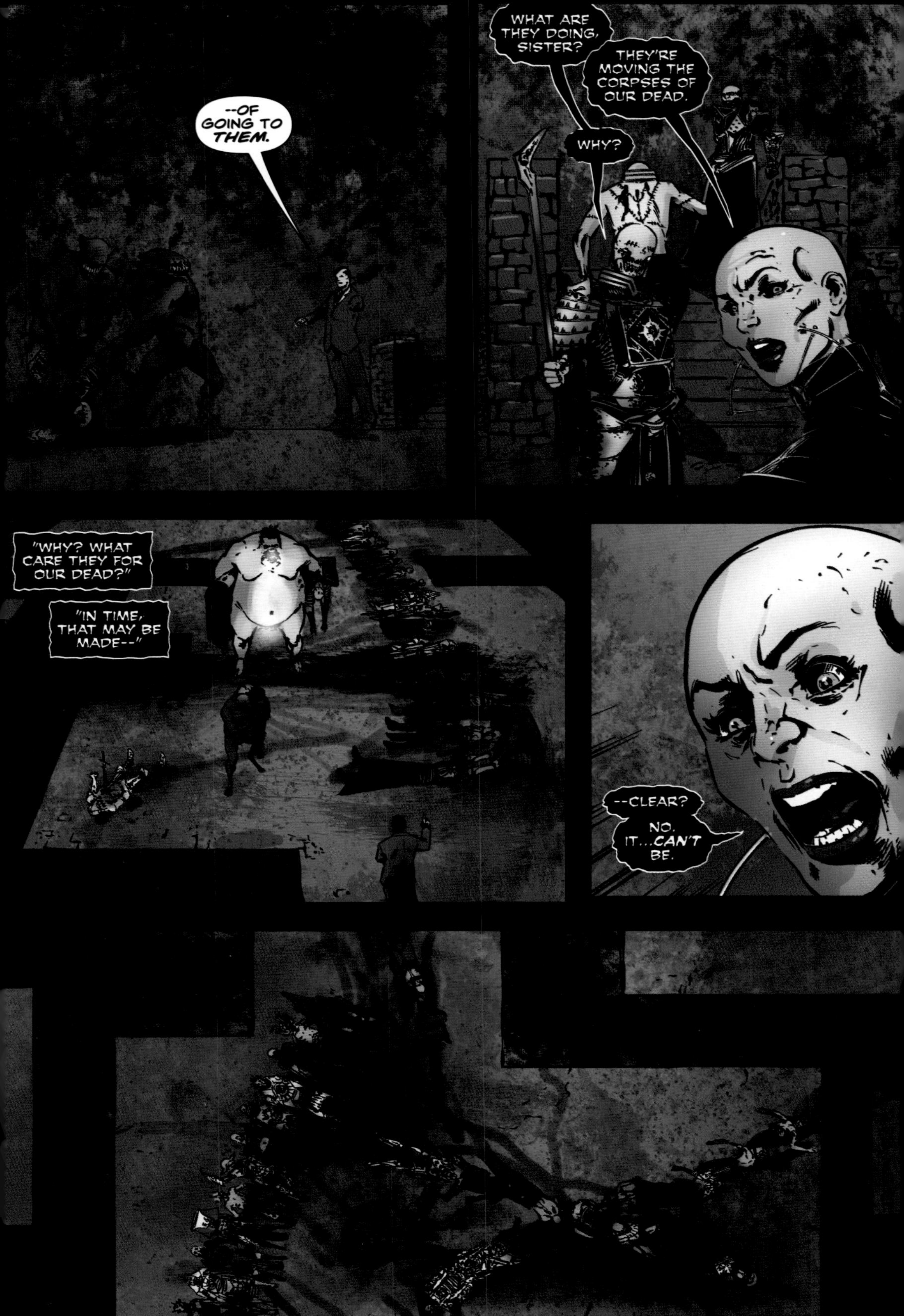
--OF GOING TO *THEM.*
WHAT ARE THEY DOING, SISTER?
THEY'RE MOVING THE CORPSES OF OUR DEAD.
WHY?
"WHY? WHAT CARE THEY FOR OUR DEAD?"
"IN TIME, THAT MAY BE MADE--"
--CLEAR?
NO. IT...*CAN'T* BE.

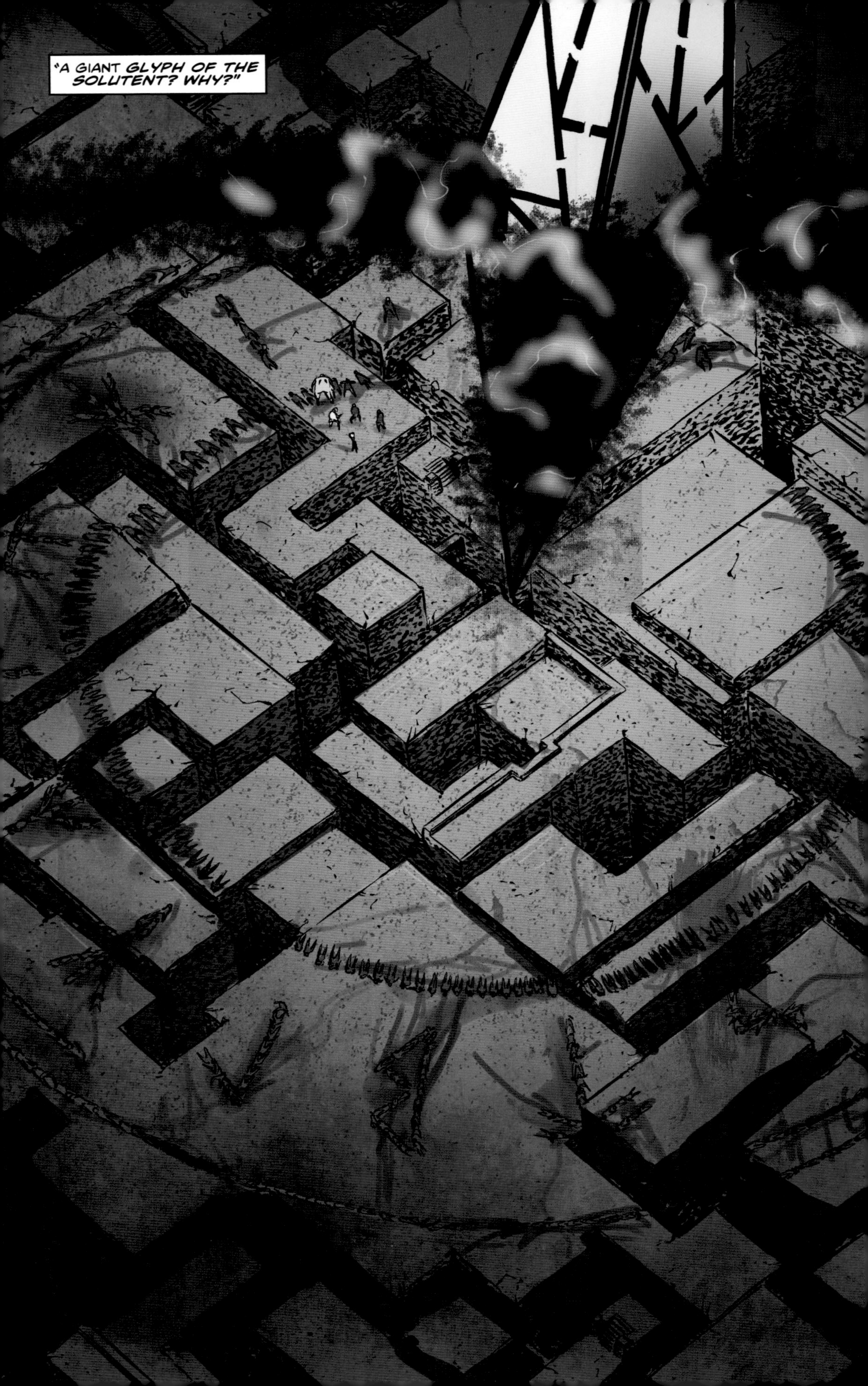
"A GIANT GLYPH OF THE SOLUTENT? WHY?"

CENOBITES GET THEIR POWER FROM LEVIATHAN. WE'RE LITERALLY CLAD IN HIS *FLESH*.

WE'RE VULNERABLE TO THE GLYPH--

THAT'S WHERE YOU GET YOUR LEATHER? DISGUSTING!

BECAUSE *LEVIATHAN'S* VULNERABLE TO IT. A GLYPH THAT *BIG*...

...THEY'VE GOTTA BE HERE TO ASSASSINATE LEVIATHAN.

WE NEED TO ACT FAST-- BEFORE THEY *FINISH* THE *GLYPH*.

THEY'RE GOING TO ASSASSINATE THE *LORD OF HELL*? AND...WE'RE ACTUALLY GOING TO *STOP* THEM?

I *STILL* HATE THIS.

IS EVERYBODY READY? THIS IS GOING TO BE *TOUGH*...

TIFFANY, WITH RESPECT--

--GOING IN *GUNS* BLAZING IS POOR TACTICS.

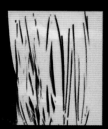

ESPECIALLY SINCE BULLETS WON'T KILL THE *ONE WITH ALL THE EYES* OR THE *FLYING DEMON*.

WHAT DO YOU SUGGEST, NORTON?

BETWEEN THE *PROTECTION TALISMANS*, THE *DEMON-KILLING KNIFE* AND THE *CENOBITE ARMY*, WE'VE GOT SOME GREAT *RESOURCES* HERE.

HOW ABOUT WE *USE* THEM?

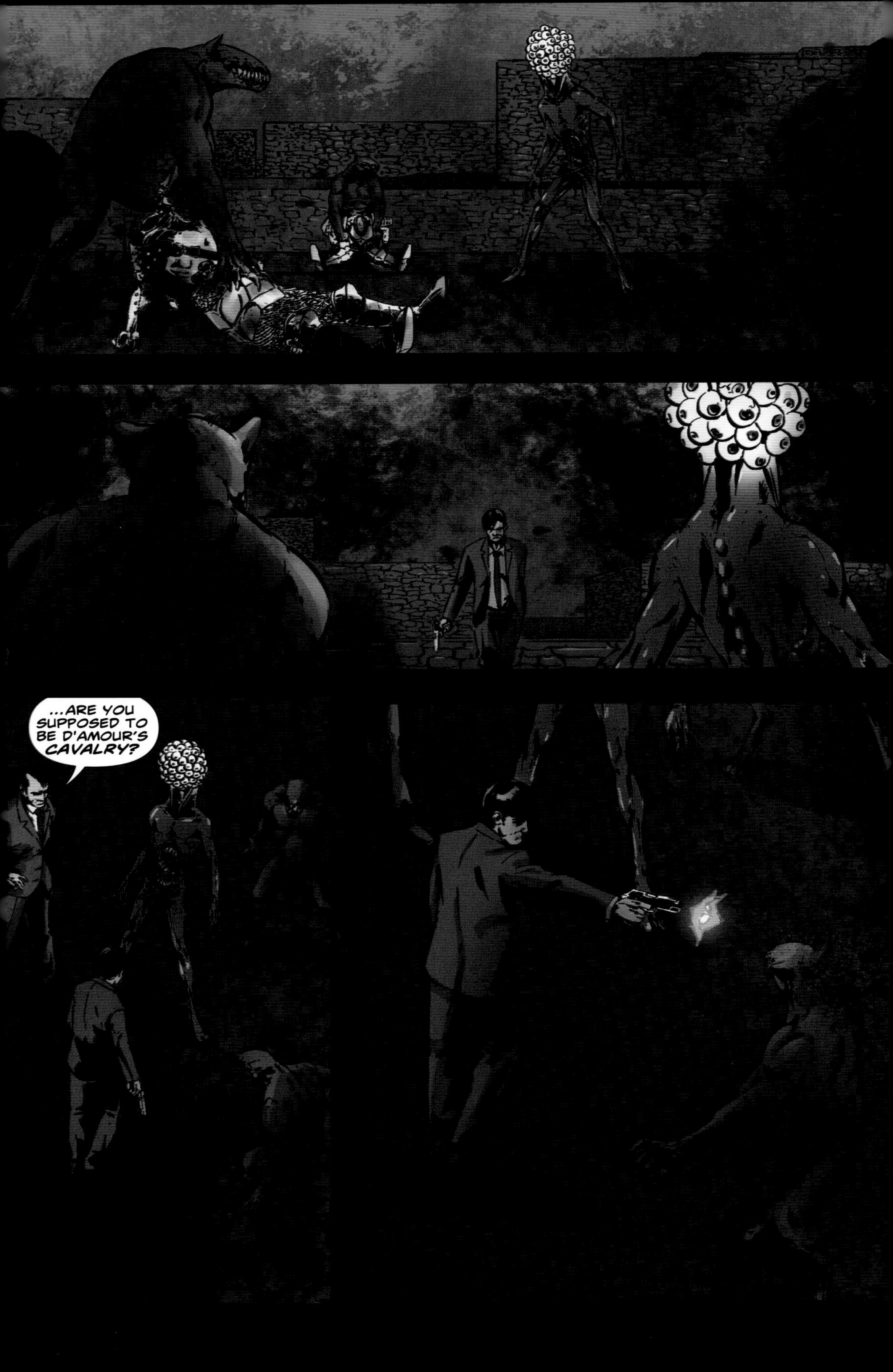
...ARE YOU SUPPOSED TO BE D'AMOUR'S CAVALRY?

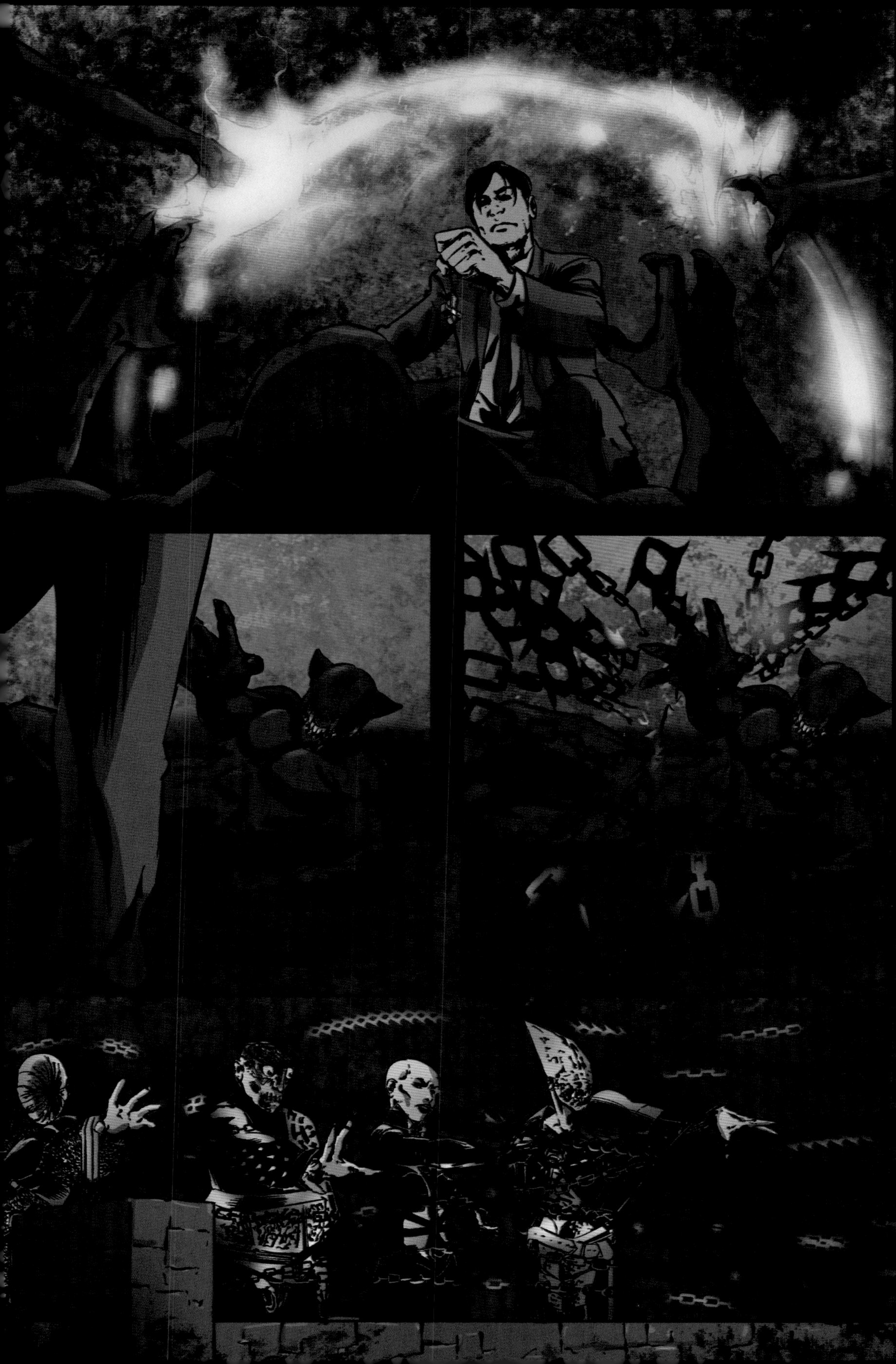

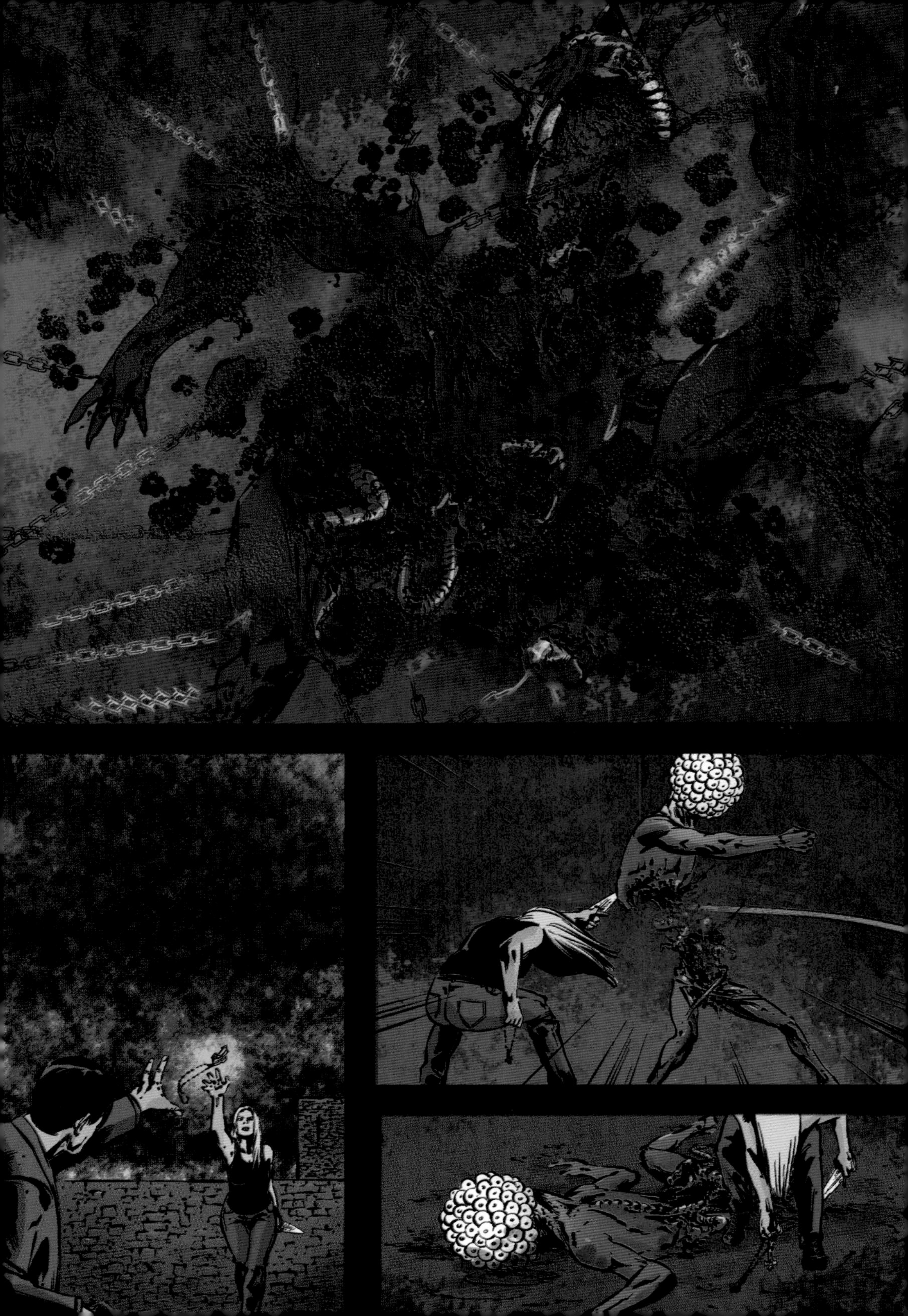

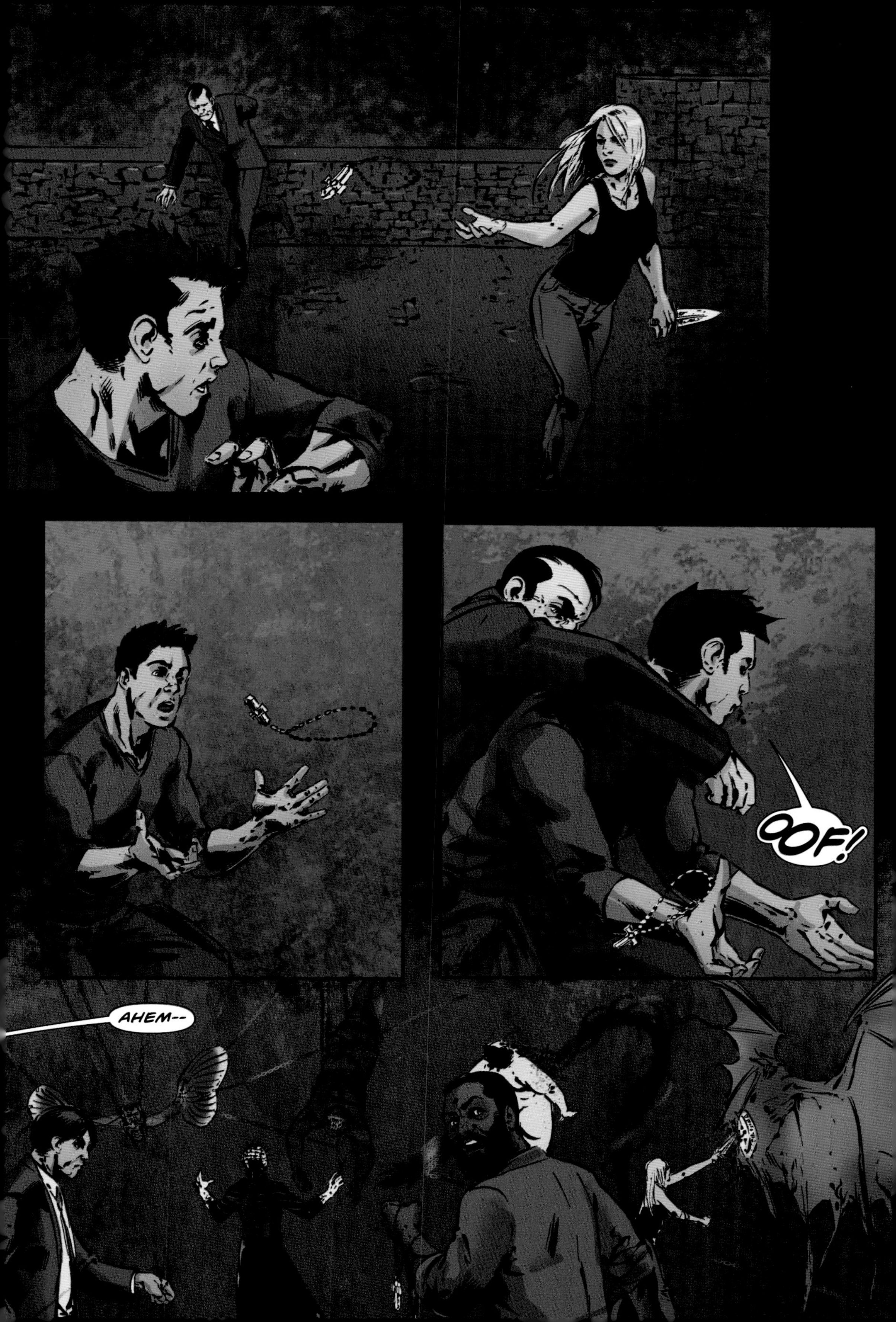
OOF!
AHEM--

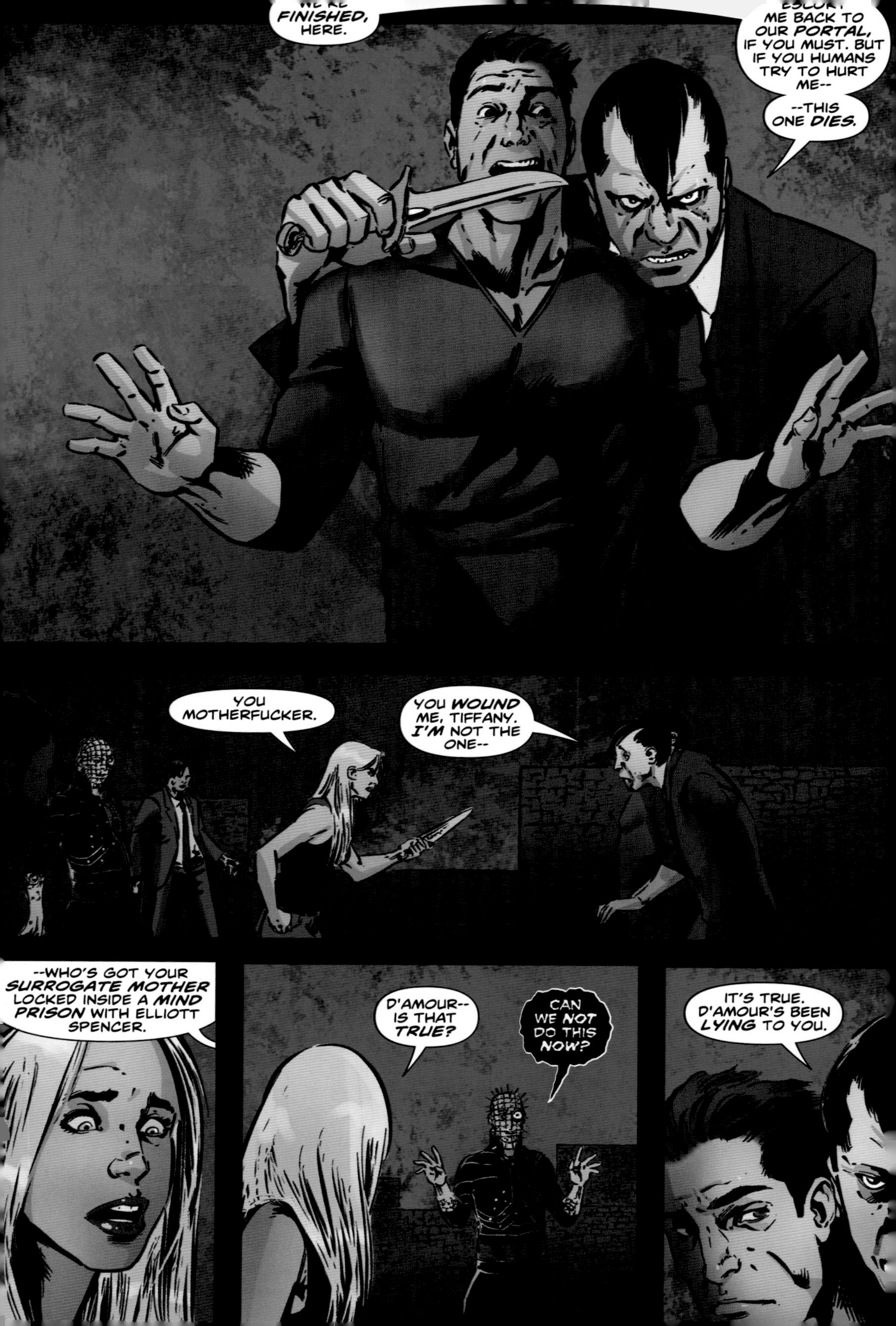
FINISHED, HERE.
ME BACK TO OUR PORTAL, IF YOU MUST. BUT IF YOU HUMANS TRY TO HURT ME--
--THIS ONE DIES.
YOU MOTHERFUCKER.
YOU WOUND ME, TIFFANY. I'M NOT THE ONE--
--WHO'S GOT YOUR SURROGATE MOTHER LOCKED INSIDE A MIND PRISON WITH ELLIOTT SPENCER.
D'AMOUR-- IS THAT TRUE?
CAN WE NOT DO THIS NOW?
IT'S TRUE. D'AMOUR'S BEEN LYING TO YOU.

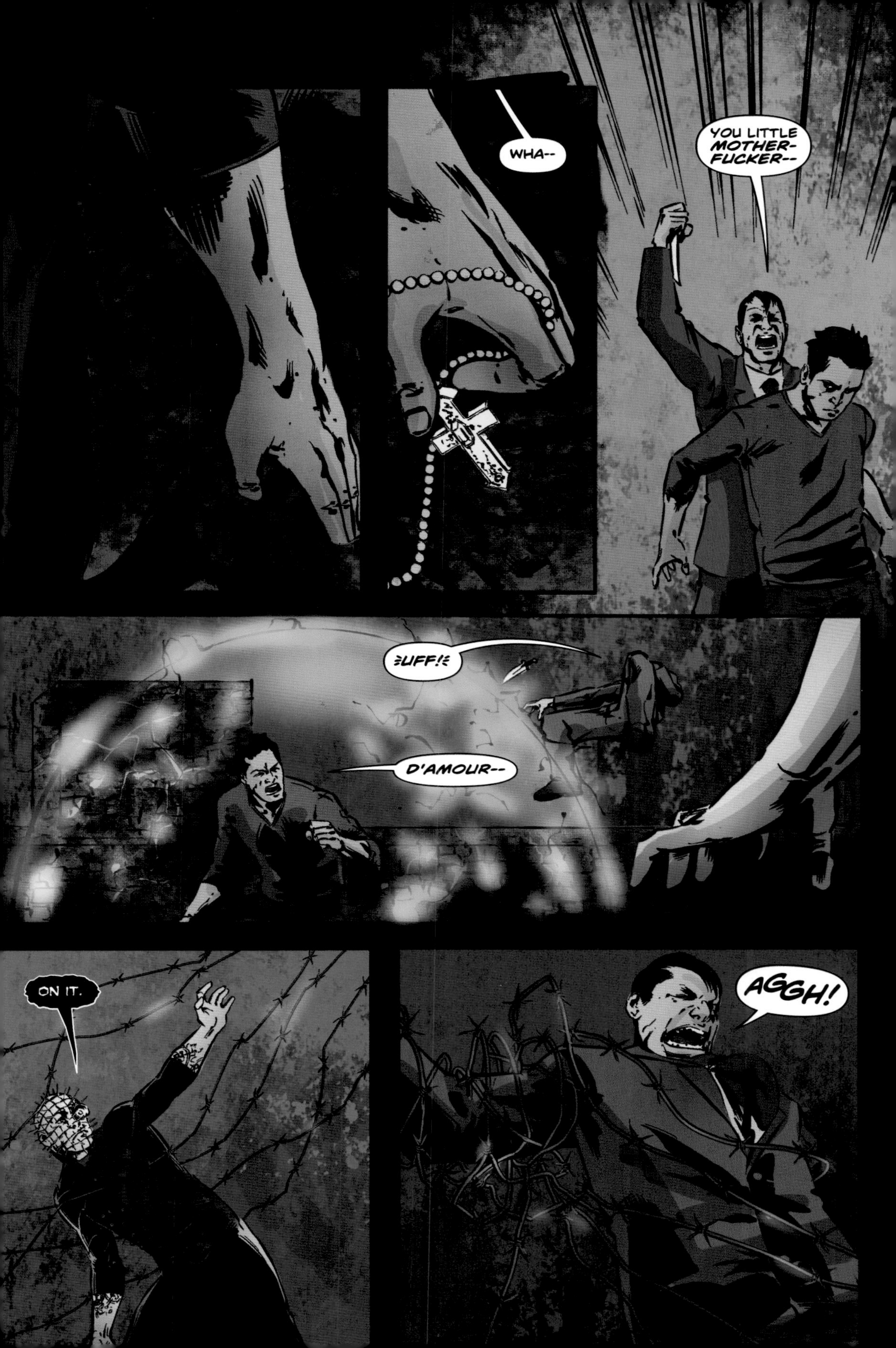
WHA--
YOU LITTLE MOTHER-FUCKER--
UFF!
D'AMOUR--
ON IT.
AGGH!

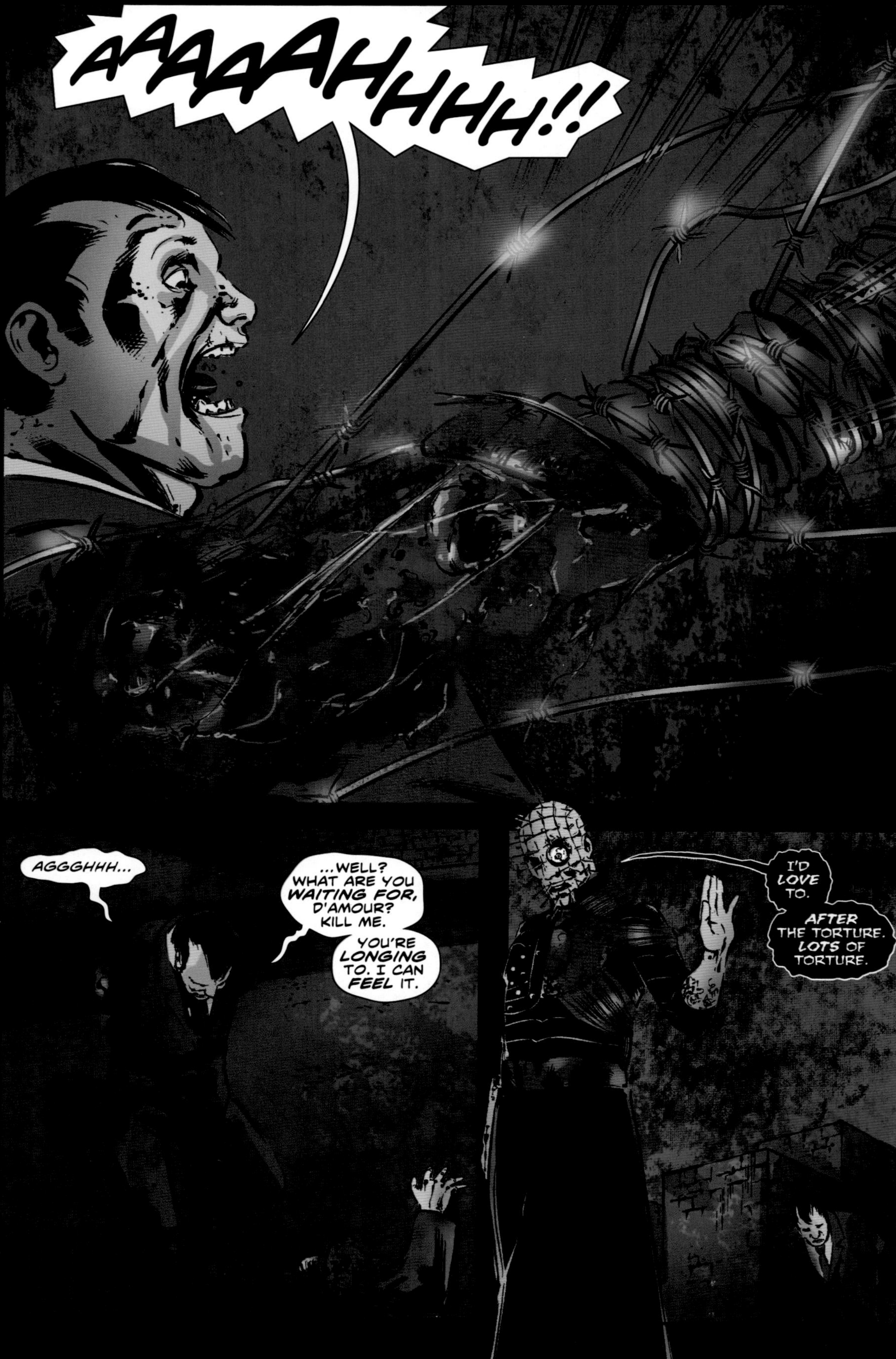
AAAAAHHHH!!
AGGGHHH...
...WELL? WHAT ARE YOU WAITING FOR, D'AMOUR? KILL ME.
YOU'RE LONGING TO. I CAN FEEL IT.
I'D LOVE TO.
AFTER THE TORTURE. LOTS OF TORTURE.

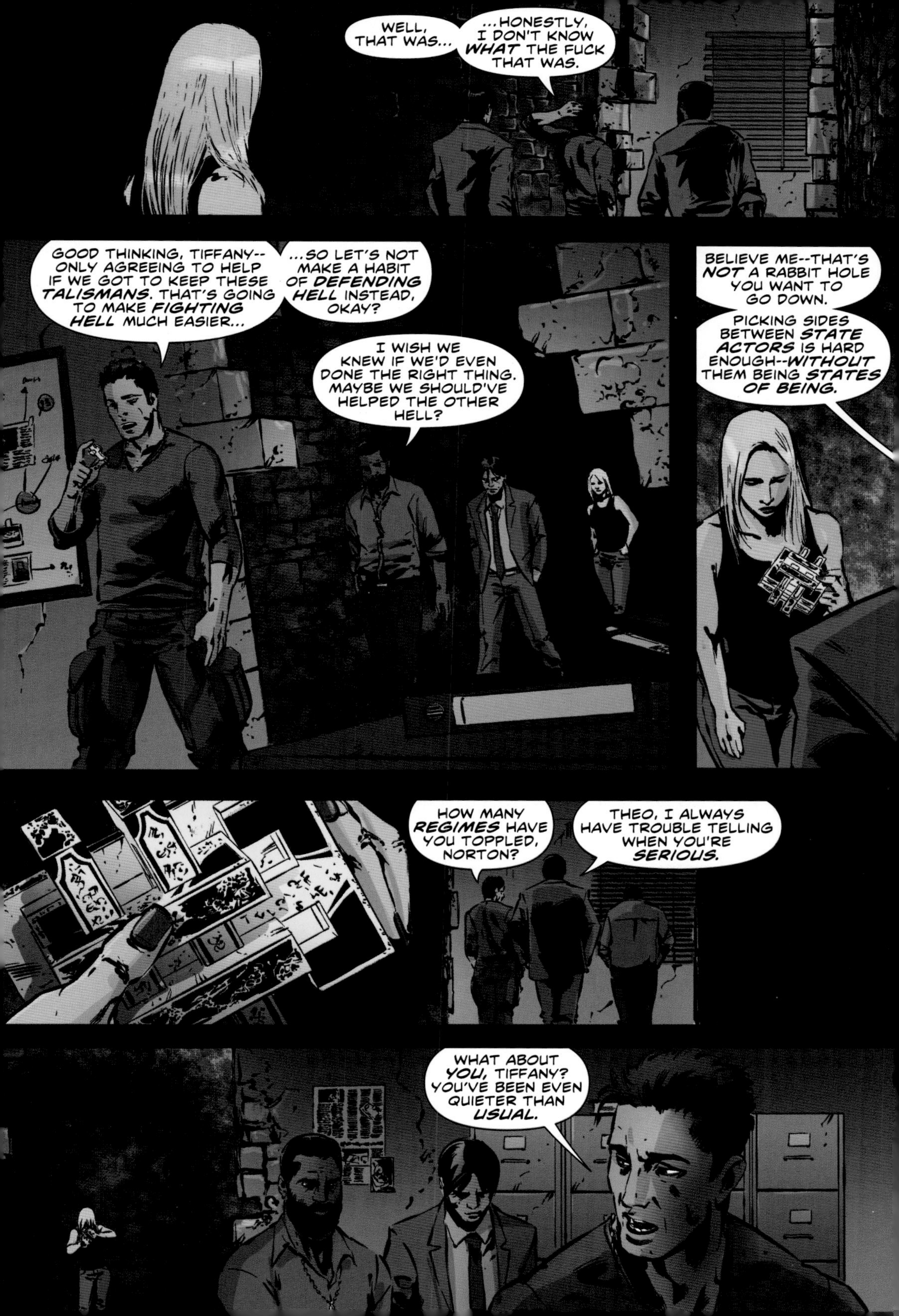
WELL, THAT WAS...
...HONESTLY, I DON'T KNOW WHAT THE FUCK THAT WAS.
GOOD THINKING, TIFFANY-- ONLY AGREEING TO HELP IF WE GOT TO KEEP THESE TALISMANS. THAT'S GOING TO MAKE FIGHTING HELL MUCH EASIER...
...SO LET'S NOT MAKE A HABIT OF DEFENDING HELL INSTEAD, OKAY?
I WISH WE KNEW IF WE'D EVEN DONE THE RIGHT THING. MAYBE WE SHOULD'VE HELPED THE OTHER HELL?
BELIEVE ME--THAT'S NOT A RABBIT HOLE YOU WANT TO GO DOWN.
PICKING SIDES BETWEEN STATE ACTORS IS HARD ENOUGH--WITHOUT THEM BEING STATES OF BEING.
HOW MANY REGIMES HAVE YOU TOPPLED, NORTON?
THEO, I ALWAYS HAVE TROUBLE TELLING WHEN YOU'RE SERIOUS.
WHAT ABOUT YOU, TIFFANY? YOU'VE BEEN EVEN QUIETER THAN USUAL.

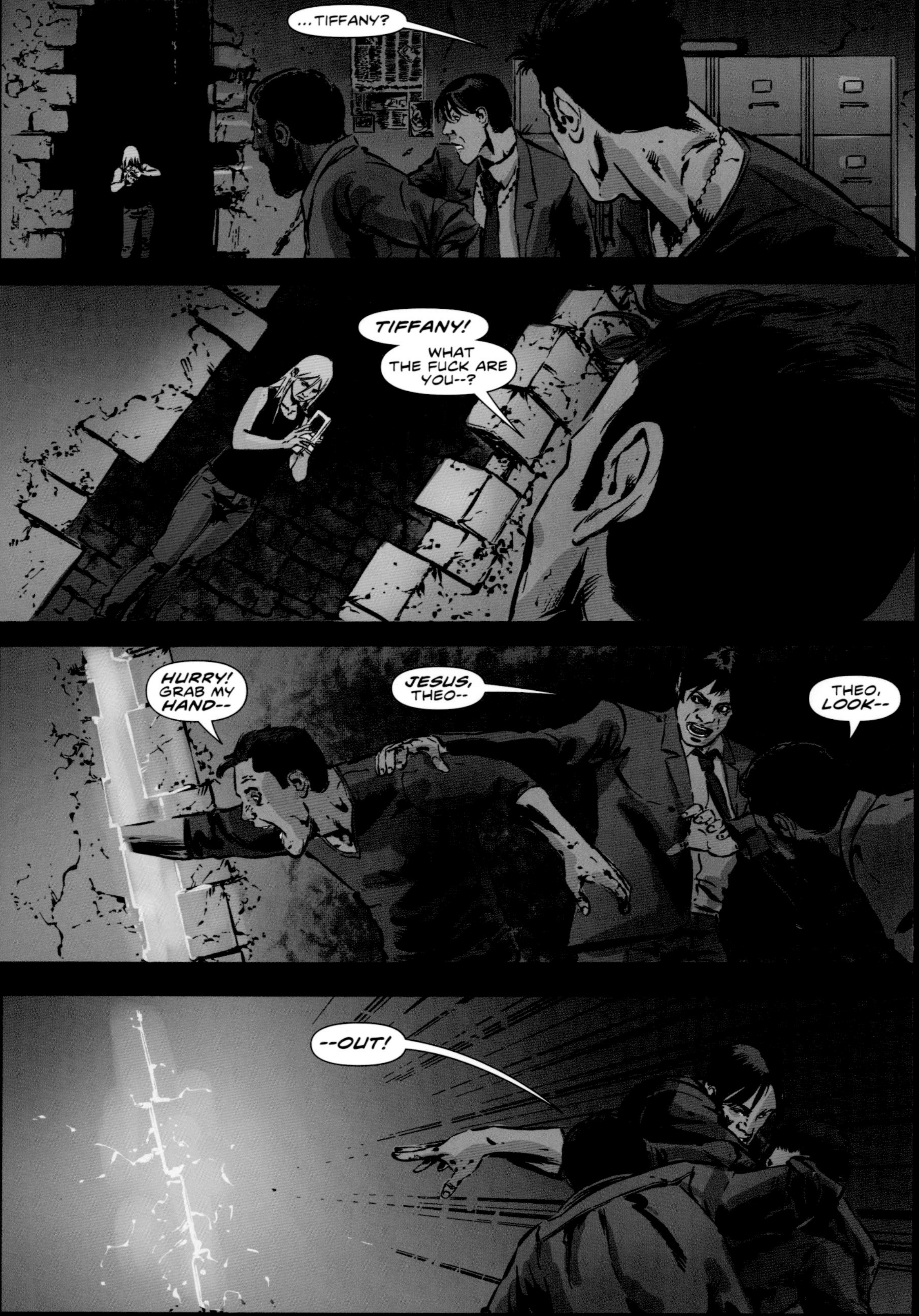
...TIFFANY?
TIFFANY! WHAT THE FUCK ARE YOU--?
HURRY! GRAB MY HAND--
JESUS, THEO--
THEO, LOOK--
--OUT!

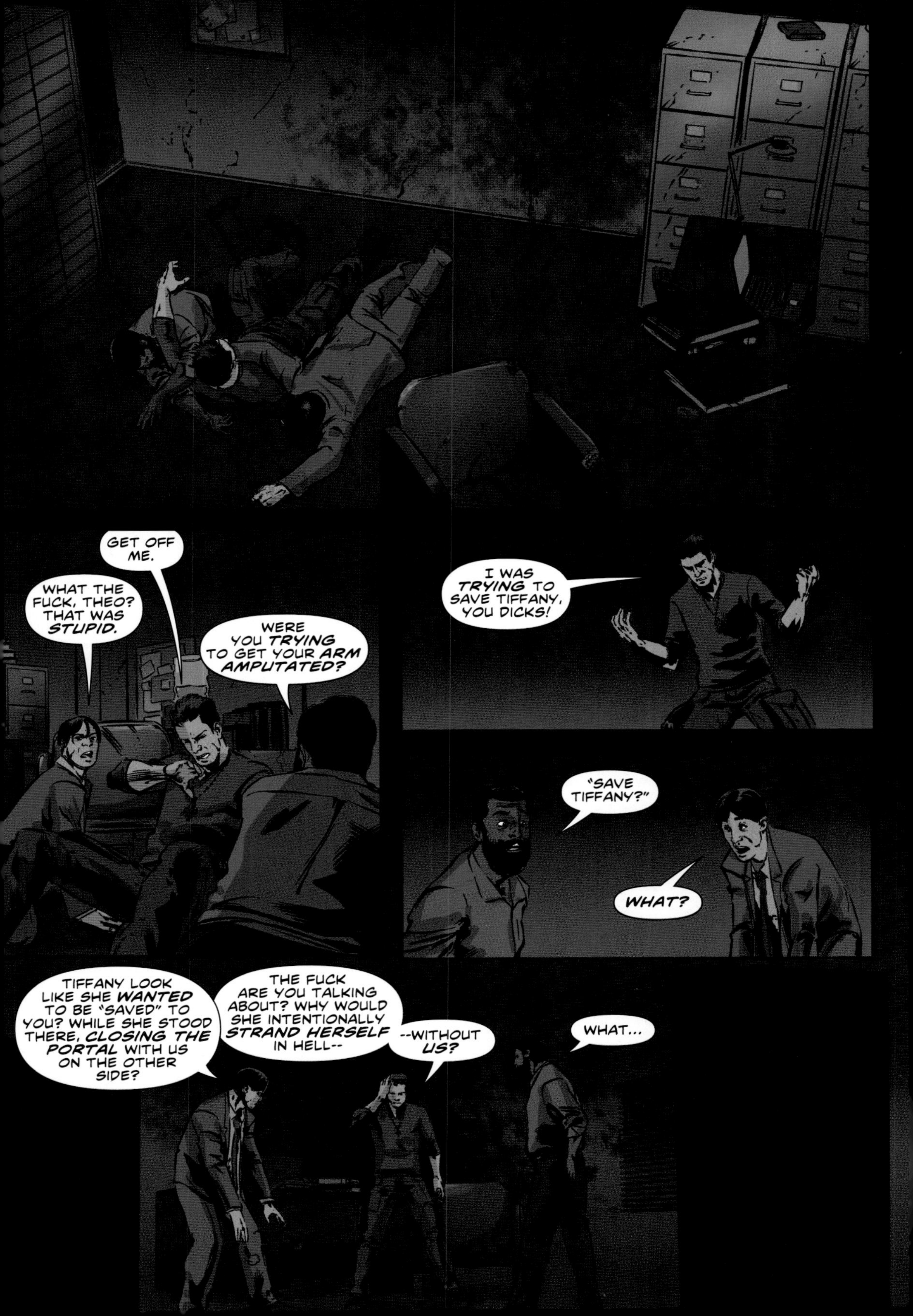
GET OFF ME.
WHAT THE FUCK, THEO? THAT WAS STUPID.
WERE YOU TRYING TO GET YOUR ARM AMPUTATED?
I WAS TRYING TO SAVE TIFFANY, YOU DICKS!
"SAVE TIFFANY?"
WHAT?
TIFFANY LOOK LIKE SHE WANTED TO BE "SAVED" TO YOU? WHILE SHE STOOD THERE, CLOSING THE PORTAL WITH US ON THE OTHER SIDE?
THE FUCK ARE YOU TALKING ABOUT? WHY WOULD SHE INTENTIONALLY STRAND HERSELF IN HELL--
--WITHOUT US?
WHAT...

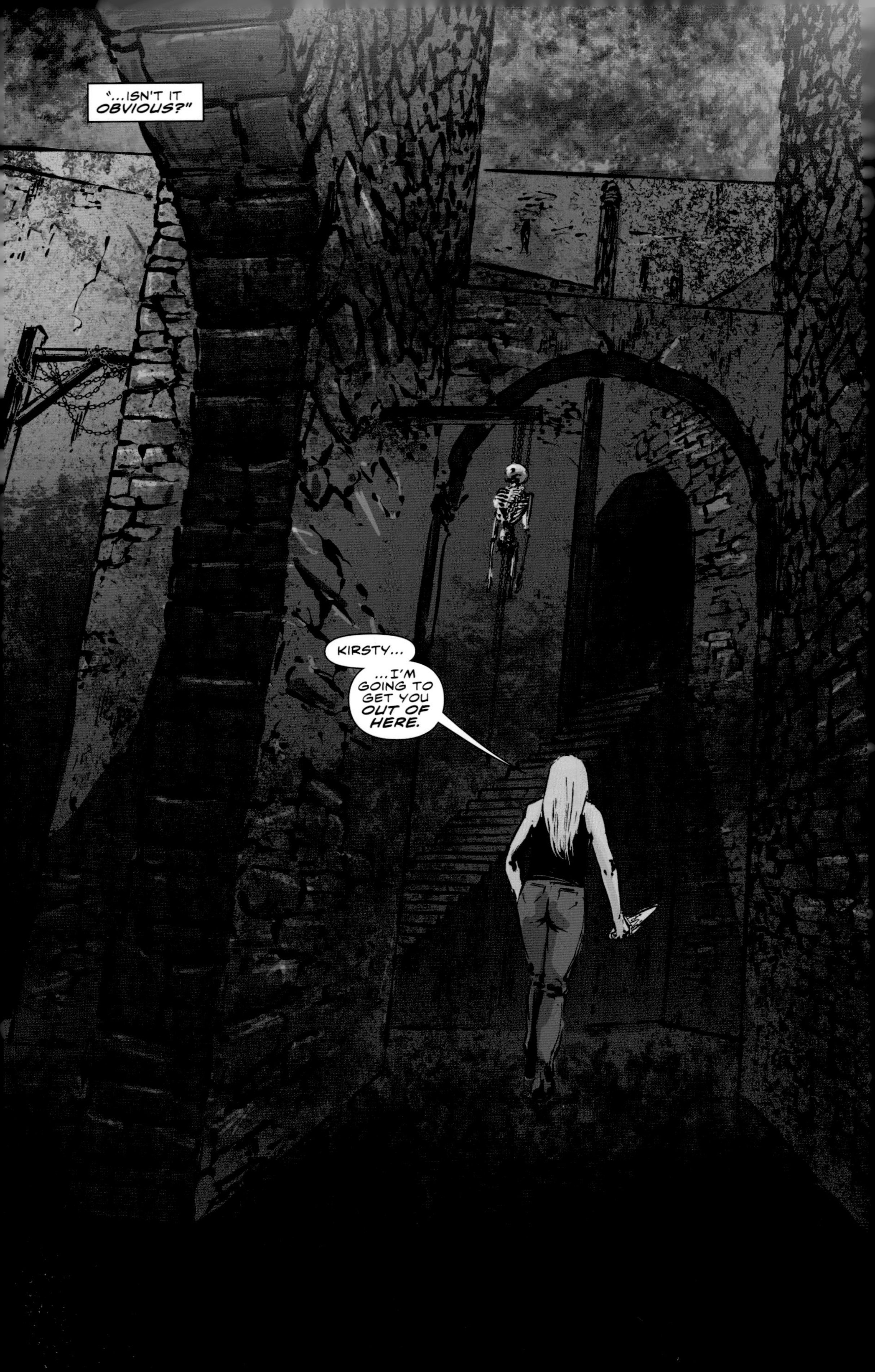
"...ISN'T IT OBVIOUS?"
KIRSTY...
...I'M GOING TO GET YOU OUT OF HERE.

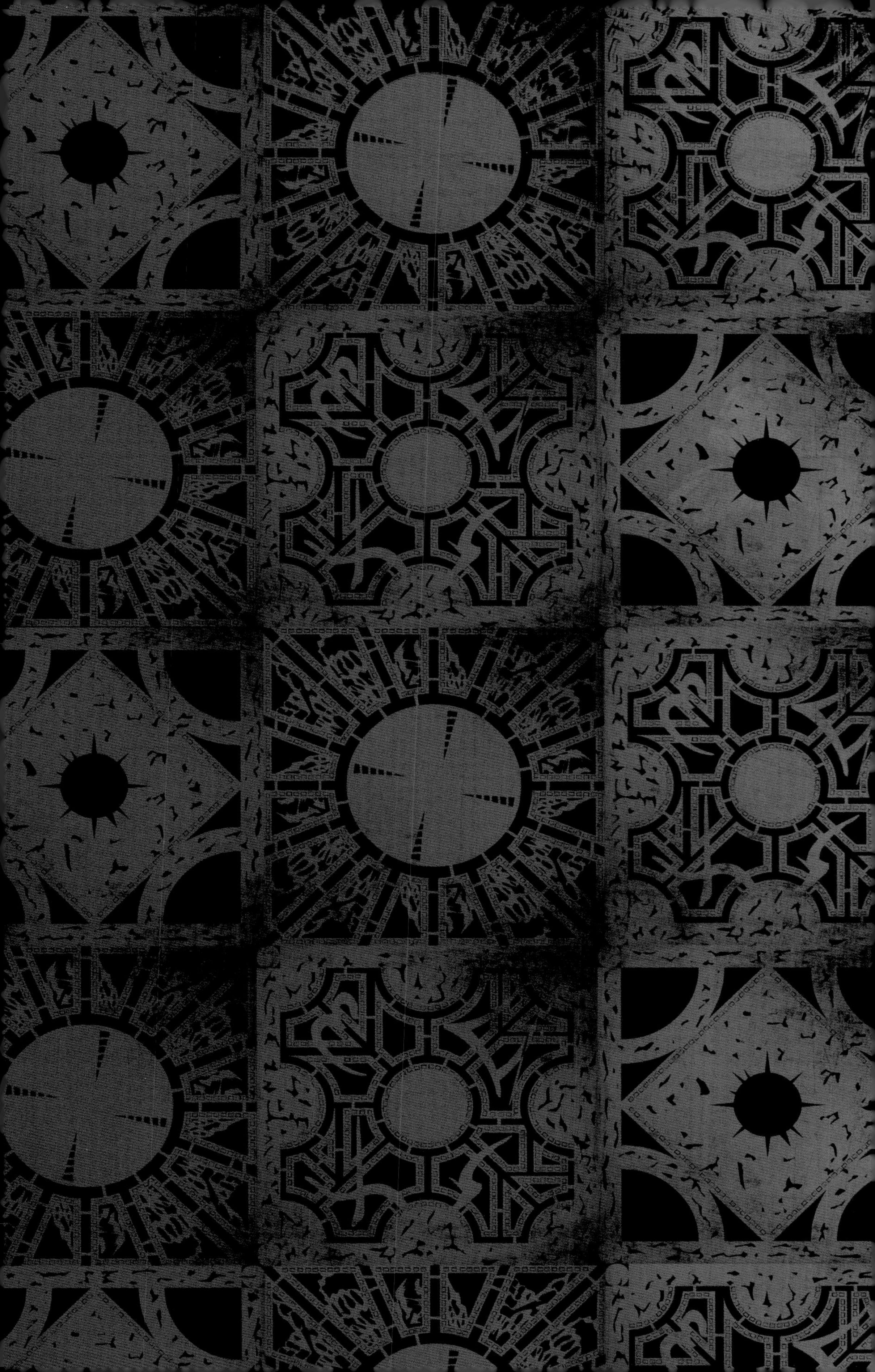

CHAPTER EIGHT

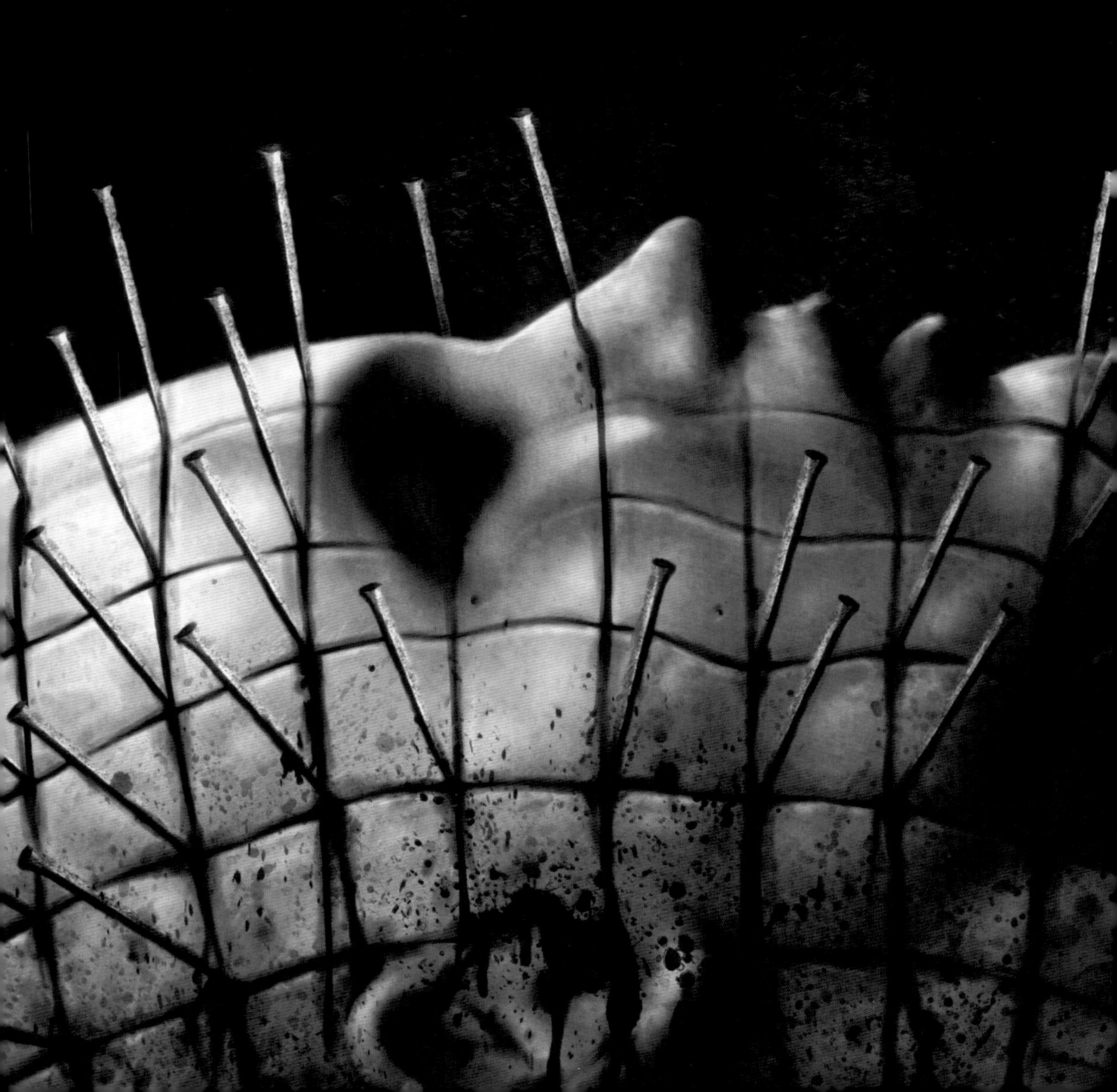

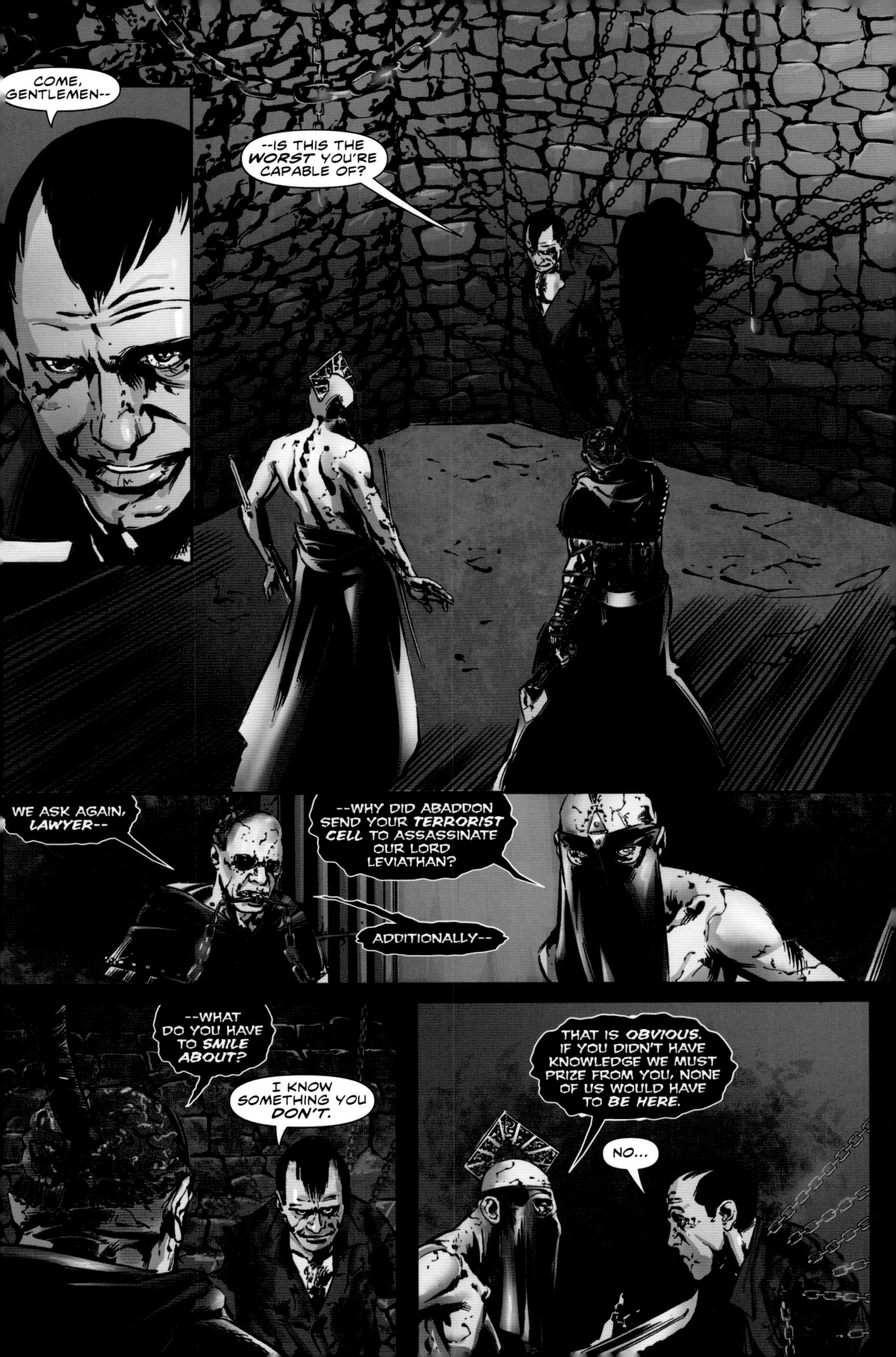

COME, GENTLEMEN--
--IS THIS THE WORST YOU'RE CAPABLE OF?
WE ASK AGAIN, LAWYER--
--WHY DID ABADDON SEND YOUR TERRORIST CELL TO ASSASSINATE OUR LORD LEVIATHAN?
ADDITIONALLY--
--WHAT DO YOU HAVE TO SMILE ABOUT?
I KNOW SOMETHING YOU DON'T.
THAT IS OBVIOUS. IF YOU DIDN'T HAVE KNOWLEDGE WE MUST PRIZE FROM YOU, NONE OF US WOULD HAVE TO BE HERE.
NO...

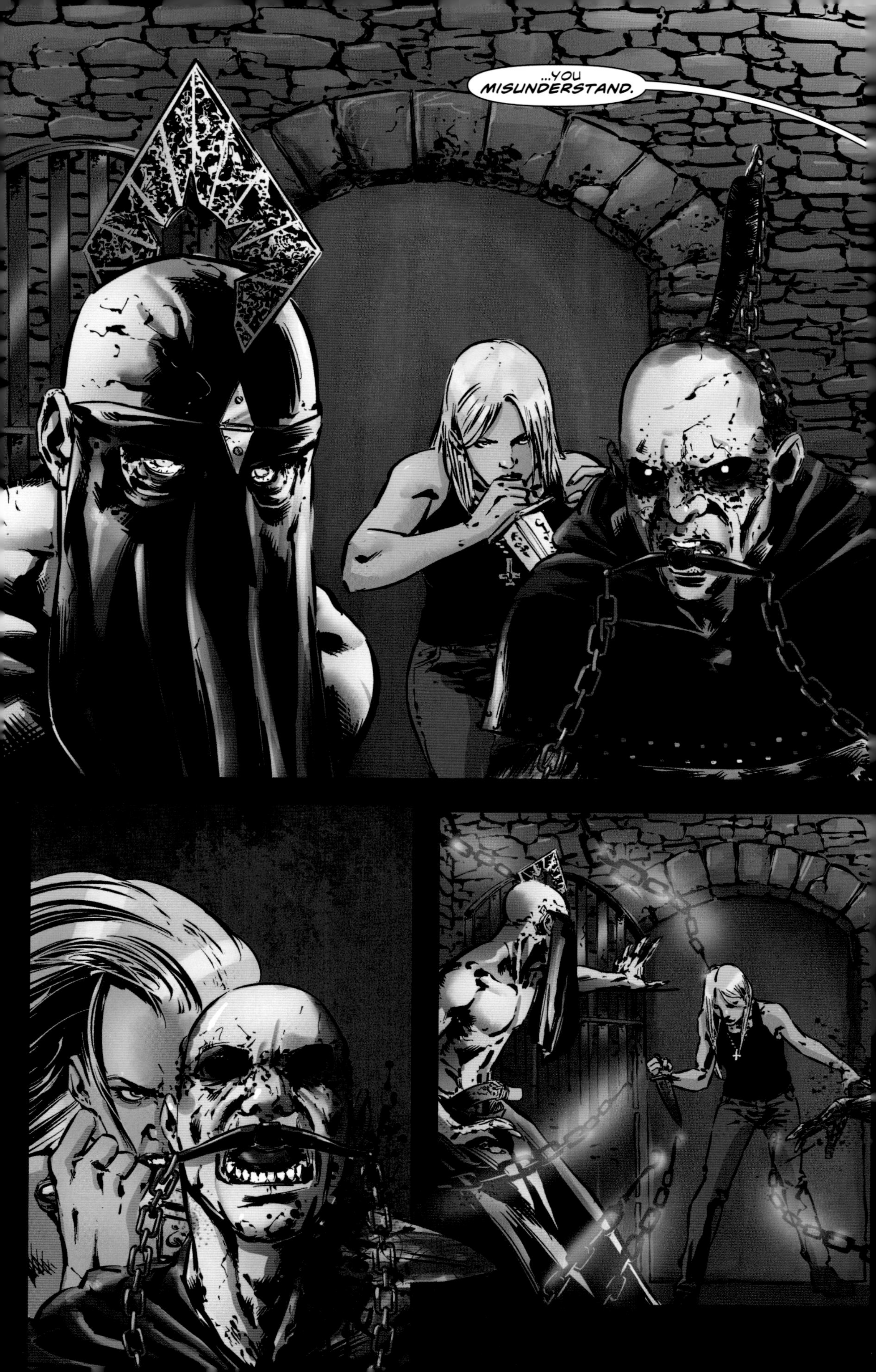
...YOU MISUNDERSTAND.

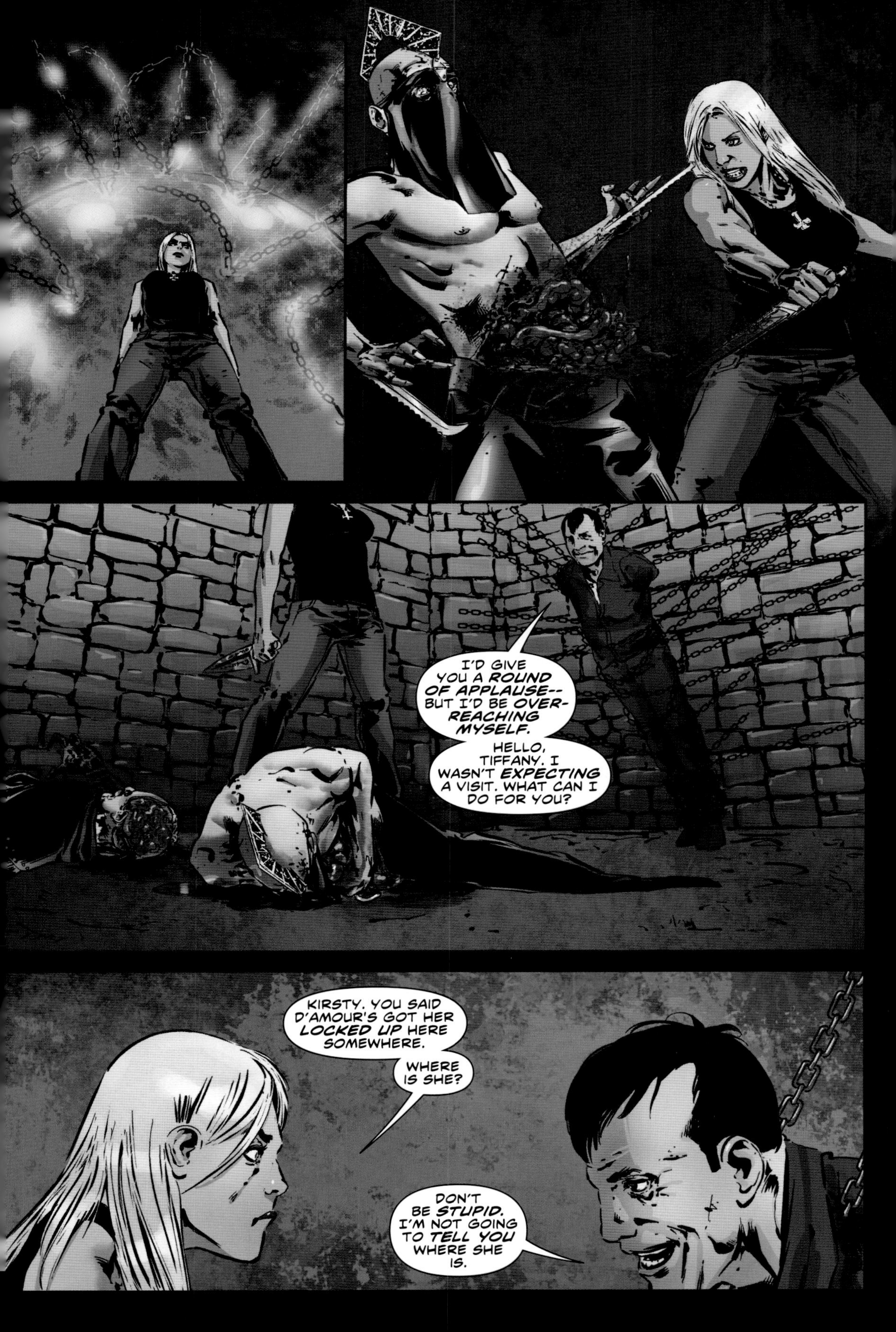
I'D GIVE YOU A ROUND OF APPLAUSE-- BUT I'D BE OVER-REACHING MYSELF.
HELLO, TIFFANY. I WASN'T EXPECTING A VISIT. WHAT CAN I DO FOR YOU?
KIRSTY. YOU SAID D'AMOUR'S GOT HER LOCKED UP HERE SOMEWHERE.
WHERE IS SHE?
DON'T BE STUPID. I'M NOT GOING TO TELL YOU WHERE SHE IS.

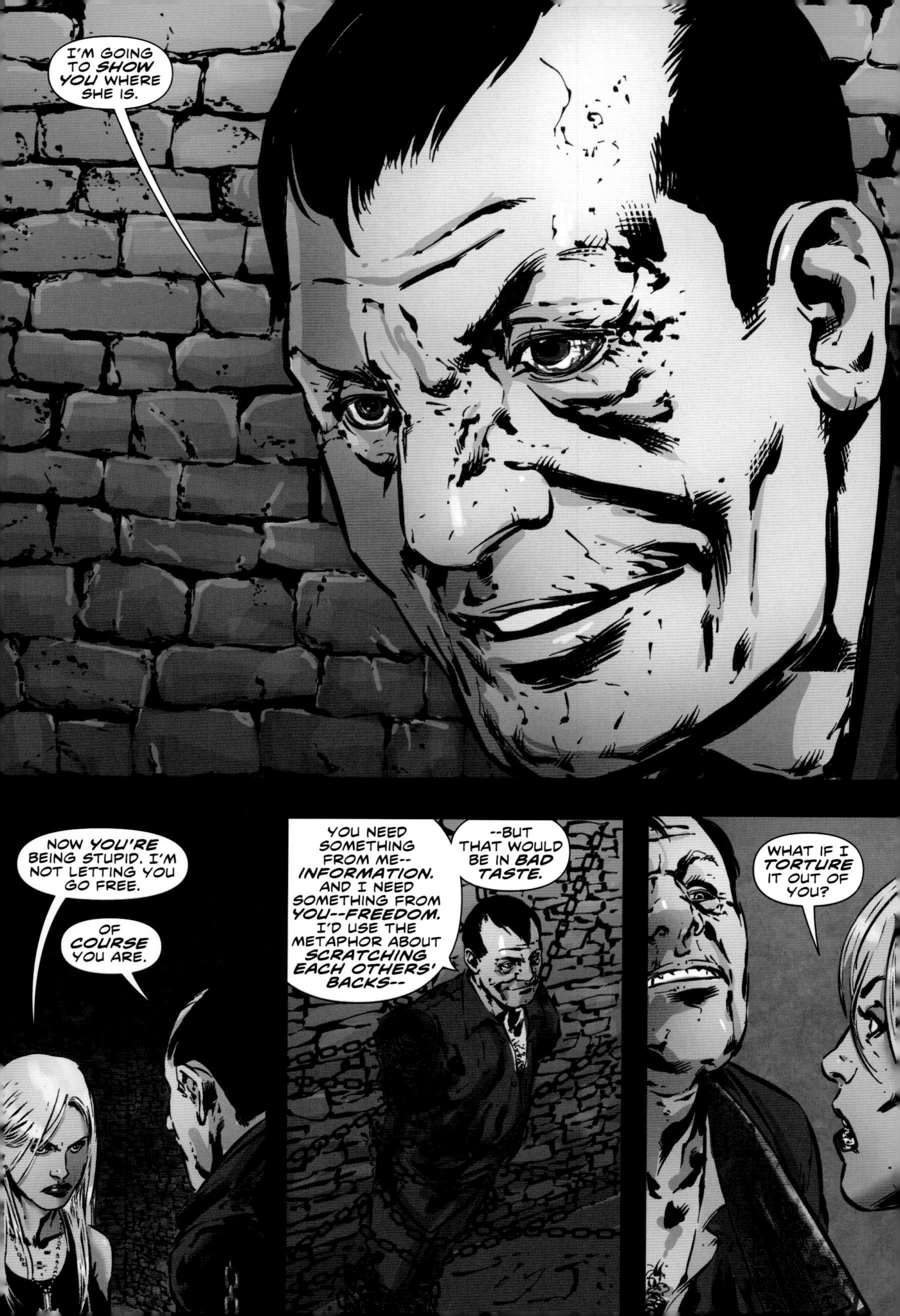
I'M GOING TO SHOW YOU WHERE SHE IS.
NOW YOU'RE BEING STUPID. I'M NOT LETTING YOU GO FREE.
OF COURSE YOU ARE.
YOU NEED SOMETHING FROM ME--INFORMATION. AND I NEED SOMETHING FROM YOU--FREEDOM. I'D USE THE METAPHOR ABOUT SCRATCHING EACH OTHERS' BACKS--
--BUT THAT WOULD BE IN BAD TASTE.
WHAT IF I TORTURE IT OUT OF YOU?

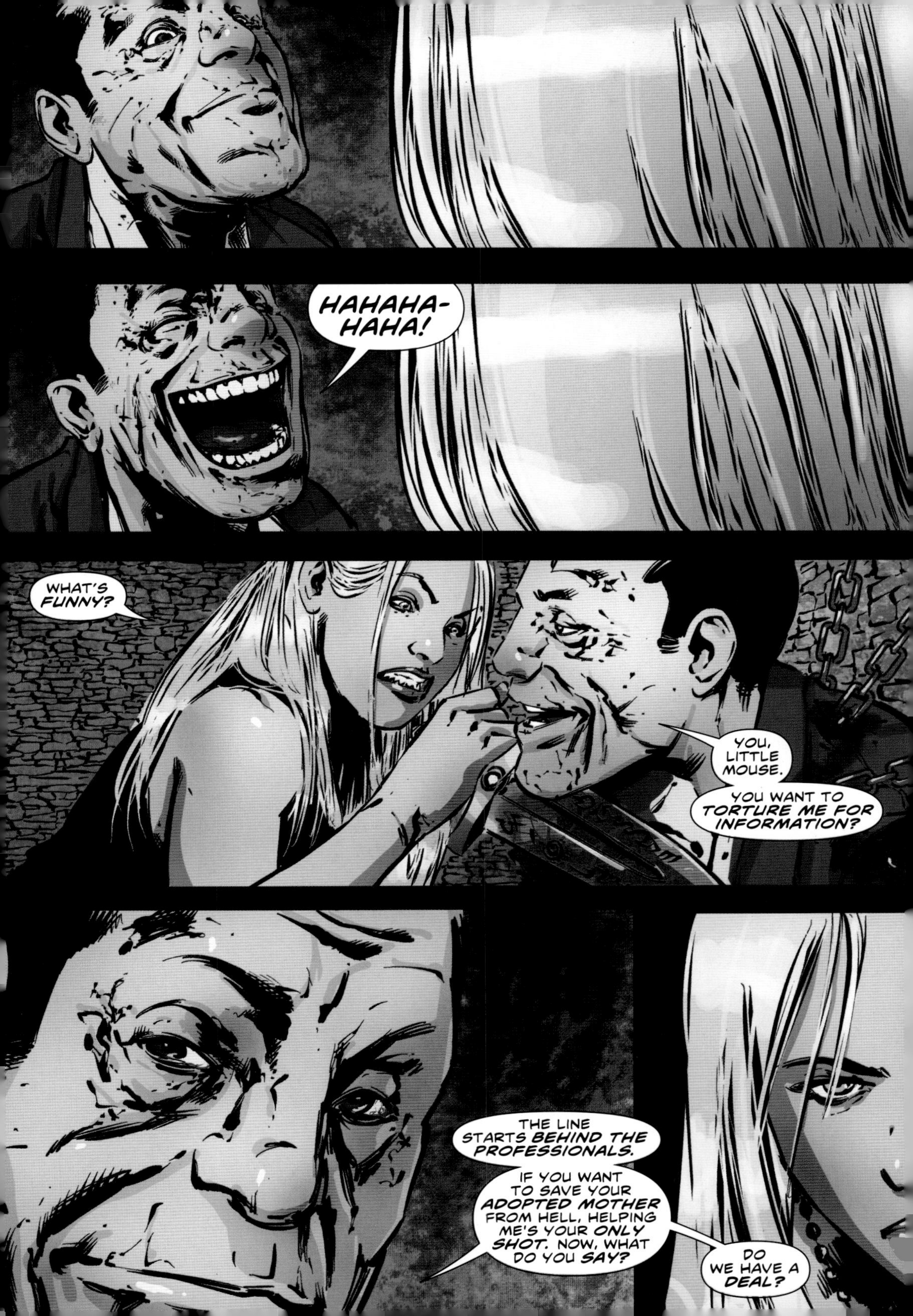
HAHAHA-HAHA!
WHAT'S FUNNY?
YOU, LITTLE MOUSE.
YOU WANT TO TORTURE ME FOR INFORMATION?
THE LINE STARTS BEHIND THE PROFESSIONALS.
IF YOU WANT TO SAVE YOUR ADOPTED MOTHER FROM HELL, HELPING ME'S YOUR ONLY SHOT. NOW, WHAT DO YOU SAY?
DO WE HAVE A DEAL?

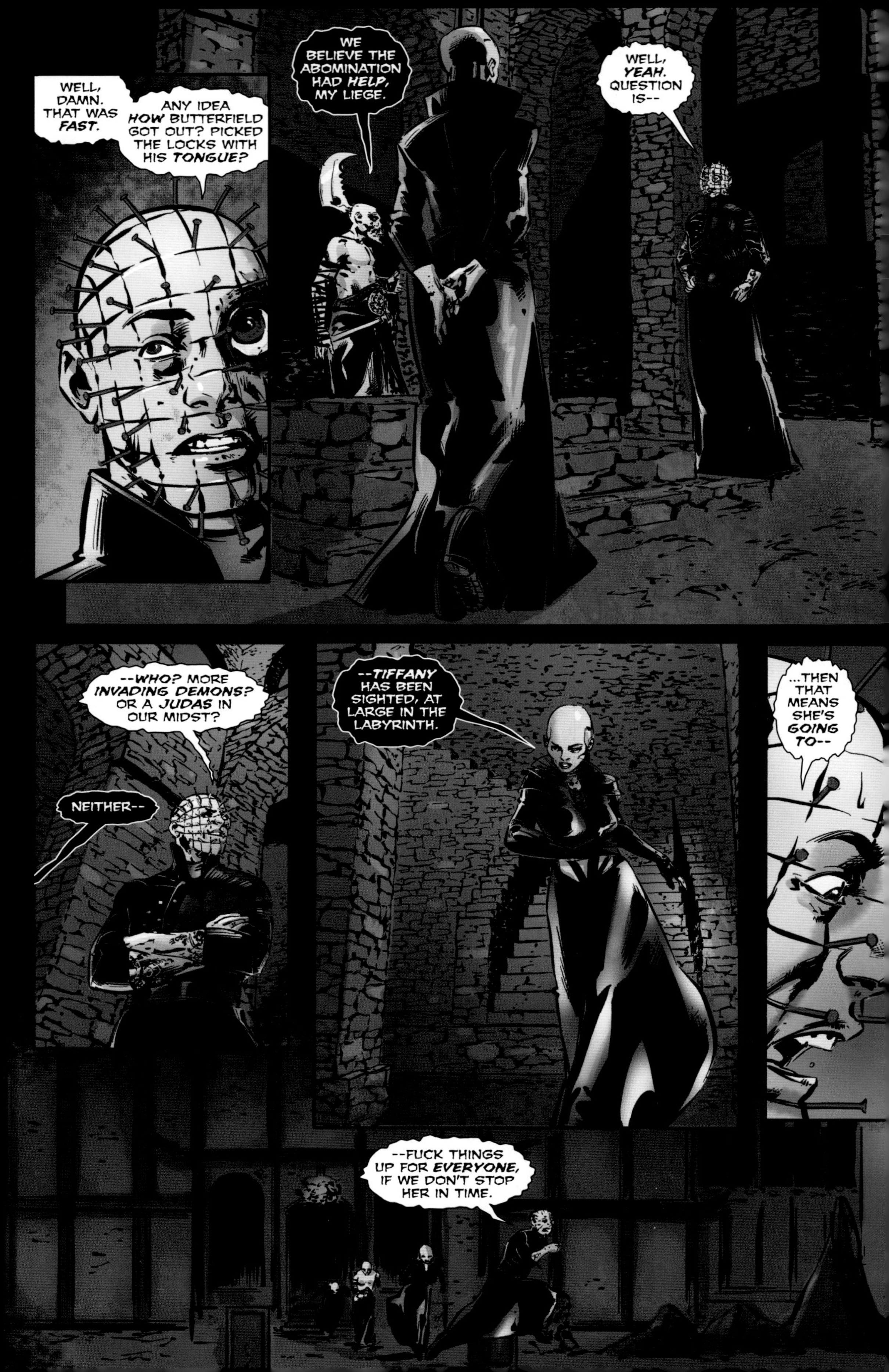
WELL, DAMN. THAT WAS FAST.
ANY IDEA HOW BUTTERFIELD GOT OUT? PICKED THE LOCKS WITH HIS TONGUE?
WE BELIEVE THE ABOMINATION HAD HELP, MY LIEGE.
WELL, YEAH. QUESTION IS--
--WHO? MORE INVADING DEMONS? OR A JUDAS IN OUR MIDST?
NEITHER--
--TIFFANY HAS BEEN SIGHTED, AT LARGE IN THE LABYRINTH.
...THEN THAT MEANS SHE'S GOING TO--
--FUCK THINGS UP FOR EVERYONE, IF WE DON'T STOP HER IN TIME.

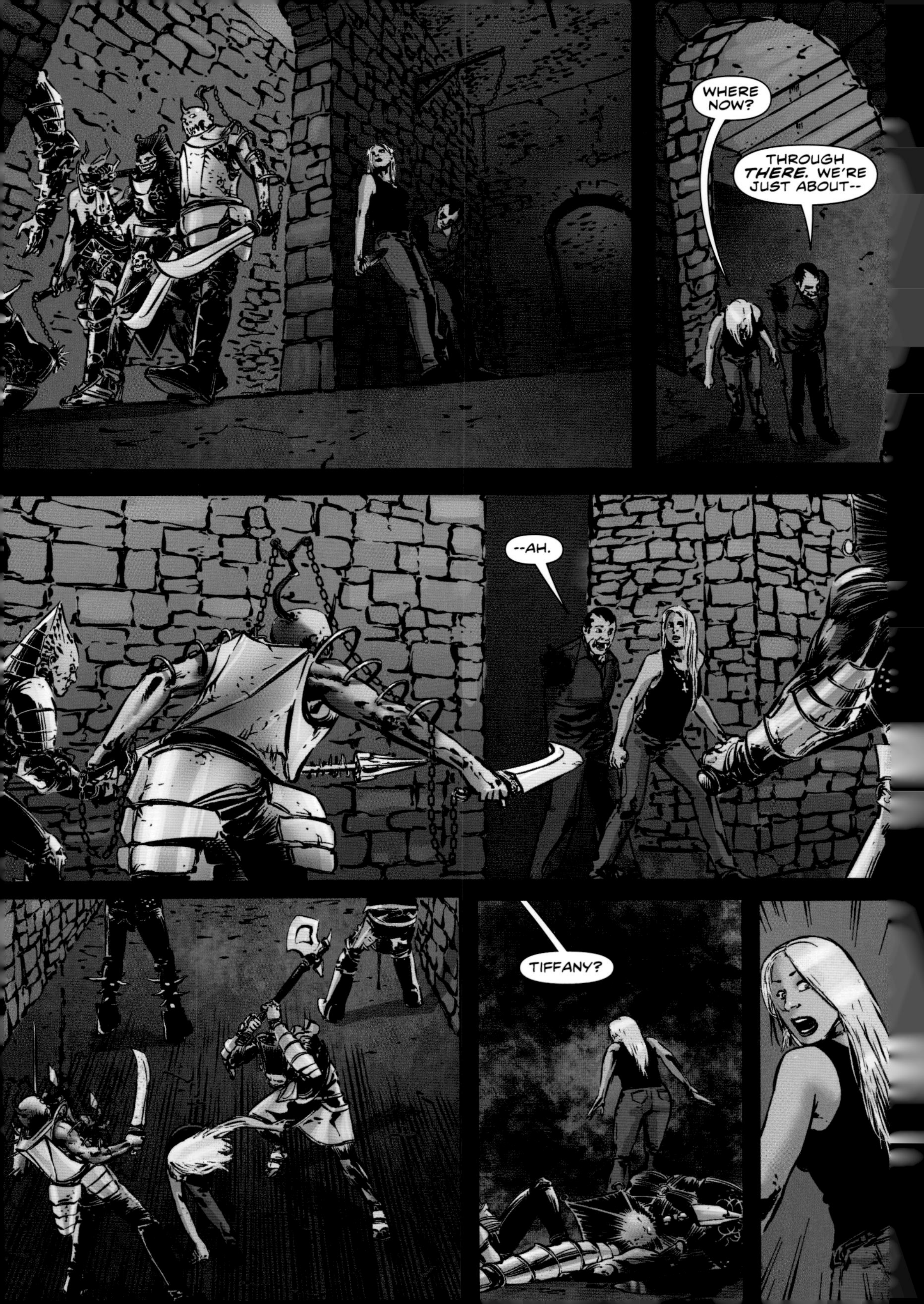
WHERE NOW?
THROUGH *THERE.* WE'RE JUST ABOUT--
--AH.
TIFFANY?

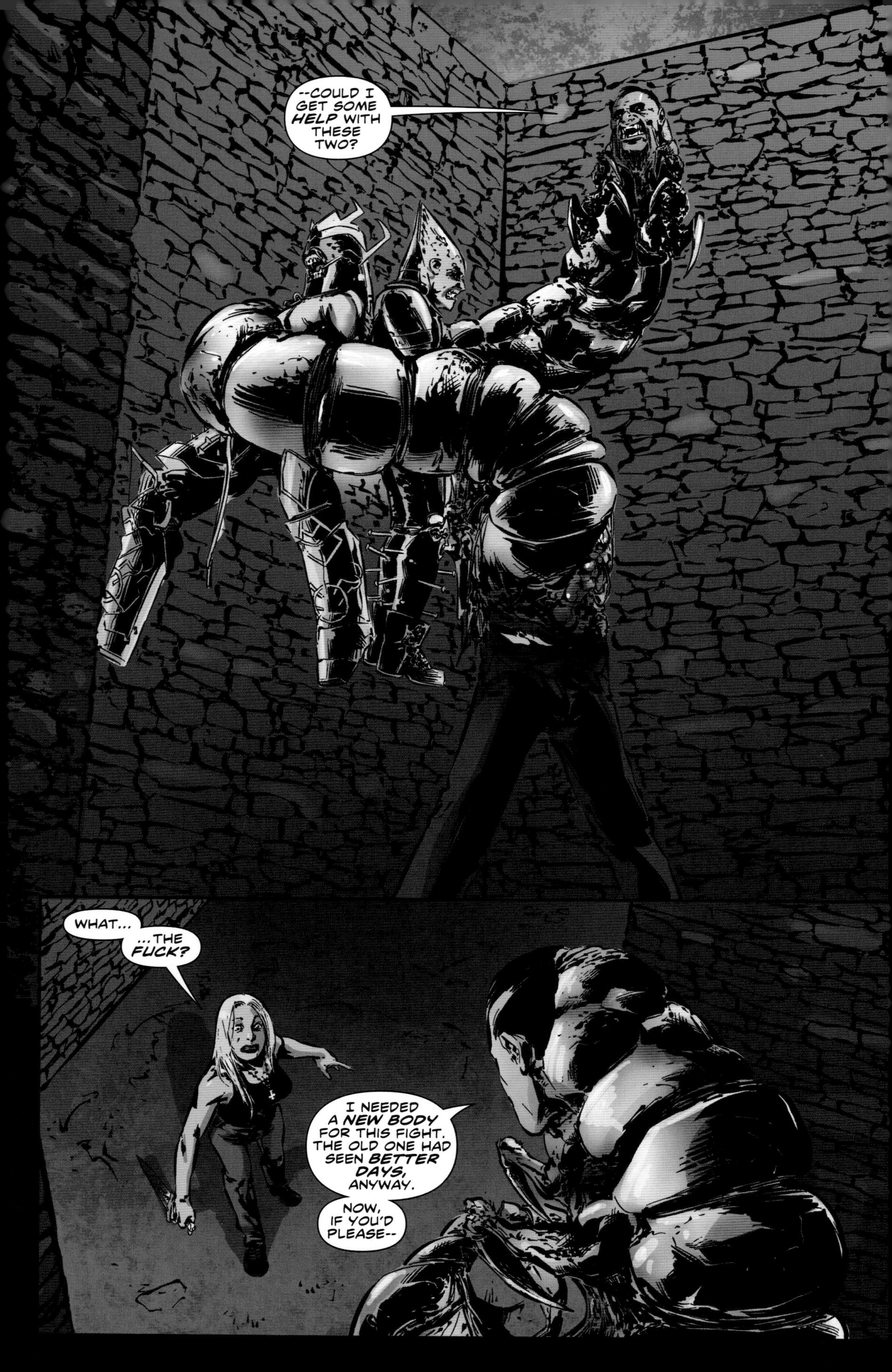
--COULD I GET SOME ***HELP*** WITH THESE TWO?
WHAT...
...THE ***FUCK?***
I NEEDED A ***NEW BODY*** FOR THIS FIGHT. THE OLD ONE HAD SEEN ***BETTER DAYS,*** ANYWAY.
NOW, IF YOU'D PLEASE--

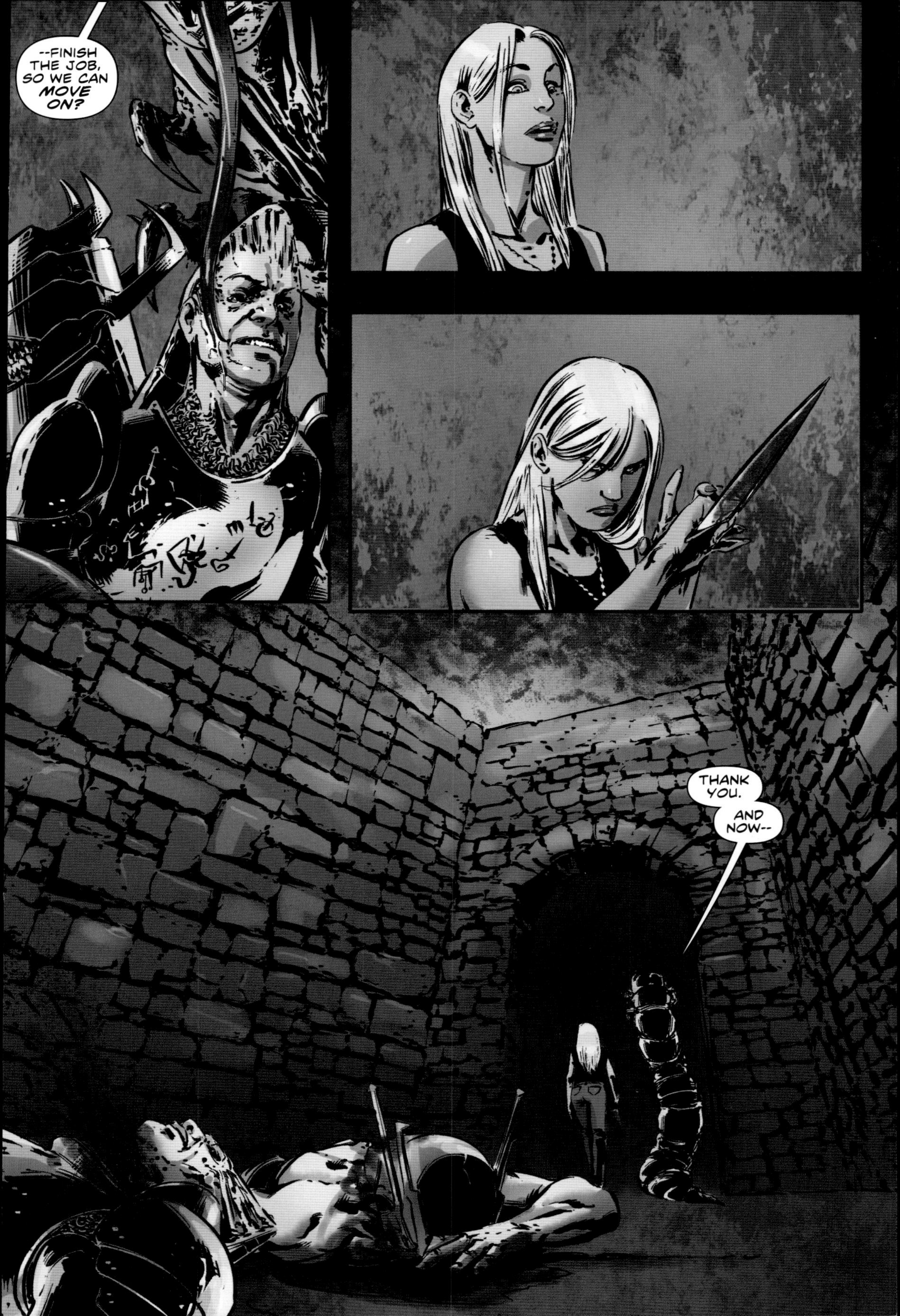
--FINISH THE JOB, SO WE CAN MOVE ON?
THANK YOU.
AND NOW--

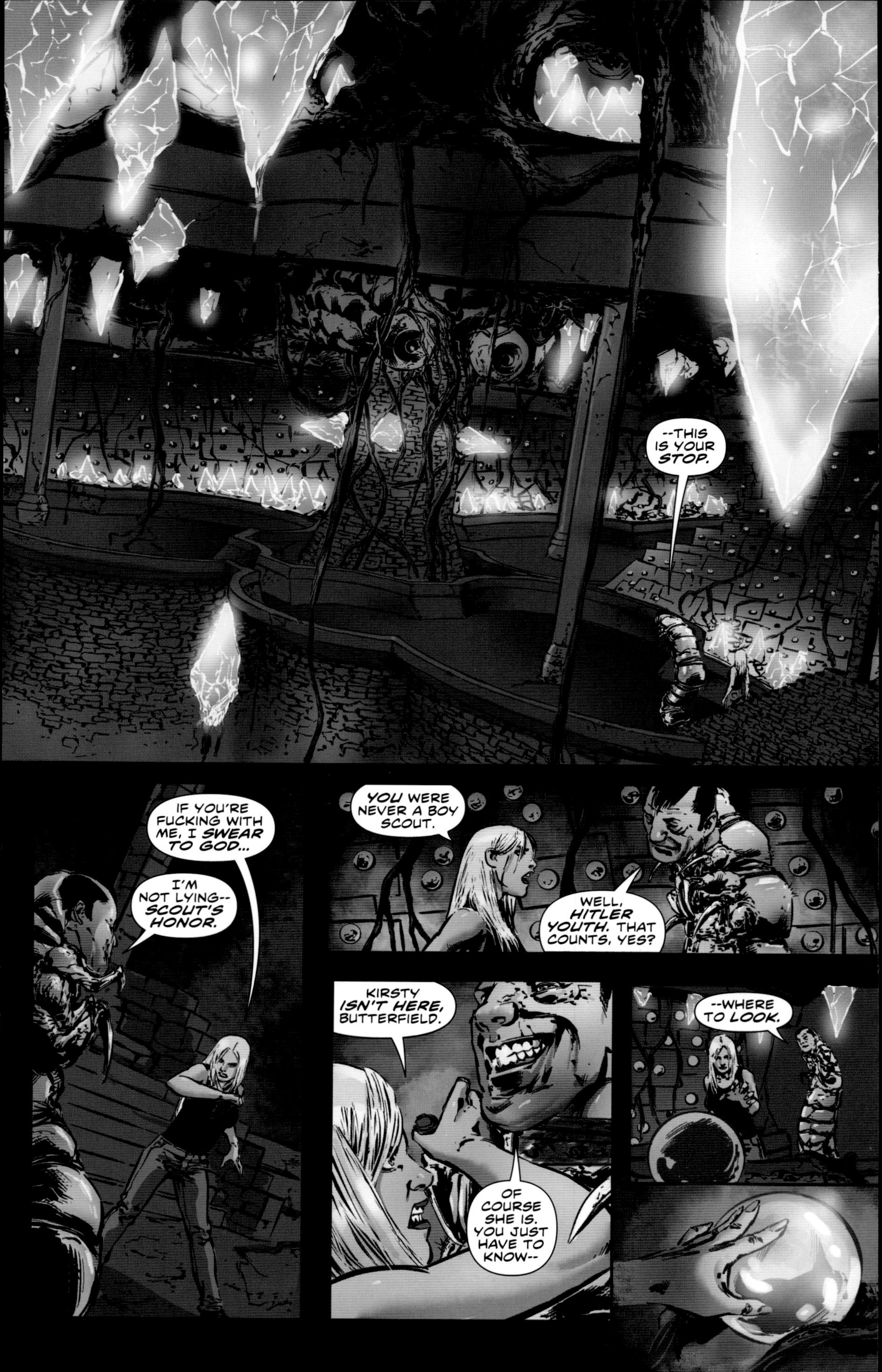
--THIS IS YOUR STOP.
IF YOU'RE FUCKING WITH ME, I SWEAR TO GOD...
I'M NOT LYING-- SCOUT'S HONOR.
YOU WERE NEVER A BOY SCOUT.
WELL, HITLER YOUTH. THAT COUNTS, YES?
KIRSTY ISN'T HERE, BUTTERFIELD.
OF COURSE SHE IS. YOU JUST HAVE TO KNOW--
--WHERE TO LOOK.

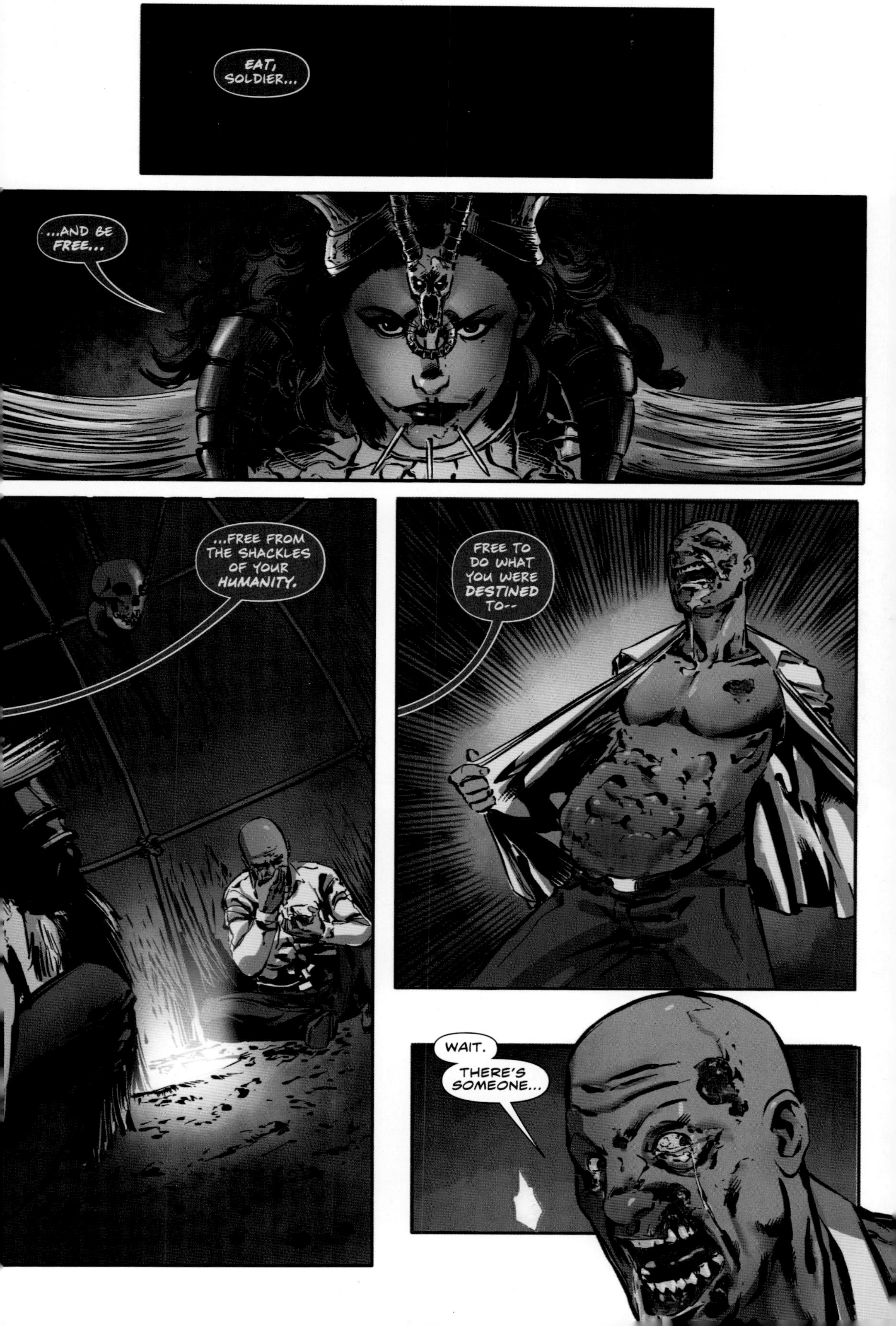
EAT, SOLDIER...
...AND BE FREE...
...FREE FROM THE SHACKLES OF YOUR HUMANITY.
FREE TO DO WHAT YOU WERE DESTINED TO--
WAIT.
THERE'S SOMEONE...

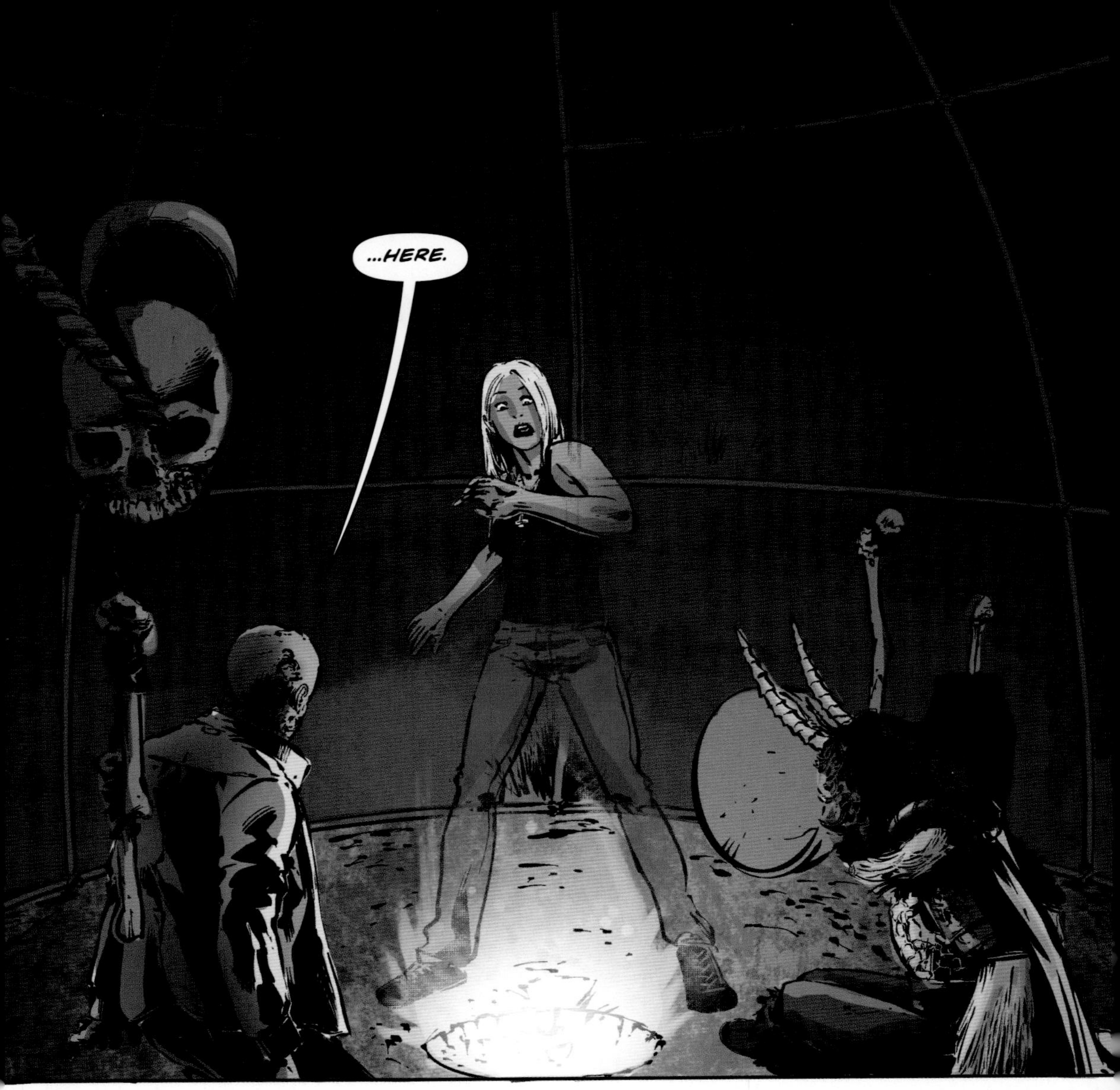
...HERE.

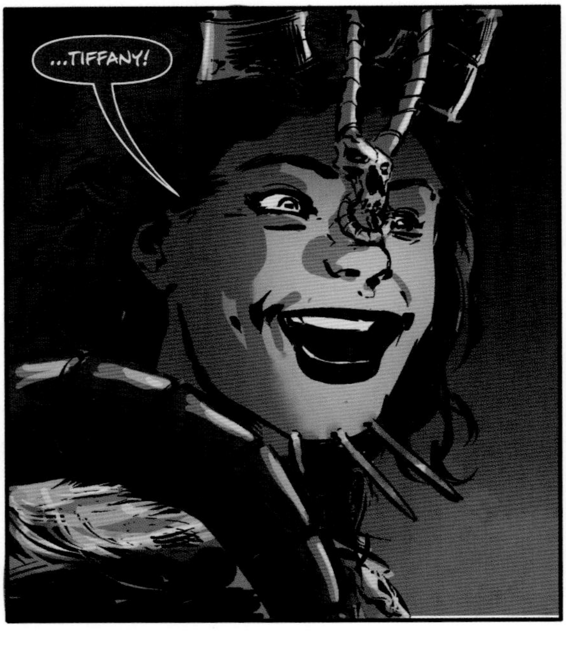
...TIFFANY!

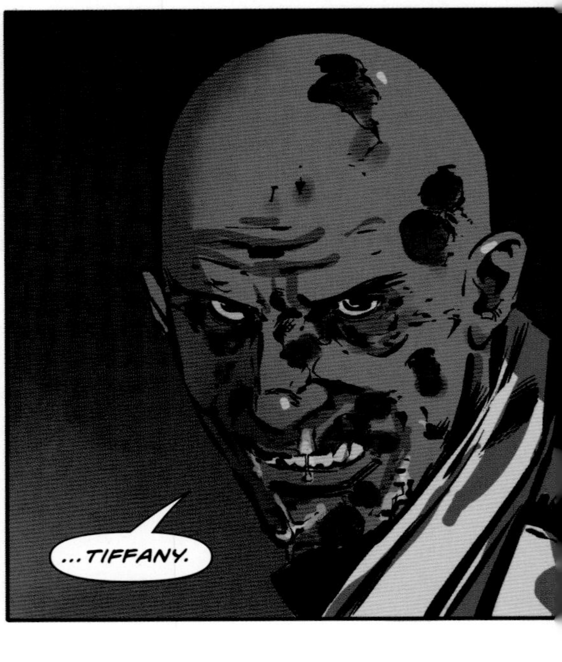
...TIFFANY.

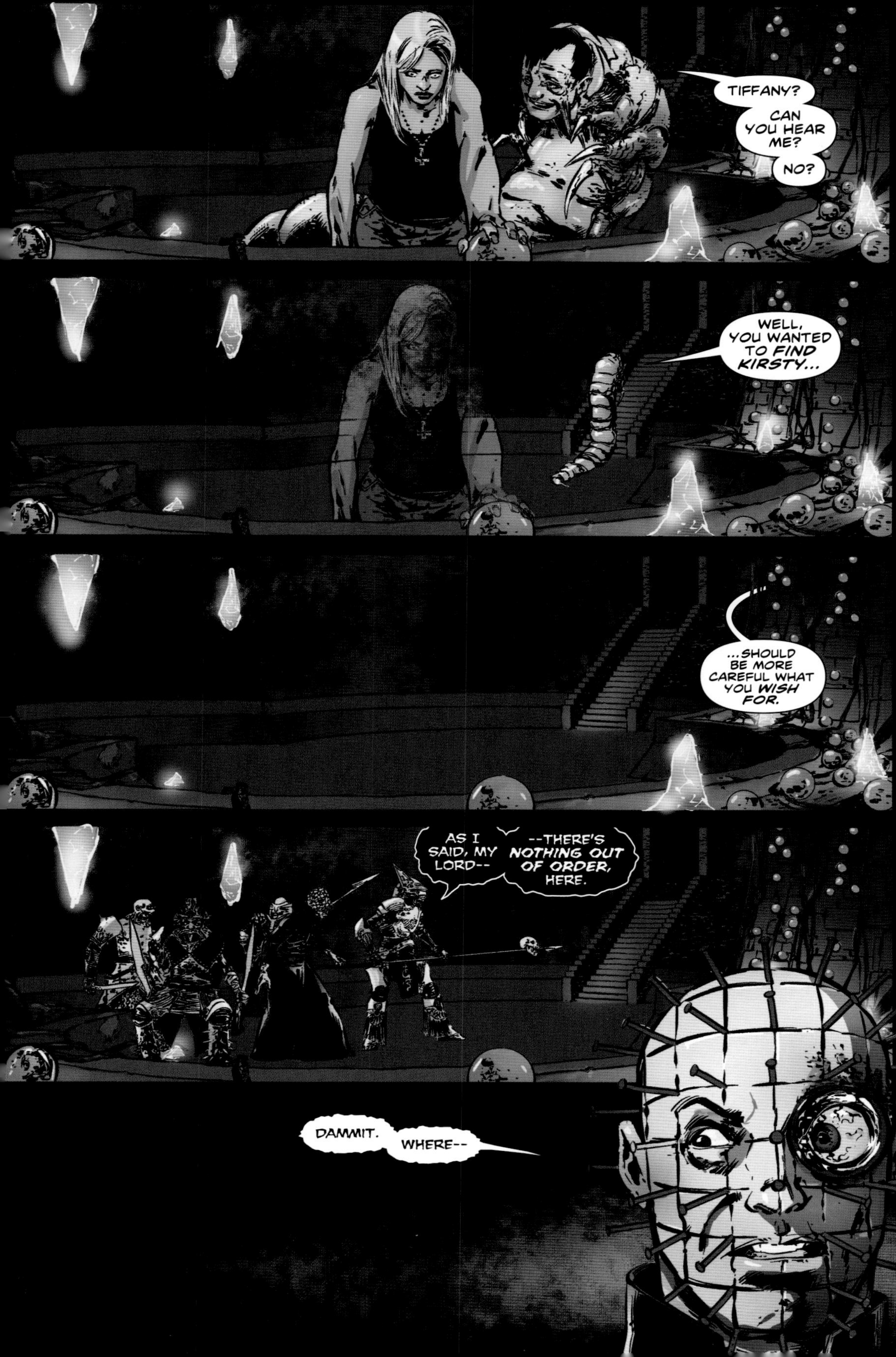

TIFFANY?
CAN YOU HEAR ME?
NO?
WELL, YOU WANTED TO FIND KIRSTY...
...SHOULD BE MORE CAREFUL WHAT YOU WISH FOR.
AS I SAID, MY LORD--
--THERE'S NOTHING OUT OF ORDER, HERE.
DAMMIT.
WHERE--

--ARE WE?

A MIND-PRISON!

IT'S ANOTHER OF LEVIATHAN'S TORTURES!

NO--WHERE ARE WE NOW? WHAT'S THIS DESERT?

ONE OF SPENCER'S MEMORIES!

HE MET A SERVANT OF SOME OTHER HELL! THAT'S WHERE HE G HIS NEW POWERS FROM! THE POWERS USED FOR HIS COU D'ETAT IN INDIA!

...SO SPENCER'S NEW POWERS--

--ARE FROM ANOTHER HELL?

YES! COME ON, WE'VE GOT TO RUN! HE'S TOO STRONG TO FIGHT!

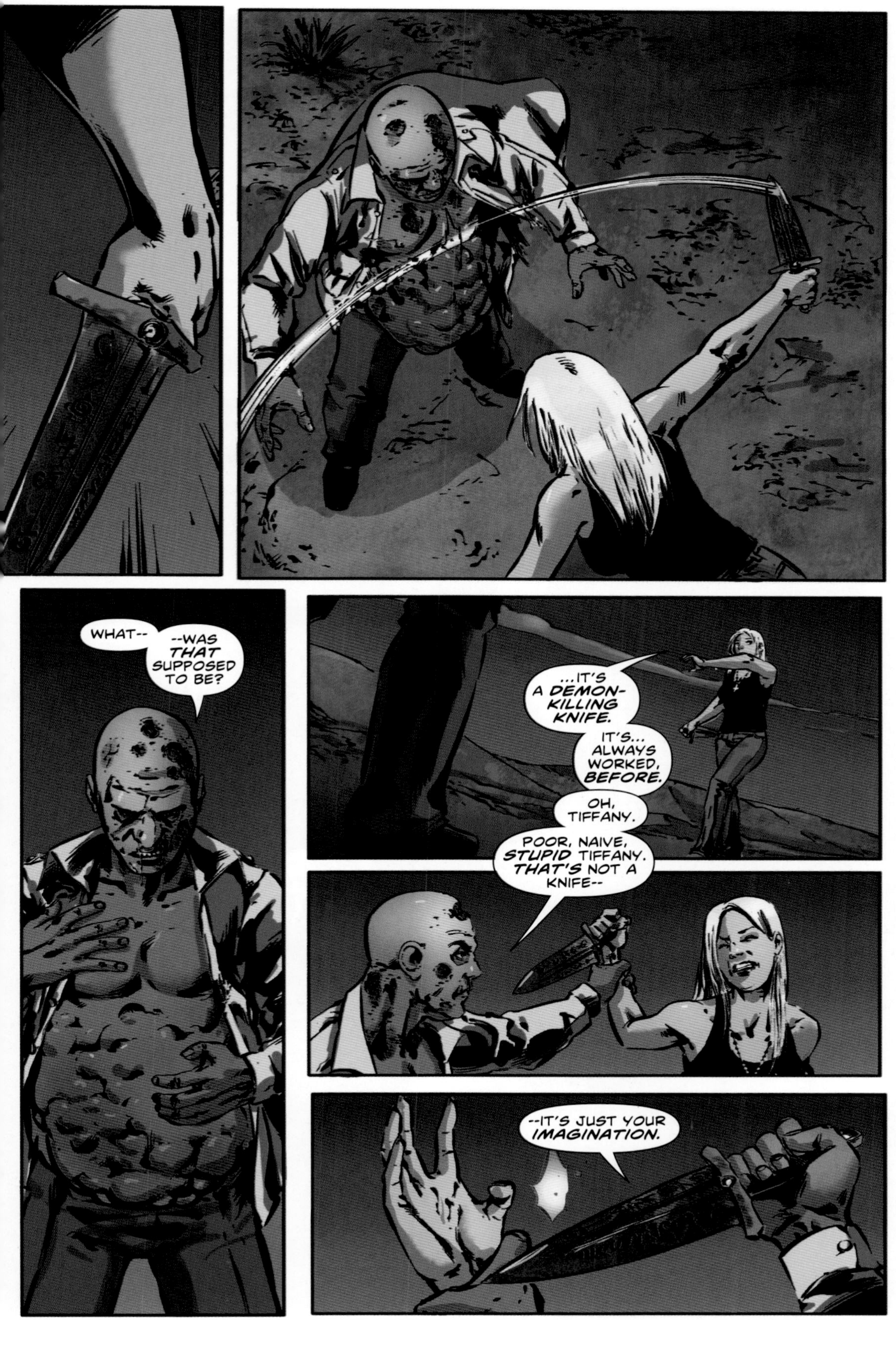
WHAT--
--WAS THAT SUPPOSED TO BE?
...IT'S A DEMON-KILLING KNIFE.
IT'S... ALWAYS WORKED, BEFORE.
OH, TIFFANY.
POOR, NAIVE, STUPID TIFFANY. THAT'S NOT A KNIFE--
--IT'S JUST YOUR IMAGINATION.

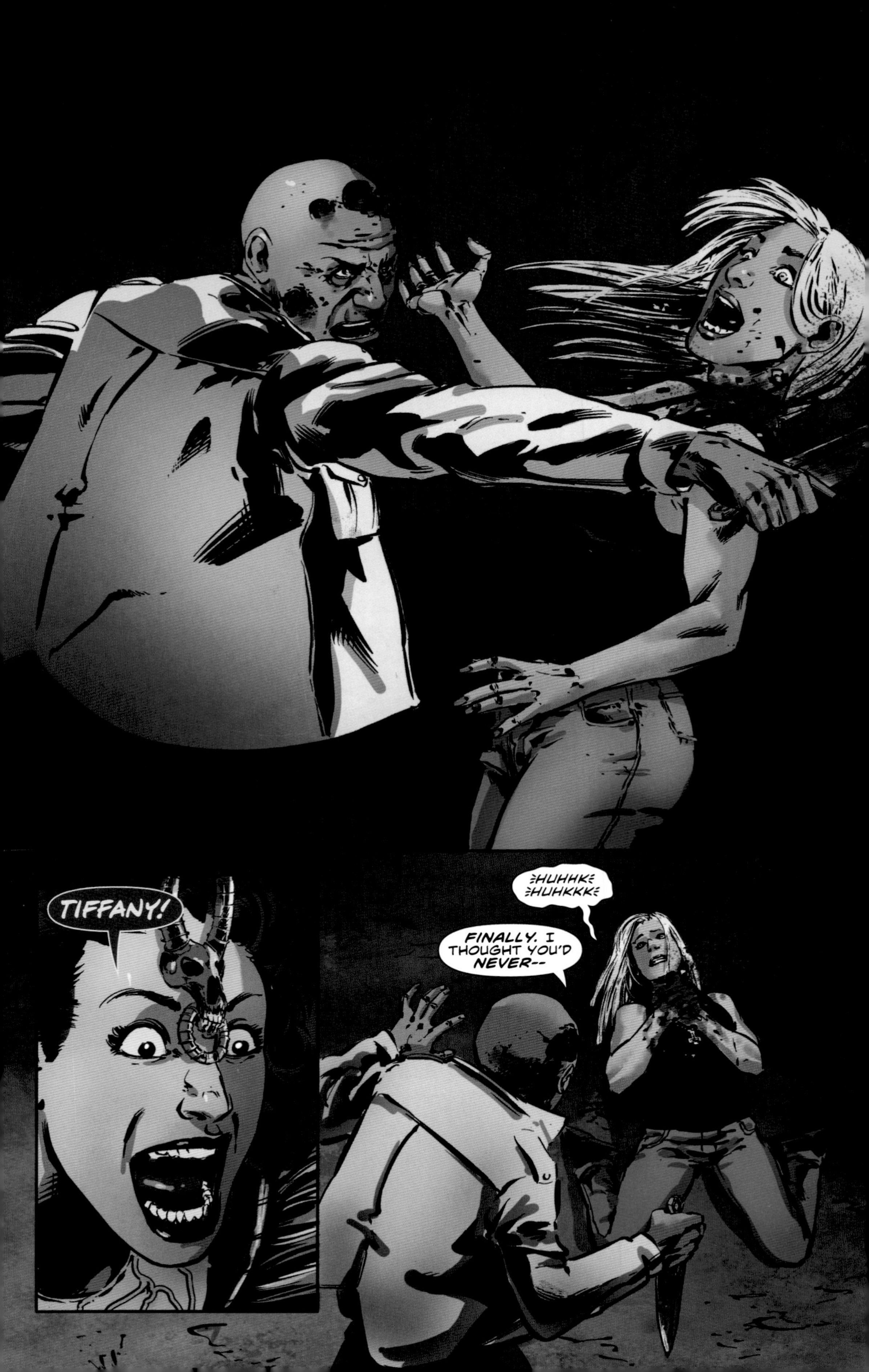
TIFFANY!
HUHHK HUHKKK
FINALLY. I THOUGHT YOU'D NEVER--

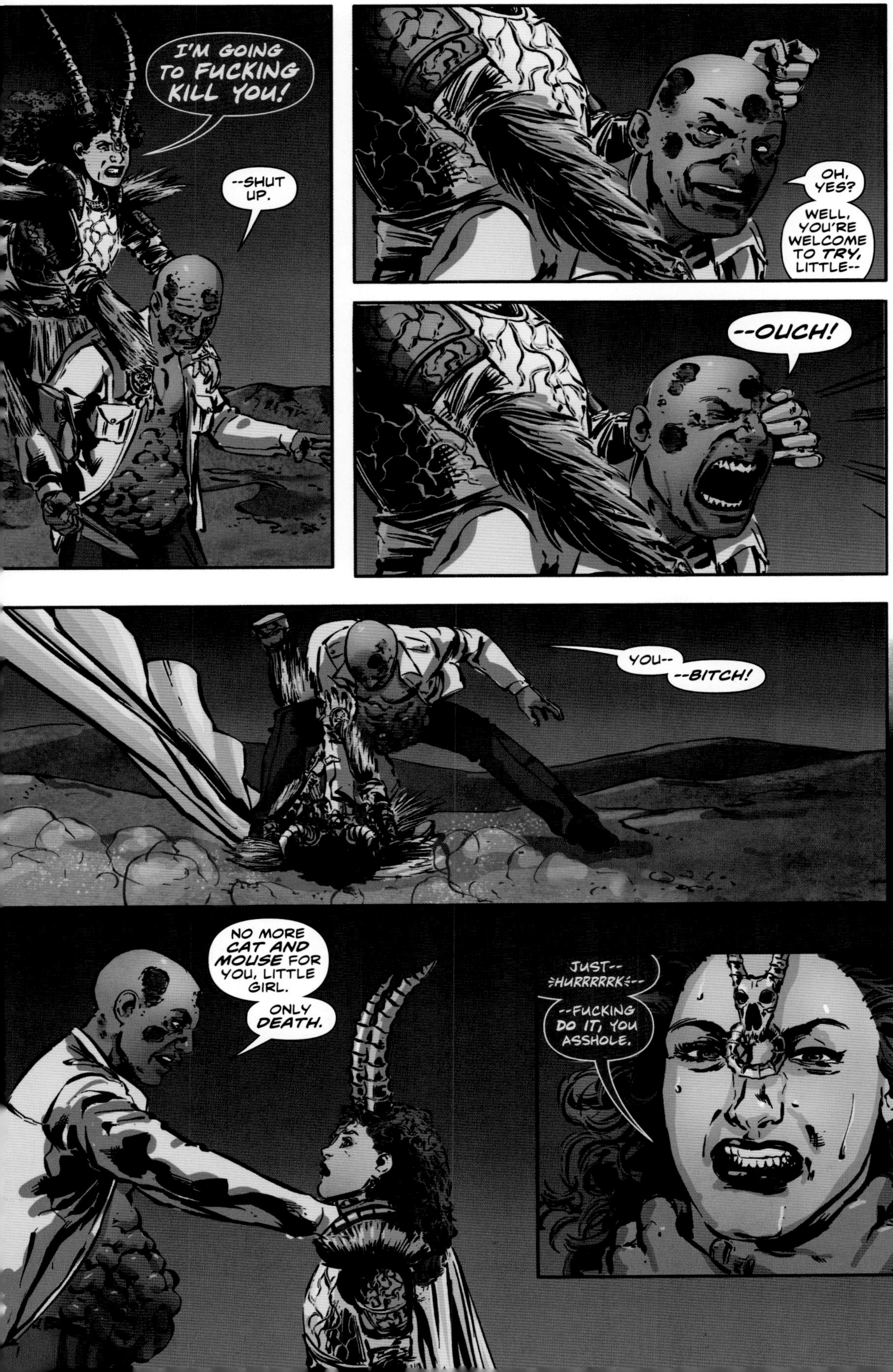
I'M GOING TO FUCKING KILL YOU!
--SHUT UP.
OH, YES?
WELL, YOU'RE WELCOME TO TRY, LITTLE--
--OUCH!
YOU--
--BITCH!
NO MORE CAT AND MOUSE FOR YOU, LITTLE GIRL.
ONLY DEATH.
JUST--
HURRRRRK--
--FUCKING DO IT, YOU ASSHOLE.

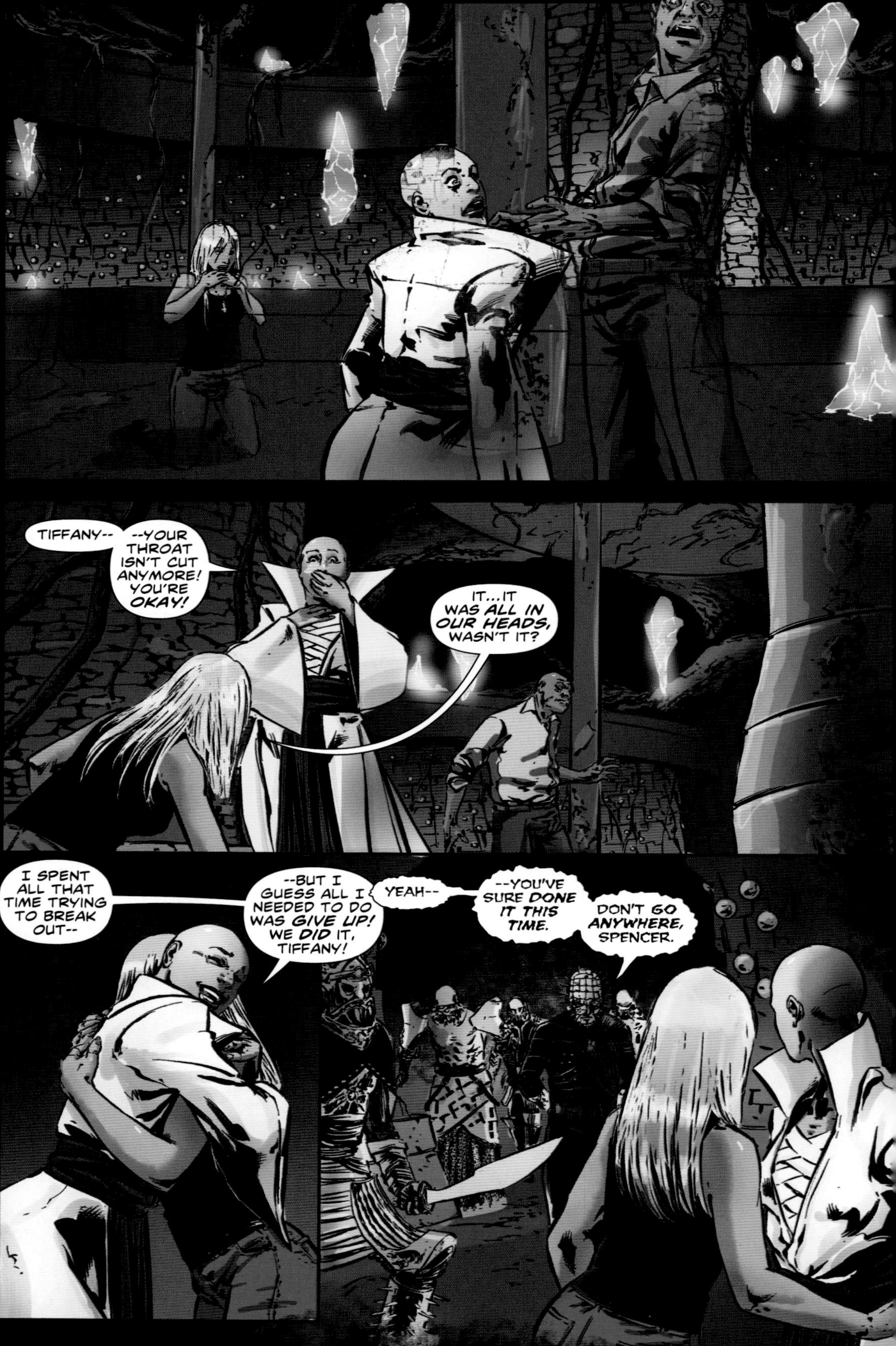
TIFFANY--
--YOUR THROAT ISN'T CUT ANYMORE! YOU'RE OKAY!
IT...IT WAS ALL IN OUR HEADS, WASN'T IT?
I SPENT ALL THAT TIME TRYING TO BREAK OUT--
--BUT I GUESS ALL I NEEDED TO DO WAS GIVE UP! WE DID IT, TIFFANY!
YEAH--
--YOU'VE SURE DONE IT THIS TIME.
DON'T GO ANYWHERE, SPENCER.

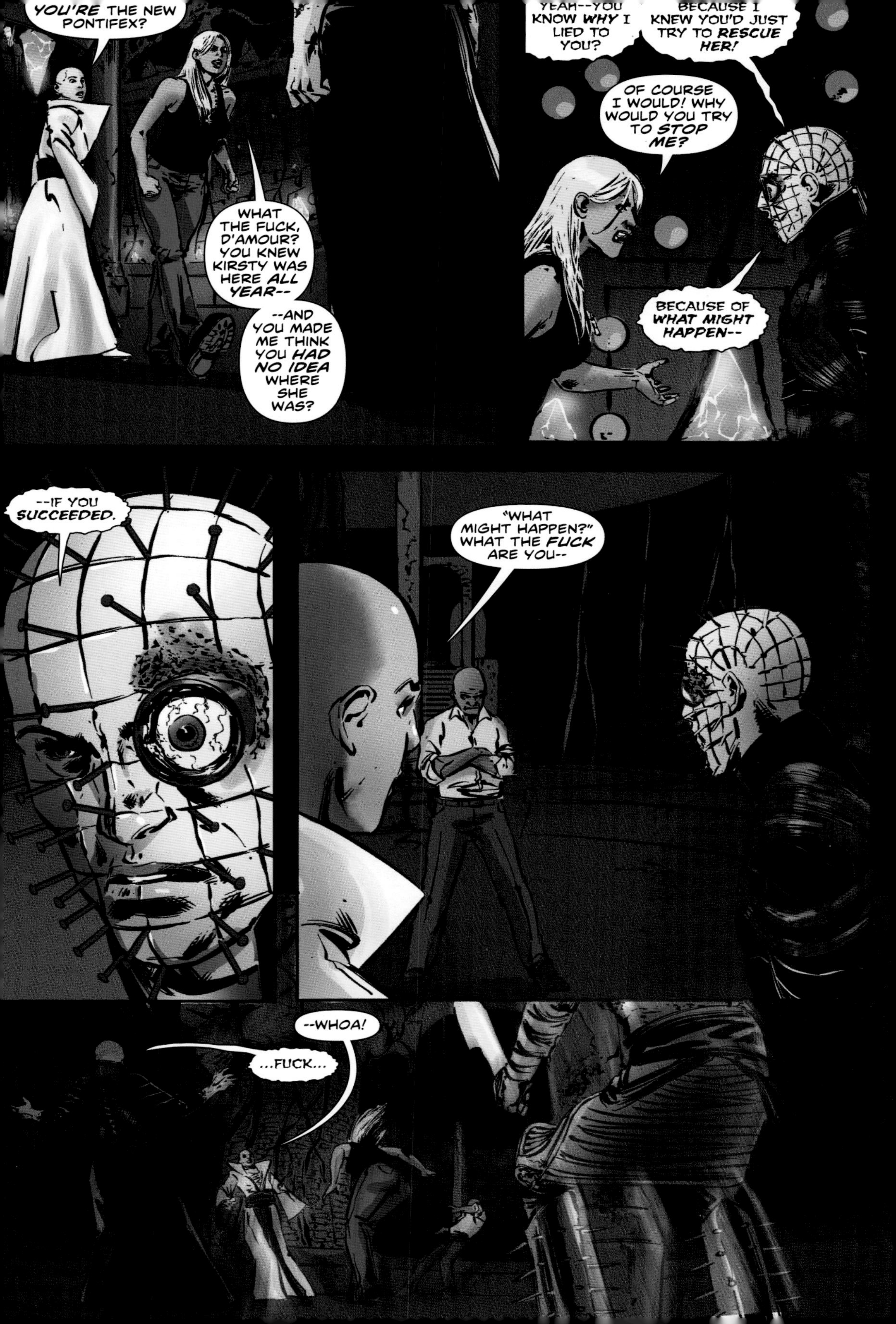
YOU'RE THE NEW PONTIFEX?
WHAT THE FUCK, D'AMOUR? YOU KNEW KIRSTY WAS HERE ALL YEAR--
--AND YOU MADE ME THINK YOU HAD NO IDEA WHERE SHE WAS?
YEAH--YOU KNOW WHY I LIED TO YOU?
BECAUSE I KNEW YOU'D JUST TRY TO RESCUE HER!
OF COURSE I WOULD! WHY WOULD YOU TRY TO STOP ME?
BECAUSE OF WHAT MIGHT HAPPEN--
--IF YOU SUCCEEDED.
"WHAT MIGHT HAPPEN?" WHAT THE FUCK ARE YOU--
--WHOA!
...FUCK...

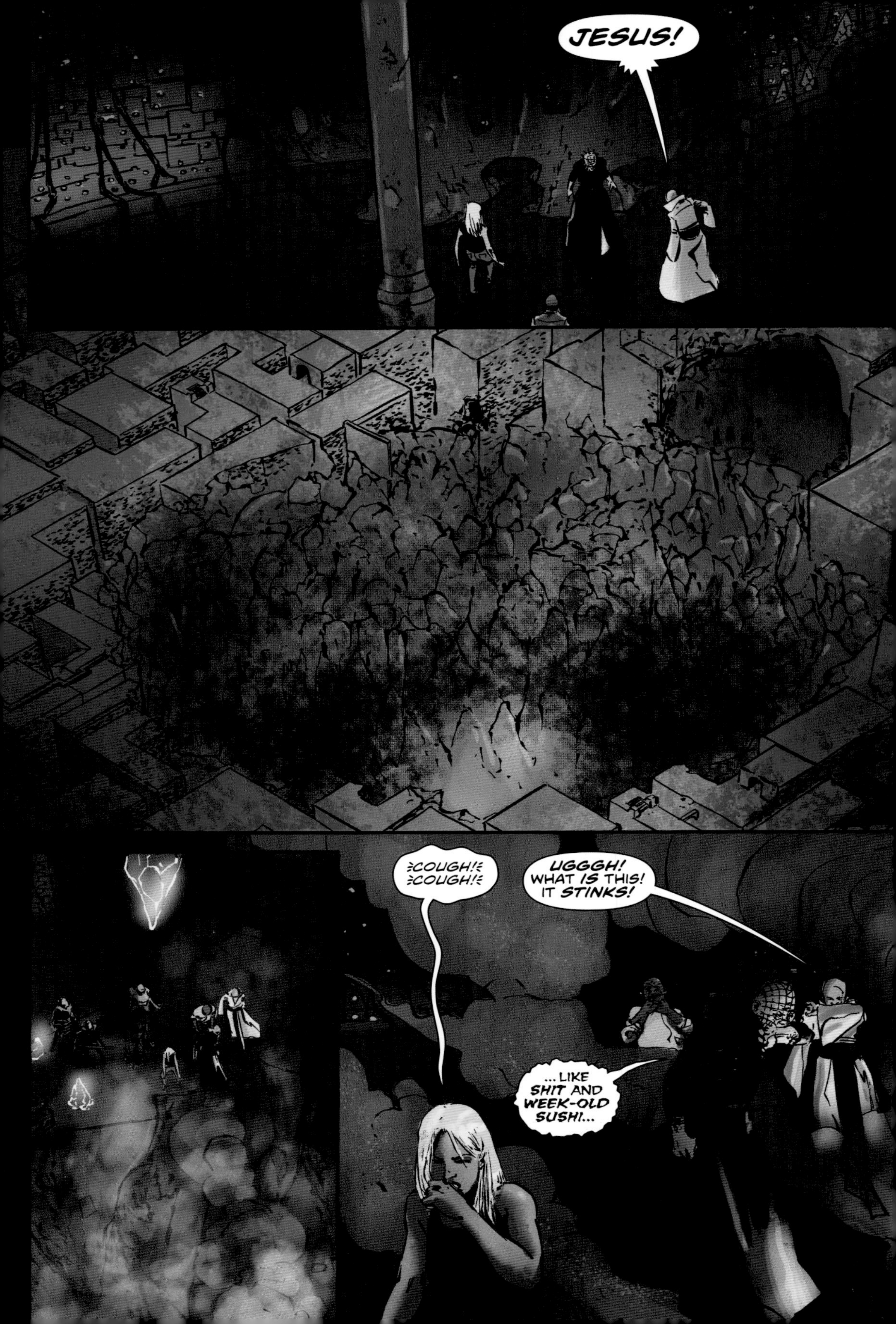
JESUS!
COUGH! COUGH!
UGGGH! WHAT IS THIS! IT STINKS!
...LIKE SHIT AND WEEK-OLD SUSHI...

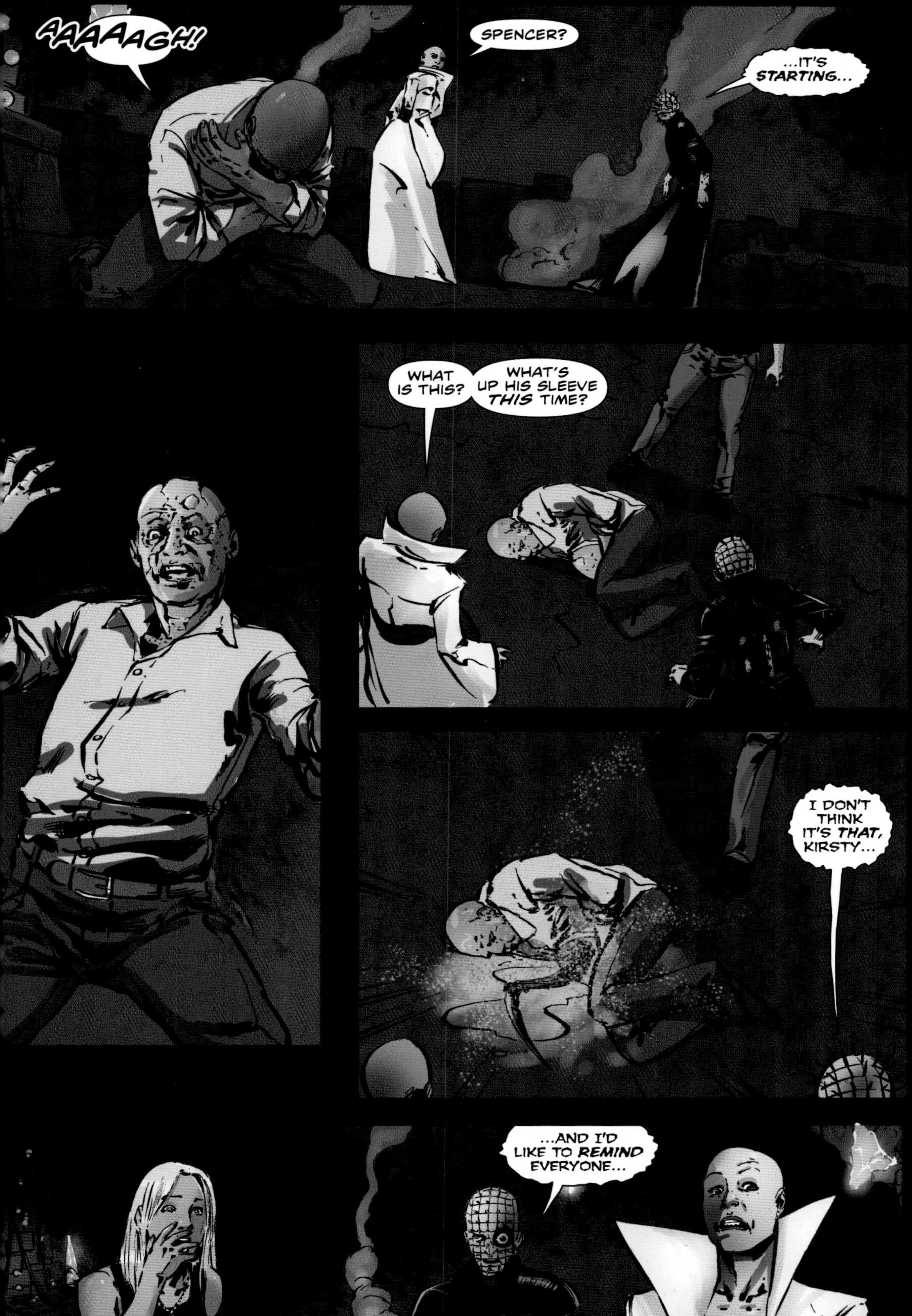
AAAAAGH!
SPENCER?
...IT'S STARTING...
WHAT IS THIS?
WHAT'S UP HIS SLEEVE THIS TIME?
I DON'T THINK IT'S THAT, KIRSTY...
...AND I'D LIKE TO REMIND EVERYONE...

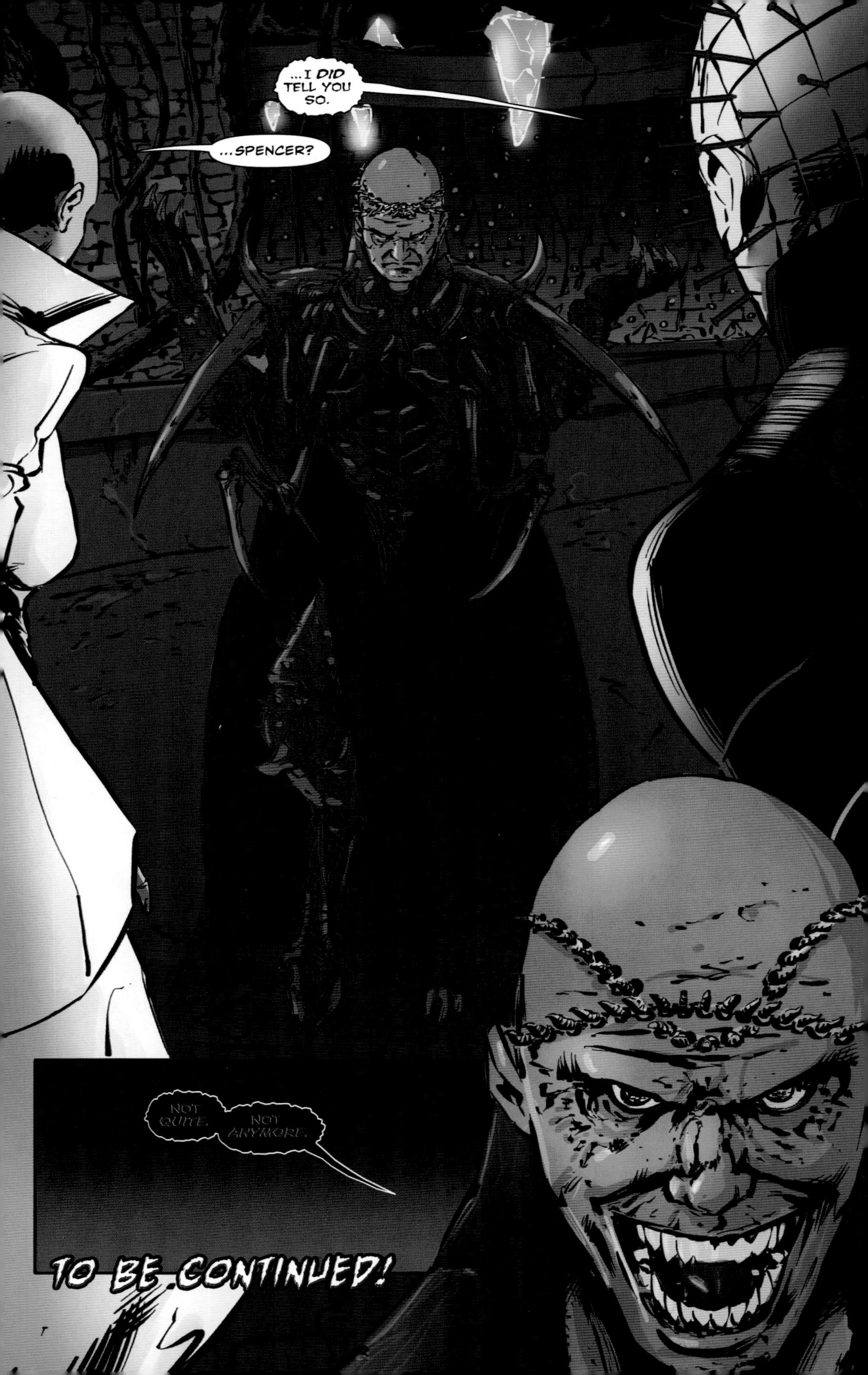
...I DID TELL YOU SO.
...SPENCER?
NOT QUITE.
NOT ANYMORE.
TO BE CONTINUED!

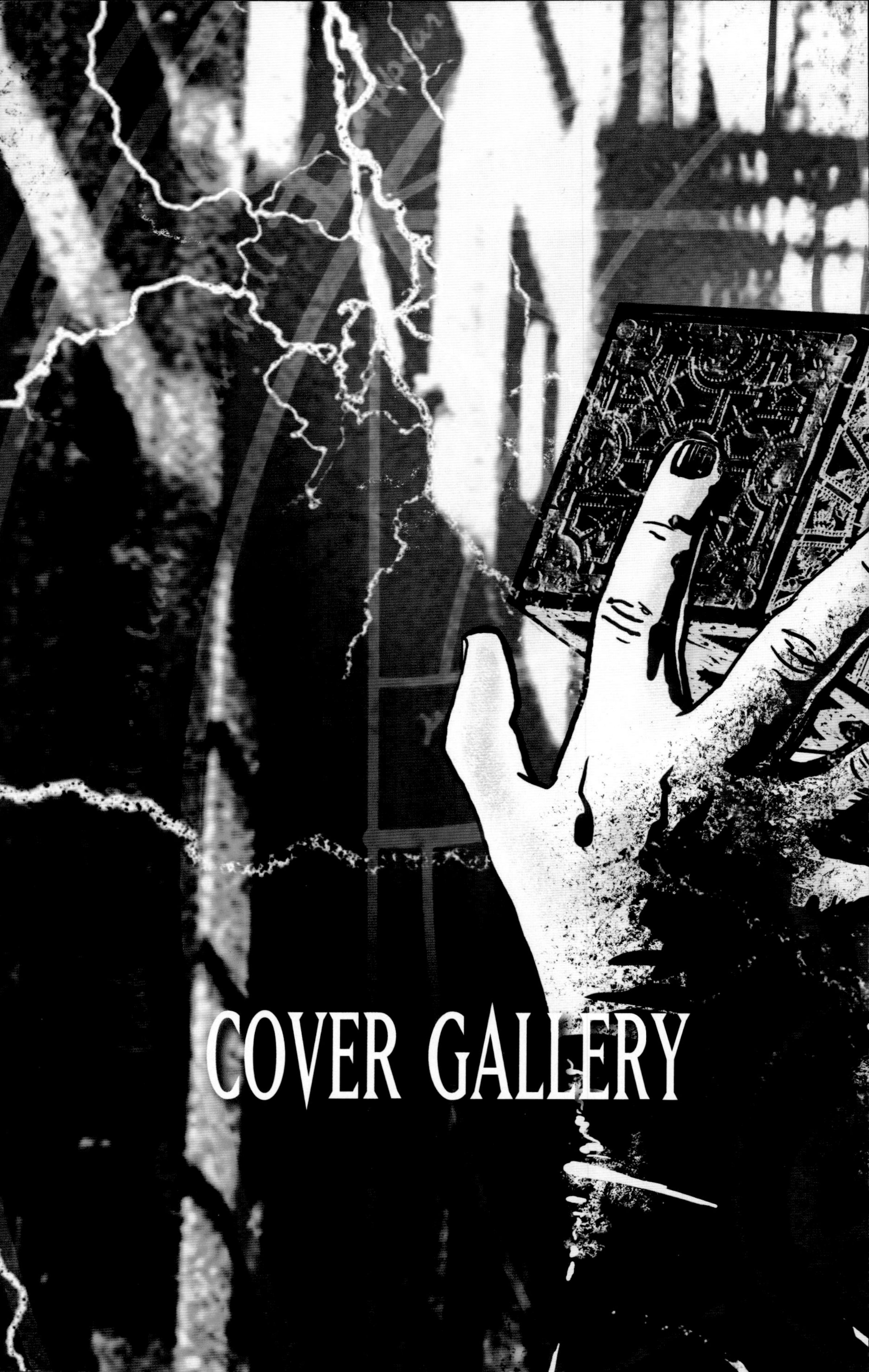
COVER GALLERY

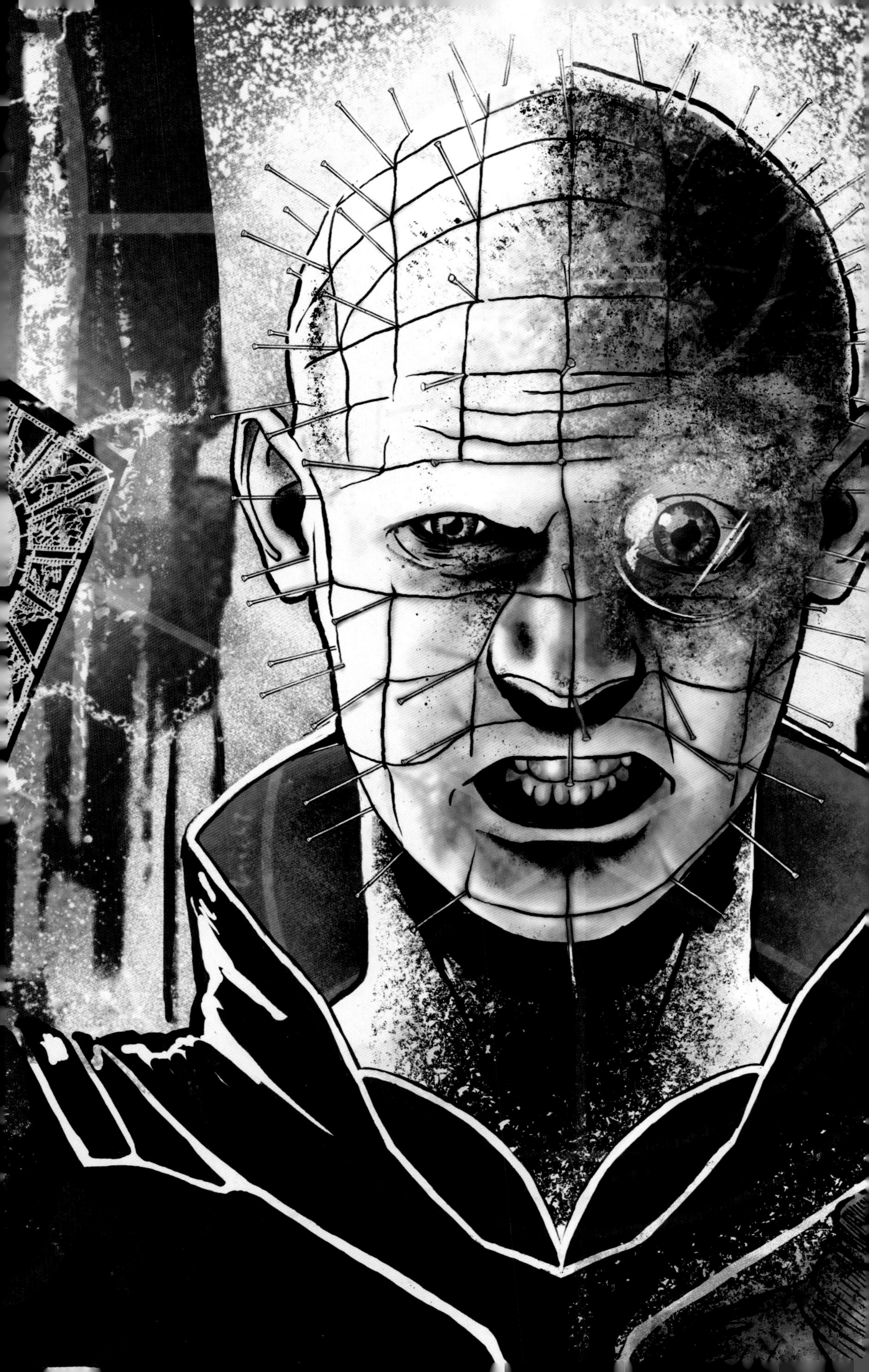

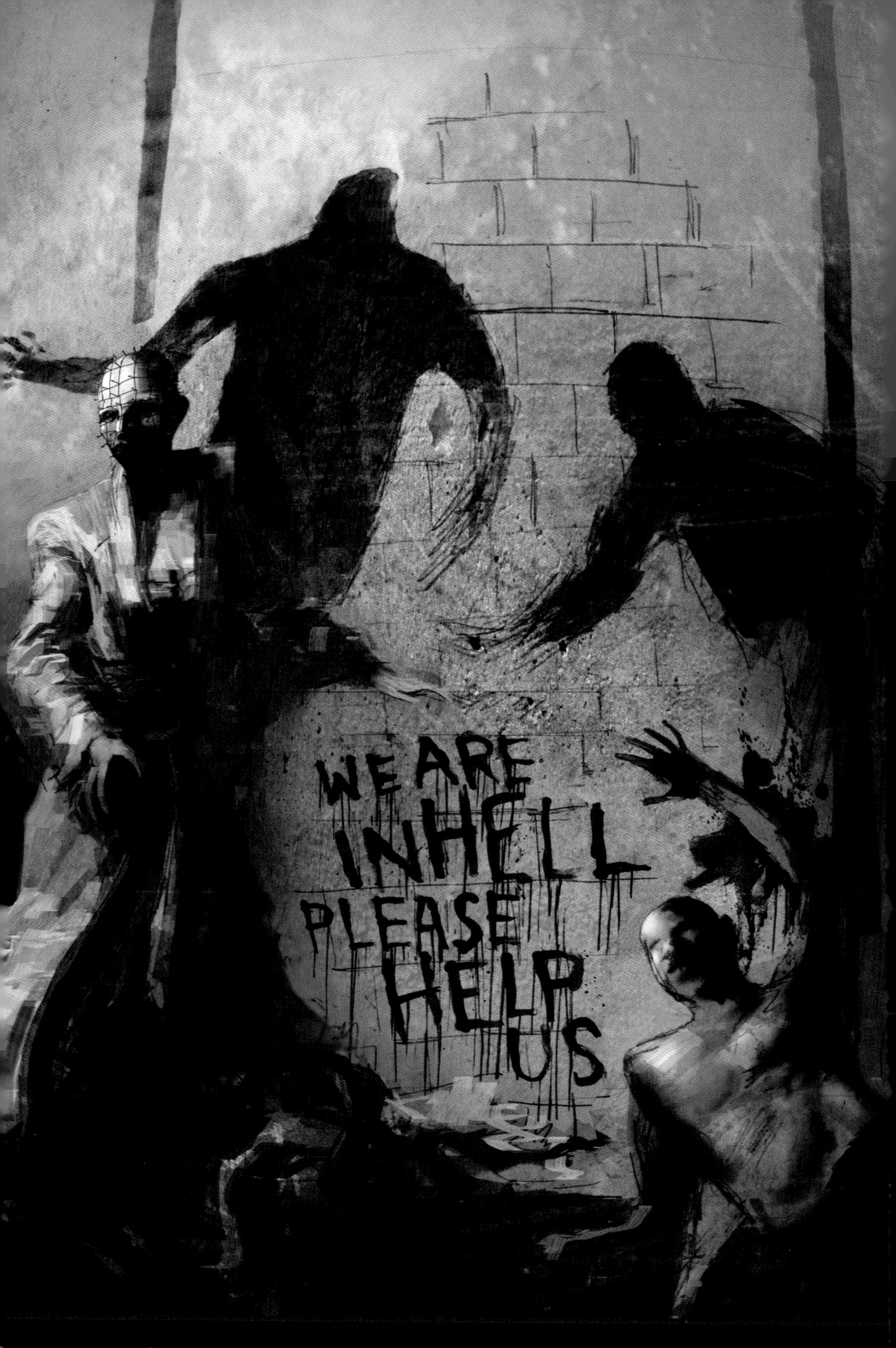
WE ARE
IN HELL
PLEASE
HELP
US
ISSUE FIVE: SAMI MAKKONEN

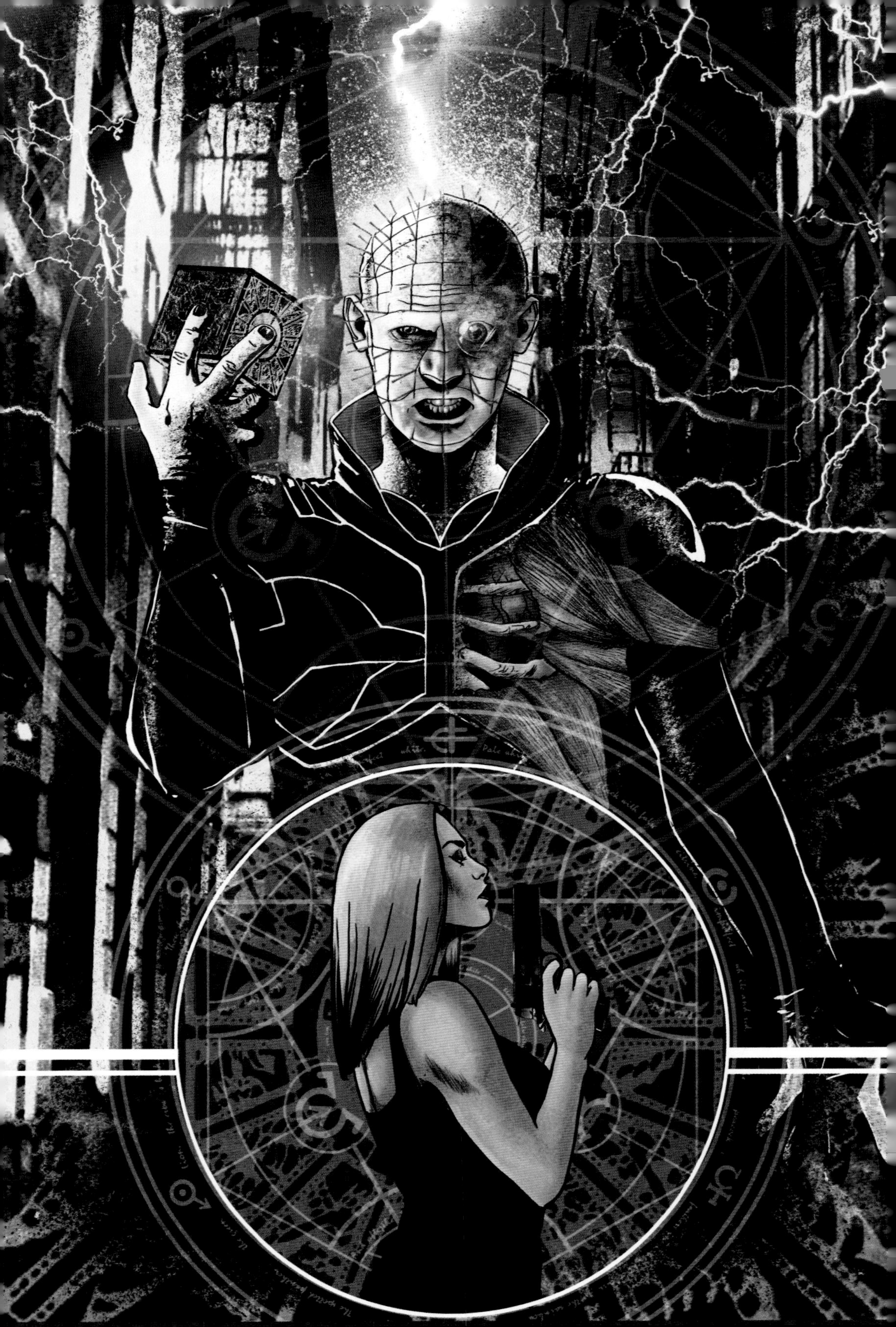

ISSUE SIX: LORENA CARVALHO

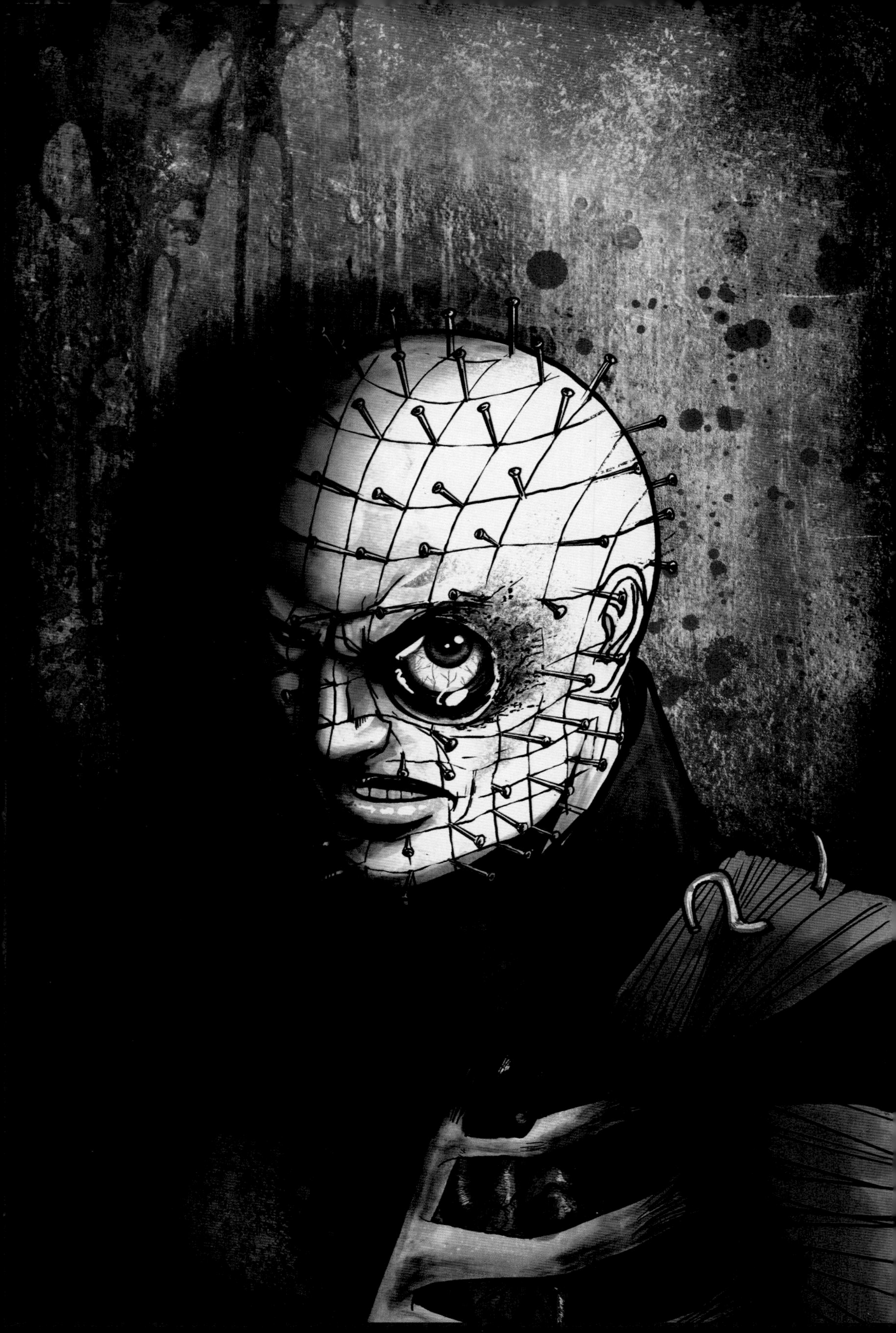

ISSUE SEVEN: LORENA CARVALHO

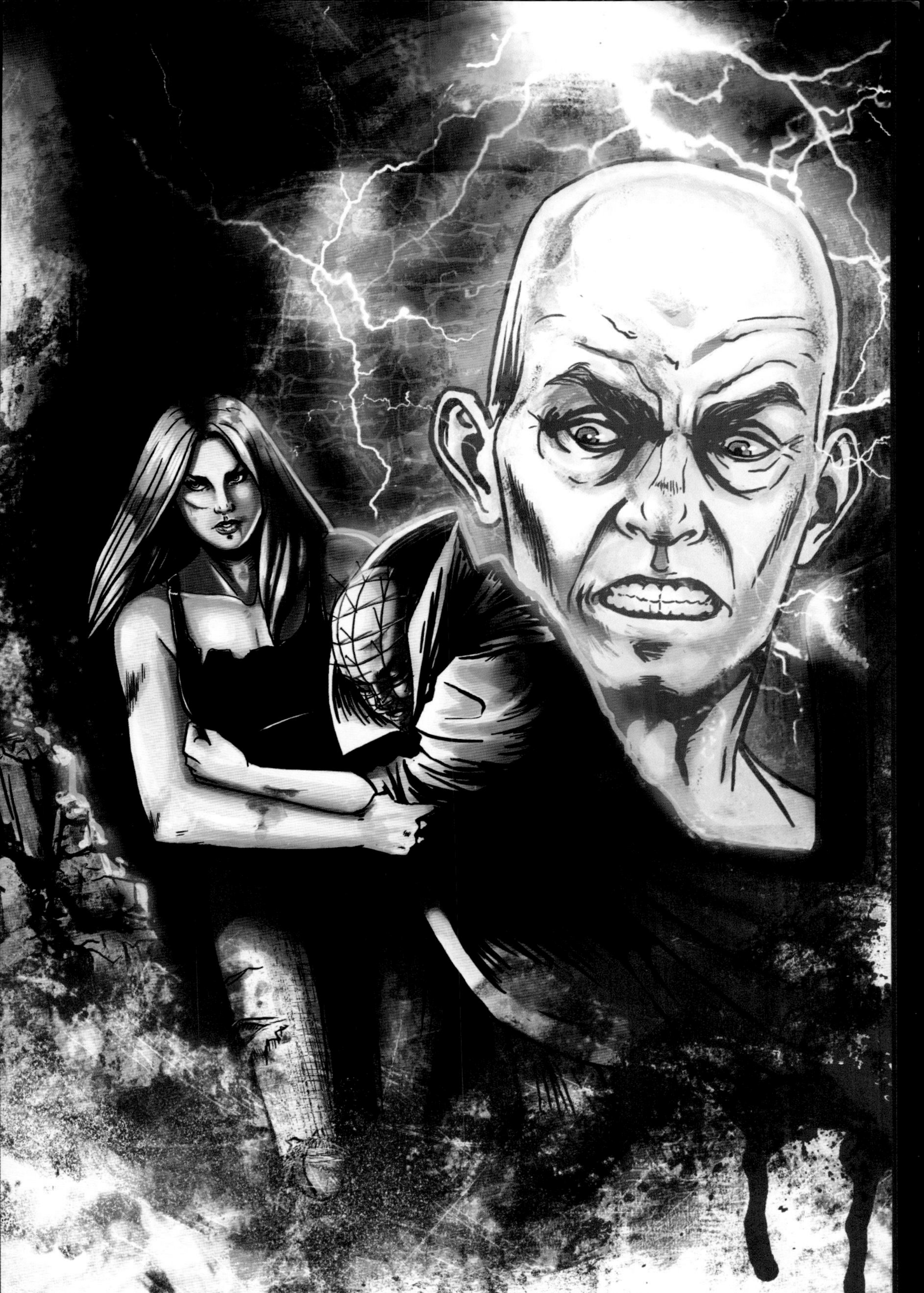

ISSUE EIGHT: LORENA CARVALHO

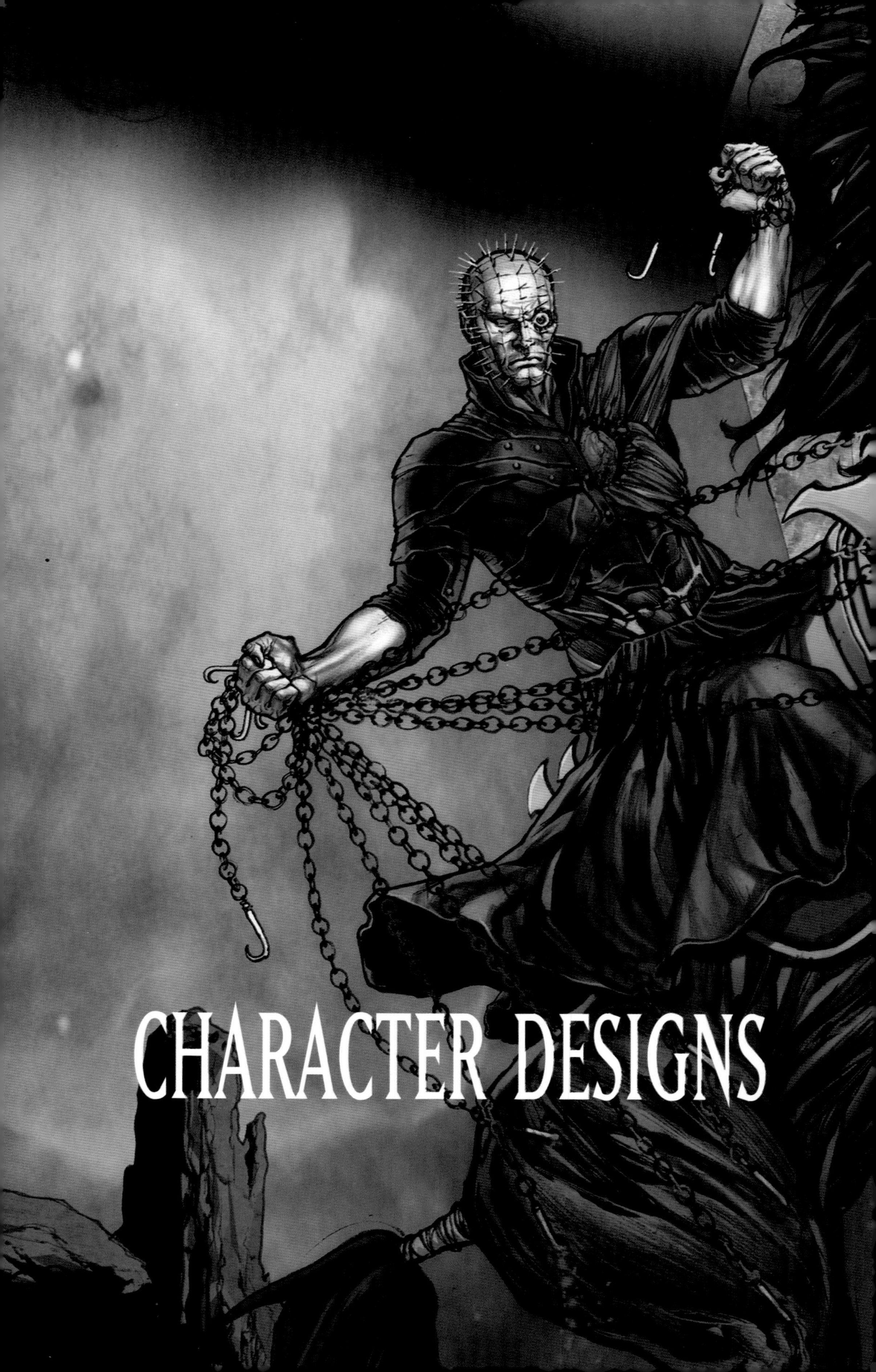

CHARACTER DESIGNS

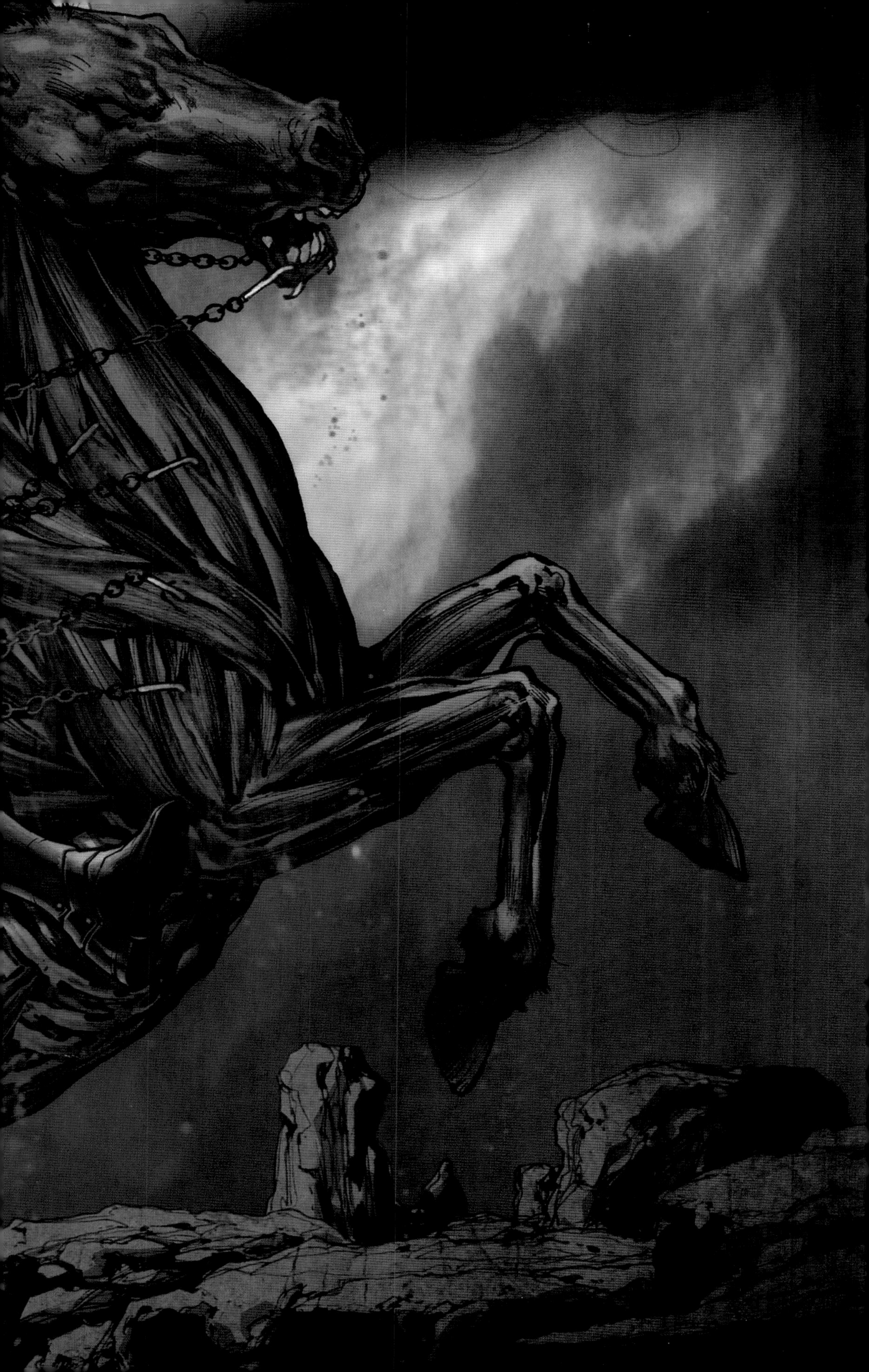

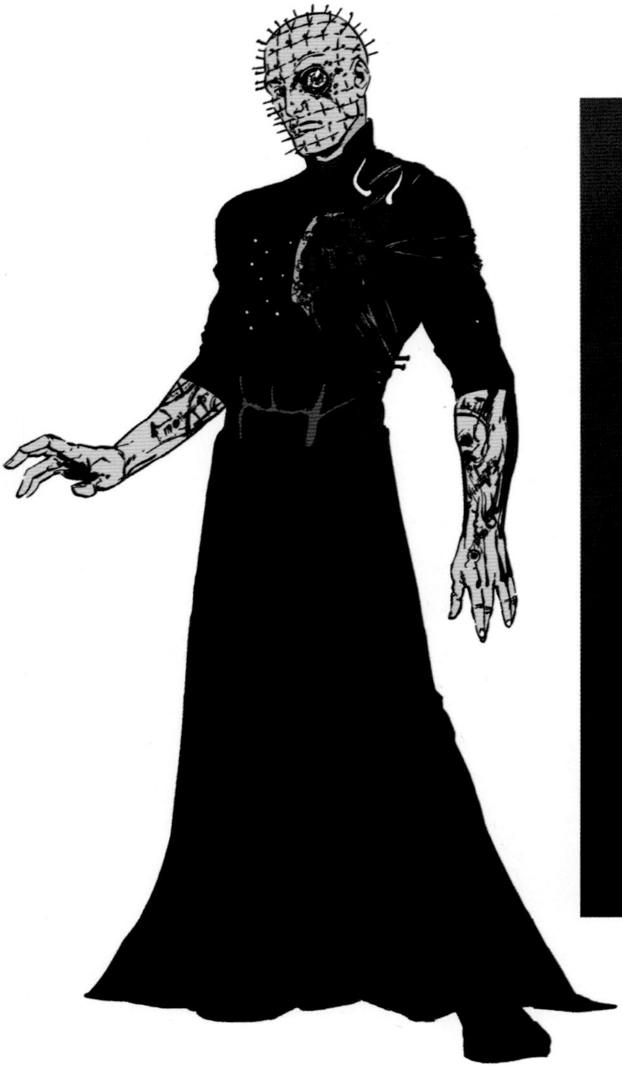

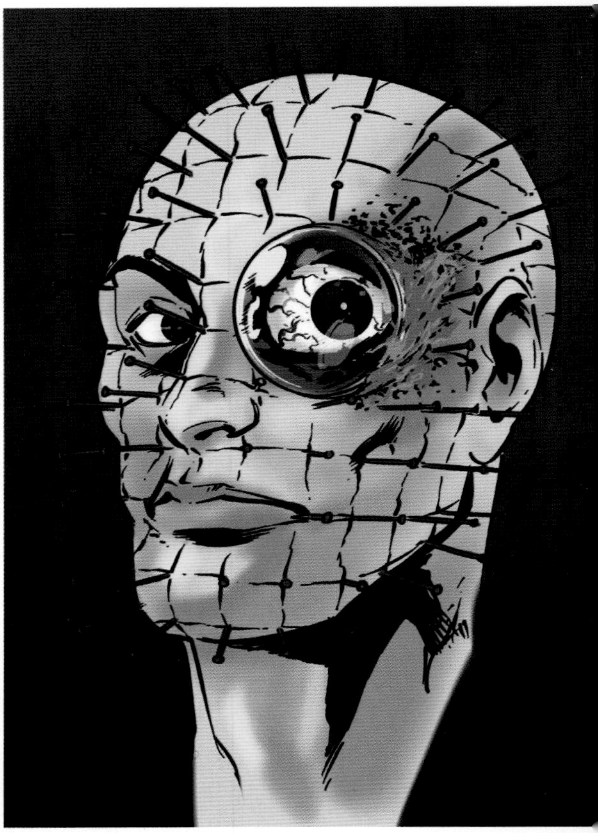

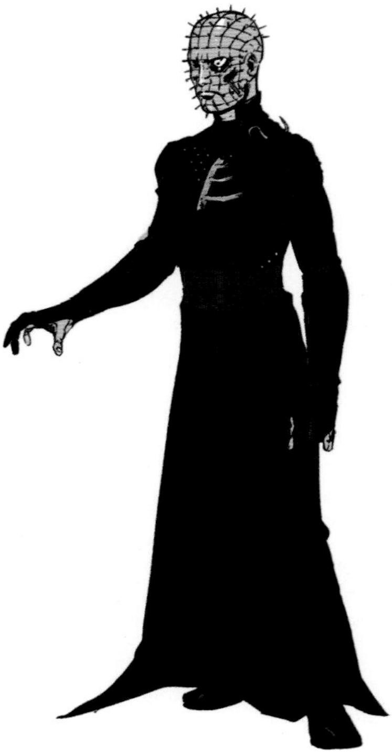

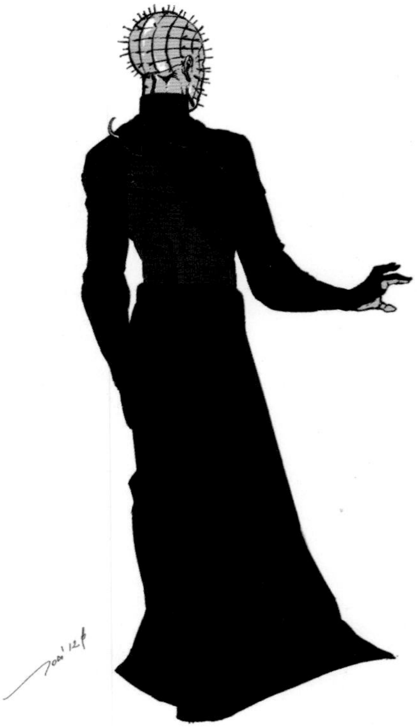

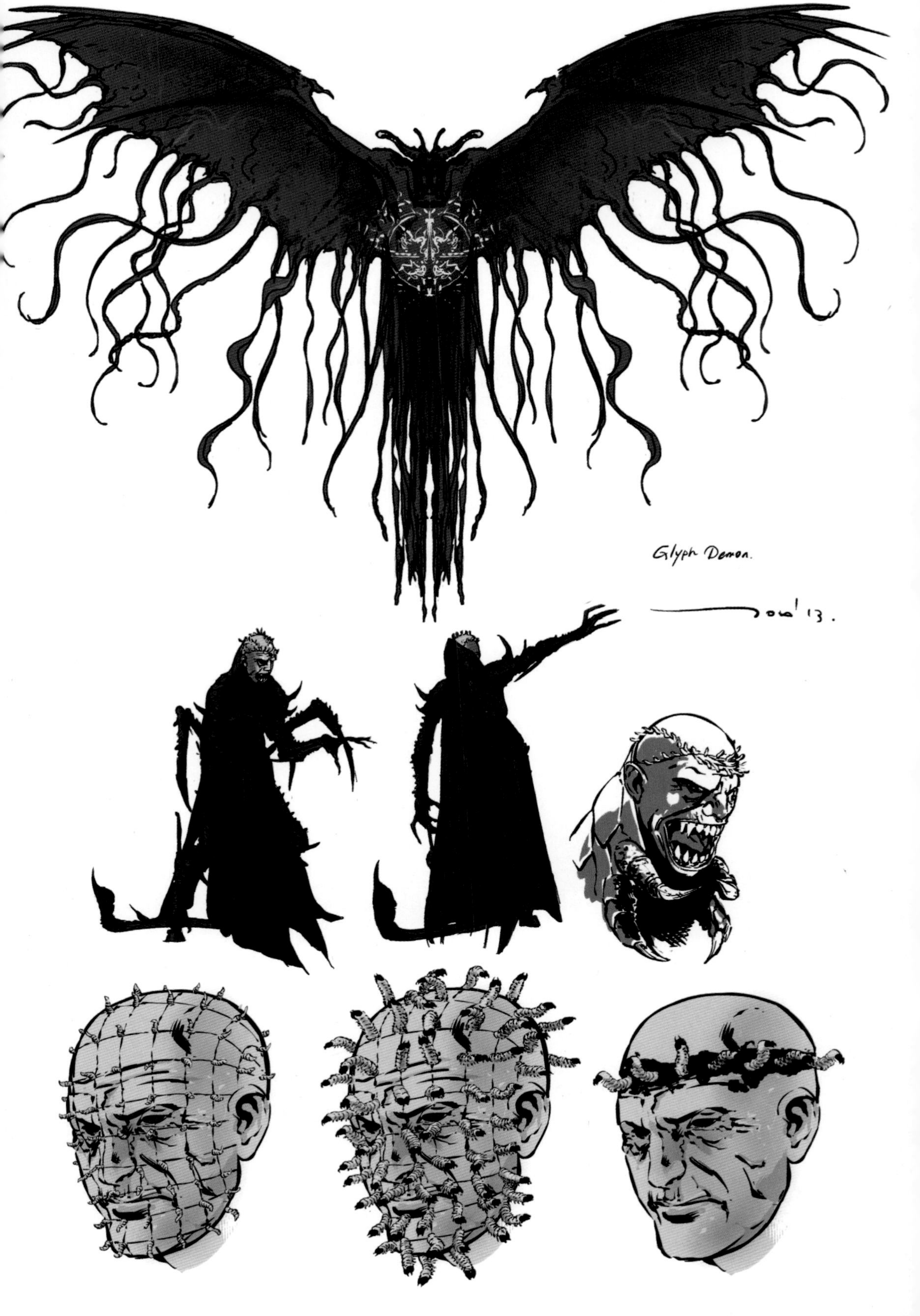
Glyph Demon.

CLIVE BARKER'S

HELLRAISER

THE DARK WATCH